LATIN LITERATURE

LATIN LITERATURE

J. W. Mackail

FREDERICK UNGAR PUBLISHING CO.
NEW YORK

Republished 1966

Reprinted from the edition of 1895

Printed in the United States of America

Library of Congress Catalog Card No. 66-16865

CONTENTS.

I.

THE REPUBLIC.

II.

THE AUGUSTAN AGE.

viii   *Contents.*

Contents.

I
THE REPUBLIC

I.

ORIGINS OF LATIN LITERATURE: EARLY EPIC AND TRAGEDY.

To the Romans themselves, as they looked back two hundred years later, the beginnings of a real literature seemed definitely fixed in the generation which passed between the first and second Punic wars. The peace of B.C. 241 closed an epoch throughout which the Roman Republic had been fighting for an assured place in the group of powers which controlled the Mediterranean world. This was now gained; and the pressure of Carthage thus removed, Rome was left free to follow the natural expansion of her colonies and her commerce. Wealth and peace are comparative terms; it was in such wealth and peace as the cessation of the long and exhausting war with Carthage brought, that a leisured class began to form itself at Rome, which not only could take a certain interest in Greek literature, but felt in an indistinct way that it was their duty, as representing one of the great civilised powers, to have a substantial national culture of their own.

That this new Latin literature must be based on that of Greece, went without saying; it was almost equally inevitable that its earliest forms should be in the shape of translations from that body of Greek poetry, epic and dramatic, which had for long established itself through all the Greek-speaking world as a common basis of culture.

Latin literature, though artificial in a fuller sense than that
of some other nations, did not escape the general law of
all literatures, that they must begin by verse before they
can go on to prose.

Up to this date, native Latin poetry had been confined,
so far as we can judge, to hymns and ballads, both of a
rude nature. Alongside of these were the popular festival-
performances, containing the germs of a drama. If the
words of these performances were ever written down (which
is rather more than doubtful), they would help to make
the notion of translating a regular Greek play come more
easily. But the first certain Latin translation was a piece
of work which showed a much greater audacity, and which
in fact, though this did not appear till long afterwards, was
much more far-reaching in its consequences. This was
a translation of the *Odyssey* into Saturnian verse by one
Andronicus, a Greek prisoner of war from Tarentum, who
lived at Rome as a tutor to children of the governing class
during the first Punic War. At the capture of his city, he
had become the slave of one of the distinguished family
of the Livii, and after his manumission was known, according to Roman custom, under the name of Lucius Livius
Andronicus.

The few fragments of his *Odyssey* which survive do not
show any high level of attainment; and it is interesting to
note that this first attempt to create a mould for Latin
poetry went on wrong, or, perhaps it would be truer to say,
on premature lines. From this time henceforth the whole
serious production of Latin poetry for centuries was a
continuous effort to master and adapt Greek structure and
versification; the *Odyssey* of Livius was the first and, with
one notable exception, almost the last sustained attempt
to use the native forms of Italian rhythm towards any
large achievement; this current thereafter sets underground,
and only emerges again at the end of the classical period.
It is a curious and significant fact that the attempt, such

as it was, was made not by a native, but by a naturalised foreigner.

The heroic hexameter was, of course, a metre much harder to reproduce in Latin than the trochaic and iambic metres of the Greek drama, the former of which especially accommodated itself without difficulty to Italian speech. In his dramatic pieces, which included both tragedies and comedies, Andronicus seems to have kept to the Greek measures, and in this he was followed by his successors. Throughout the next two generations the production of dramatic literature was steady and continuous. Gnaeus Naevius, the first native Latin poet of consequence, beginning to produce plays a few years later than Andronicus, continued to write busily till after the end of the second Punic War, and left the Latin drama thoroughly established. Only inconsiderable fragments of his writings survive ; but it is certain that he was a figure of really great distinction. Though not a man of birth himself, he had the skill and courage to match himself against the great house of the Metelli. The Metelli, it is true, won the battle ; Naevius was imprisoned, and finally died in exile ; but he had established literature as a real force in Rome. Aulus Gellius has preserved the splendid and haughty verses which he wrote to be engraved on his own tomb —

> *Immortales mortales si foret fas flere*
> *Flerent divae Camenae Naevium poetam ;*
> *Itaque postquam est Orci traditus thesauro*
> *Obliti sunt Romai loquier lingua Latina.*

The Latin Muses were, indeed, then in the full pride and hope of a vigorous and daring youth. The greater part of Naevius' plays, both in tragedy and comedy, were, it is true, translated or adapted from Greek originals ; but alongside of these, — the *Danae*, the *Iphigenia*, the *Andromache*, which even his masculine genius can hardly have made more than pale reflexes of Euripides — were new creations, "plays of the purple stripe," as they came to be called, where he wakened a tragic note from the legendary or actual history of the Roman race. His *Alimonium Romuli et Remi*, though it may have borrowed much from the kindred Greek legends of Danae or Melanippe, was one of the foundation-stones of a new national literature; in the tragedy of *Clastidium*, the scene was laid in his own days, and the action turned on one of the great victories won by those very Metelli whom, in a single stinging line, he afterwards held up to the ridicule of the nation.

In his advanced years, Naevius took a step of even greater consequence. Turning from tragedy to epic, he did not now, like Andronicus, translate from the Greek, but launched out on the new venture of a Roman epic. The Latin language was not yet ductile enough to catch the cadences of the noble Greek hexameter; and the native Latin Saturnian was the only possible alternative. How far he was successful in giving modulation or harmony to this rather cumbrous and monotonous verse, the few extant fragments of the *Bellum Punicum* hardly enable us to determine; it is certain that it met with a great and continued success, and that, even in Horace's time, it was universally read. The subject was not unhappily chosen: the long struggle between Rome and Carthage had, in the great issues involved, as well as in its abounding dramatic incidents and thrilling fluctuations of fortune, many elements of the heroic, and almost of the superhuman; and in his interweaving of this great pageant of history with the ancient legends of both cities, and his connecting it, through the story of Aeneas, with the war of Troy itself, Naevius showed a constructive power of a very high order. It is, doubtless, possible to make too much of the sweeping statements made in the comments of Macrobius and Servius on the earlier parts of the *Aeneid* — "this passage is all taken from Naevius;" "all this passage is simply conveyed from Naevius' *Punic War*." Yet there is no doubt that

Virgil owed him immense obligations; though in the details
of the war itself we can recognise little in the fragments
beyond the dry and disconnected narrative of the rhyming
chronicler. Naevius laid the foundation of the Roman
epic; he left it at his death — in spite of the despondent
and perhaps jealous criticism which he left as his epitaph —
in the hands of an abler and more illustrious successor.

Quintus Ennius, the first of the great Roman poets, and
a figure of prodigious literary fecundity and versatility, was
born at a small town of Calabria about thirty years later
than Naevius, and, though he served as a young man in the
Roman army, did not obtain the full citizenship till fifteen
years after Naevius' death. For some years previously he
had lived at Rome, under the patronage of the great Scipio
Africanus, busily occupied in keeping up a supply of
translations from the Greek for use on the Roman stage.
The easier circumstances of his later life do not seem to
have in any way diminished his fertility or the care which
he lavished on the practice of his art. He was the first
instance in the Western world of the pure man of letters.
Alongside of his strictly literary production, he occupied
himself diligently with the technique of composition —
grammar, spelling, pronunciation, metre, even an elementary
system of shorthand. Four books of miscellaneous translations from popular Greek authors familiarised the reading
public at Rome with several branches of general literature
hitherto only known to scholars. Following the demand
of the market, he translated comedies, seemingly with
indifferent success. But his permanent fame rested on two
great bodies of work, tragic and epic, in both of which he
far eclipsed his predecessors.

We possess the names, and a considerable body of fragments, of upwards of twenty of his tragedies; the greater
number of the fragments being preserved in the works of
Cicero, who was never tired of reading and quoting him.
As is usual with such quotations, they throw light more on

his mastery of phrase and power of presenting detached thoughts, than on his more strictly dramatic qualities. That mastery of phrase is astonishing. From the silver beauty of the moonlit line from his *Melanippe* —

> *Lumine sic tremulo terra et cava caerula candent,*

to the thunderous oath of Achilles —

> *Per ego deum sublimas subices*
> *Umidas, unde oritur imber sonitu saevo et spiritu*

they give examples of almost the whole range of beauty of which the Latin language is capable. Two quotations may show his manner as a translator. The first is a fragment of question and reply from the splendid prologue to the *Iphigenia at Aulis*, one of the most thrilling and romantic passages in Attic poetry —

> Agam. *Quid nocti' videtur in altisono*
> *Caeli clupeo?*
> Senex. *Temo superat*
> *Cogens sublime etiam atque etiam*
> *Noctis iter.*

What is singular here is not that the mere words are wholly different from those of the original, but that in the apparently random variation Ennius produces exactly the same strange and solemn effect. This is no accident: it is genius. Again, as a specimen of his manner in more ordinary narrative speeches, we may take the prologue to his *Medea*, where the well-known Greek is pretty closely followed —

> *Utinam ne in nemore Pelio securibus*
> *Caesa cecidisset abiegna ad terram trabes,*
> *Neve inde navis inchoandae exordium*
> *Coepisset, quae nunc nominatur nomine*
> *Argo, quia Argivi in ea dilecti viri*

Vecti petebant pellem inauratam arietis
Colchis, imperio regis Peliae, per dolum :
Nam nunquam era errans mea domo ecferret pedem
Medea, animo aegra, amore saevo saucia.

At first reading these lines may seem rather stiff and
ungraceful to ears familiar with the liquid lapse of the
Euripidean iambics; but it is not till after the second or
even the third reading that one becomes aware in them of
a strange and austere beauty of rhythm which is distinctively
Italian. Specially curious and admirable is the use of
elision, in the eighth, for instance, and even more so in the
fifth line, so characteristic alike of ancient and modern
Italy. In Latin poetry Virgil was its last and greatest
master; its gradual disuse in post-Virgilian poetry, like its
absence in the earlier hexameters of Cicero, was fatal to the
music of the verse, and with its reappearance in the early
Italian poetry of the Middle Ages that music once more
returns.

It was in his later years, and after long practice in many
literary forms, that Ennius wrote his great historical epic,
the eighteen books of *Annales*, in which he recorded the
legendary and actual history of the Roman State from the
arrival of Aeneas in Italy down to the events of his own day.
The way here had been shown him by Naevius; but in the
interval, chiefly owing to Ennius' own genius and industry,
the literary capabilities of the language had made a very
great advance. It is uncertain whether Ennius made
any attempt to develop the native metres, which in his predecessor's work were still rude and harsh; if he did, he must
soon have abandoned it. Instead, he threw himself on the
task of moulding the Latin language to the movement of
the splendid Greek hexameter; his success in the enterprise
was so conclusive that the question between the two forms
was never again raised. The *Annales* at once became a
classic; until dislodged by the *Aeneid*, they remained the

foremost and representative Roman poem, and even in the centuries which followed, they continued to be read and admired, and their claim to the first eminence was still supported by many partisans. The sane and lucid judgment of Quintilian recalls them to their true place ; in a felicitous simile he compares them to some sacred grove of aged oaks, which strikes the senses with a solemn awe rather than with the charm of beauty. Cicero, who again and again speaks of Ennius in terms of the highest praise, admits that defect of finish on which the Augustan poets lay strong but not unjustified stress. The noble tribute of Lucretius, " as our Ennius sang in immortal verse, he who first brought down from lovely Helicon a garland of evergreen leaf to sound and shine throughout the nations of Italy," was no less than due from a poet who owed so much to Ennius in manner and versification.

It is not known when the *Annales* were lost ; there are doubtful indications of their existence in the earlier Middle Ages. The extant fragments, though they amount only to a few hundred lines, are sufficient to give a clear idea of the poet's style and versification, and of the remarkable breadth and sagacity which made the poem a storehouse of civil wisdom for the more cultured members of the ruling classes at Rome, no less than a treasury of rhythm and phrase for the poets. In the famous single lines like —

> *Non cauponantes bellum sed belligerantes,*

or —

> *Quem nemo ferro potuit superare nec auro,*

or —

> *Ille vir haud magna cum re sed plenu' fidei,*

or the great —

> *Moribus antiquis res stat Romana virisque*

Ennius expressed, with even greater point and weight than Virgil himself, the haughty virtue, the keen and

narrow political instinct, by which the small and struggling
mid-Italian town grew to be arbitress of the world ; not
Lucretius with his vast and melancholy outlook over a
world where patriotism did not exist for the philosopher,
not Virgil with his deep and charmed broodings over the
mystery and beauty of life and death, struck the Roman
note so exclusively and so certainly.

The success of the Latin epic in Ennius' hands was
indeed for the period so complete that it left no room for
further development ; for the next hundred years the *Annales*
remained not only the unique, but the satisfying achievement
in this kind of poetry, and it was only when a new wave of
Greek influence had brought with it a higher and more
refined standard of literary culture, that fresh progress could
be attained or desired. It was not so with tragedy. So
long as the stage demanded fresh material, it continued to
be supplied, and the supply only ceased when, as had
happened even in Greece, the acted drama dwindled away
before the gaudier methods of the music-hall. Marcus
Pacuvius, the nephew of Ennius, wrote plays for the thirty
years after his uncle's death, which had an even greater
vogue ; he is placed by Cicero at the head of Roman
tragedians. The plays have all perished, and even the
fragments are lamentably few ; we can still trace in them,
however, the copiousness of fancy and richness of phrase
which was marked as his distinctive quality by the great
critic Varro. Only one Roman play (on Lucius Aemilius
Paulus, the conqueror of Pydna *) is mentioned among his
pieces ; and this, though perhaps accidental, may indicate
that tragedy had not really pushed its roots deep enough
at Rome, and was destined to an early decay. Inexhaustible
as is the life and beauty of the old Greek mythology, it was

* One of the great speeches in this play was probably made use of
by Livy in his account of the address of Paulus to the people after his
triumph in 167 B.C., which has again been turned into noble tragic
verse by Fitzgerald, *Literary Remains*, vol. ii. p. 483.

impossible that a Roman audience should be content to
listen for age after age to the stories of Atalanta and
Antiope, Pentheus and Orestes, while they had a new
national life and overwhelming native interests of their
own. The Greek tragedy tended more and more to
become the merely literary survival that it was in France
under Louis Quatorze, that it has been in our own day
in the hands of Mr. Arnold or Mr. Swinburne. But one
more poet of remarkable genius carries on its history into
the next age.

Lucius Accius of Pisaurum produced one of his early
plays in the year 140 B.C., on the same occasion when one
of his latest was produced by Pacuvius, then an old man of
eighty. Accius reached a like age himself; Cicero as a
young man knew him well, and used to relate incidents of
the aged poet's earlier life which he had heard from his own
lips. For the greater part of the fifty years which include
Sulla and the Gracchi, Accius was the recognised literary
master at Rome, president of the college of poets which
held its meetings in the temple of Minerva on the Aventine,
and associating on terms of full equality with the most
distinguished statesman. A doubtful tradition mentions
him as having also written an epic, or at least a narrative
poem, called *Annales*, like that of Ennius; but this in all
likelihood is a distorted reflection of the fact that he
handed down and developed the great literary tradition left
by his predecessor. The volume of his dramatic work was
very great; the titles are preserved of no less than forty-five
tragedies. In general estimation he brought Roman tragedy
to its highest point. The fragments show a grace and
fancy which we can hardly trace in the earlier tragedians.

Accius was the last, as he seems to have been the
greatest, of his race. Tragedy indeed continued, as we
shall see, to be written and even to be acted. The literary
men of the Ciceronian and Augustan age published their
plays as a matter of course; Varius was coupled by his

contemporaries with Virgil and Horace ; and the lost *Medea* of Ovid, like the never-finished *Ajax* of Augustus, would be at the least a highly interesting literary document. But the new age found fresh poetical forms into which it could put its best thought and art ; while a blow was struck directly at the roots of tragedy by the new invention, in the hands of Cicero and his contemporaries, of a grave, impassioned, and stately prose.

II.

GREAT as was the place occupied in the culture of the Greek world by Homer and the Attic tragedians, the Middle and New Comedy, as they culminated in Menander, exercised an even wider and more pervasive influence. A vast gap lay between the third and fifth centuries before Christ. Aeschylus, and even Sophocles, had become ancient literature in the age immediately following their own. Euripides, indeed, continued for centuries after his death to be a vital force of immense moment; but this force he owed to the qualities in him that make his tragedy transgress the formal limits of the art, to pass into the wider sphere of the human comedy, with its tears and laughter, its sentiment and passions. From him to Menander is in truth but a step; but this step was of such importance that it was the comedian who became the Shakespeare of Greece. *Omnem vitae imaginem expressit* are the words deliberately used of him by the greatest of Roman critics.

When, therefore, the impulse towards a national literature began to be felt at Rome, comedy took its place side by side with tragedy and epic as part of the Greek secret that had to be studied and mastered; and this came the more naturally that a sort of comedy in rude but definite forms was already native and familiar. Dramatic improvisations were, from an immemorial antiquity, a regular feature of

14

Italian festivals. They were classed under different heads, which cannot be sharply distinguished. The *Satura* seems to have been peculiarly Latin; probably it did not differ deeply or essentially from the two other leading types that arose north and south of Latium, and were named from the little country towns of Fescennium in Etruria, and Atella in Campania. But these rude performances hardly rose to the rank of literature; and here, as elsewhere, the first literary standard was set by laborious translations from the Greek.

We find, accordingly, that the earlier masters—Andronicus, Naevius, Ennius—all wrote comedies as well as tragedies, of the type known as *palliata*, or "dressed in the Greek mantle," that is to say, freely translated or adapted from Greek originals. After Ennius, this still continued to be the more usual type; but the development of technical skill now results in two important changes. The writers of comedy become, on the whole and broadly speaking, distinct from the writers of tragedy; and alongside of the *palliata* springs up the *togata*, or comedy of Italian dress, persons, and manners.

As this latter form of Latin comedy has perished, with the exception of trifling fragments, it may be dismissed here in few words. Its life was comprised in less than a century. Titinius, the first of the writers of the *fabula togata* of whom we have any certain information, was a contemporary of Terence and the younger Scipio; a string of names, which are names and nothing more, carries us down to the latest and most celebrated of the list, Lucius Afranius. His middle-class comedies achieved a large and a long-continued popularity; we hear of performances of them being given even a hundred years after his death, and Horace speaks with gentle sarcasm of the enthusiasts who put him on a level with Menander. With his contemporary Quinctius Atta (who died B.C. 77, in the year of the abortive revolution after the death of Sulla), he owed much of his success to the admirable acting of Roscius, who created a stage tradition that lasted long after his own time. To the mass of the people, comedy (though it did not err in the direction of over-refinement) seemed tame by comparison with the shows and pageants showered on them by the ruling class as the price of their suffrages. As in other ages and countries, fashionable society followed the mob. The young man about town, so familiar to us from the brilliant sketches of Ovid, accompanies his mistress, not to comedies of manners, but to the more exciting spectacles of flesh and blood offered by the ballet-dancers and the gladiators. Thus the small class who occupied themselves with literature had little counteracting influence pressed on them to keep them from the fatal habit of perpetually copying from the Greek ; and adaptations from the Attic New Comedy, which had been inevitable and proper enough as the earlier essays of a tentative dramatic art, remained the staple of an art which thus cut itself definitely away from nature.

That we possess, in a fairly complete form, the works of two of the most celebrated of these playwrights, and of their many contemporaries and successors nothing but trifling fragments, is due to a chance or a series of chances which we cannot follow, and from which we must not draw too precise conclusions. Plautus was the earliest, and apparently the most voluminous, of the writers who devoted themselves wholly to comedy. Between him and Terence a generation intervenes, filled by another comedian, Caecilius, whose works were said to unite much of the special excellences of both ; while after the death of Terence his work was continued on the same lines by Turpilius and others, and dwindled away little by little into the early Empire. But there can be no doubt that Plautus and Terence fully represent the strength and weakness of the Latin *palliata*. Together with the eleven plays of Aristophanes, they have been in fact, since the beginning of the Middle Ages, the sole representatives of ancient, and the sole models of modern comedy.

Titus Maccius Plautus was born of poor parents, in the little Umbrian town of Sarsina, in the year 254 B.C., thus falling midway in age between Naevius and Ennius. Somehow or other he drifted to the capital, to find employment as a stage-carpenter. He alternated his playwriting with the hardest manual drudgery; and though the inexhaustible animal spirits which show themselves in his writing explain how he was able to combine extraordinary literary fertility with a life of difficulty and poverty, it must remain a mystery how and when he picked up his education, and his surprising mastery of the Latin language both in metre and diction. Of the one hundred and thirty comedies attributed to him, two-thirds were rejected as spurious by Varro, and only twenty-one ranked as certainly genuine. These last are extant, with the exception of one, called *The Carpet-Bag*, which was lost in the Middle Ages; some of them, however, exist, and probably existed in Varro's time, only in abridged or mutilated stage copies.

The constructive power shown in these pieces is, of course, less that of Plautus himself than of his Greek originals, Philemon, Diphilus, and Menander. But we do not want modern instances to assure us that, in adapting a play from one language to another, merely to keep the plot unimpaired implies more than ordinary qualities of skill or conscientiousness. When Plautus is at his best — in the *Aulularia Bacchides*, or *Rudens*, and most notably in the *Captivi* — he has seldom been improved upon either in the interest of his action or in the copiousness and vivacity of his dialogue.

Over and above his easy mastery of language, Plautus has a further claim to distinction in the wide range of his manner. Whether he ever went beyond the New Comedy of Athens for his originals, is uncertain; but within it he ranges freely over the whole field, and the twenty extant

plays include specimens of almost every kind of play to
which the name of comedy can be extended. The first
on the list, the famous *Amphitruo*, is the only surviving
specimen of the burlesque. The Greeks called this kind of
piece ἱλαροτραγῳδία — a term for which *tragédie-bouffe* would
be the nearest modern equivalent; *tragico-comoedia* is the
name by which Plautus himself describes it in the prologue.
The *Amphitruo* remains, even now, one of the most masterly
specimens of this kind. The version of Molière, in which
he did little by way of improvement on his original, has
given it fresh currency as a classic; but the French play
gives but an imperfect idea of the spirit and flexibility of
the dialogue in Plautus' hands.

Of a very different type is the piece which comes next the
Amphrituo in acknowledged excellence, the *Captivi*. It is
a comedy of sentiment, without female characters, and
therefore without the coarseness which (as one is forced to
say with regret) disfigures some of the other plays. The
development of the plot has won high praise from all critics,
and justifies the boast of the epilogue, *Huiusmodi paucas
poetae reperiunt comoedias*. But the praise which the author
gives to his own piece —

> *Non pertractate facta est neque item ut ceterae,*
> *Neque spurcidici insunt versus immemorabiles,*
> *Hic neque periurus leno est nec meretrix mala*
> *Neque miles gloriosus —*

is really a severe condemnation of two other groups of
Plautine plays. The *Casina* and the *Truculentus* (the
latter, as we know from Cicero, a special favourite with its
author) are studies in pornography which only the unflagging
animal spirits of the poet can redeem from being disgust-
ing; and the *Asinaria, Curculio*, and *Miles Gloriosus* are
broad farces with the thinnest thread of plot. The last
depends wholly on the somewhat forced and exaggerated
character of the title-rôle; as the *Pseudolus*, a piece with

rather more substance, does mainly on its *periurus leno*,
Ballio, a character who reminds one of Falstaff in his entire
shamelessness and inexhaustible vocabulary.

A different vein, the domestic comedy of middle-class
life, is opened in one of the most quietly successful of
his pieces, the *Trinummus*, or *Threepenny-bit*. In spite of
all the characters being rather fatiguingly virtuous in their
sentiments, it is full of liveliness, and not without graceful-
ness and charm. After the riotous scenes of the lighter
plays, it is something of a comfort to return to the good
sense and good feeling of respectable people. It forms an
interesting contrast to the *Bacchides*, a play which returns
to the world of the bawd and harlot, but with a brilliance
of intrigue and execution that makes it rank high among
comedies.

Two other plays are remarkable from the fact that,
though neither in construction nor in workmanship do they
rise beyond mediocrity, the leading motive of the plot in
one case and the principal character in the other are inventions of unusual felicity. The Greek original of both
is unknown; but to it, no doubt, rather than to Plautus
himself, we are bound to ascribe the credit of the *Aulularia*
and *Menaechmi*. The *Aulularia*, or *Pot of Gold*, a commonplace story of middle-class life, is a mere framework for the
portrait of the old miser, Euclio — in itself a sketch full of
life and brilliance, and still more famous as the original
of Molière's Harpagon, which is closely studied from it.
The *Menaechmi*, or *Comedy of Errors*, without any great
ingenuity of plot or distinction of character, rests securely
on the inexhaustible opportunities of humour opened up
by the happy invention of the twin-brothers who had lost
sight of one another from early childhood, and the con-
fusions that arise when they both find themselves in the
same town.

There is yet one more of the Plautine comedies which
deserves special notice, as conceived in a different vein

and worked out in a different tone from all those already
mentioned — the charming romantic comedy called *Rudens,*
or *The Cable,* though a more fitting name for it would be
The Tempest. Though not pitched in the sentimental key
of the *Captivi,* it has a higher, and, in Latin literature,
a rarer, note. By a happy chance, perhaps, rather than
from any unwonted effort of skill, this translation of the
play of Diphilus has brought with it something of the unique
and unmistakeable Greek atmosphere — the atmosphere of
the *Odyssey,* of the fisher-idyl of Theocritus, of the hundreds
of little poems in the Greek Anthology that bear clinging
about their verses the faint murmur and odour of the sea.
The scene is laid near Cyrene, on the strange rich African
coast; the prologue is spoken, not by a character in the
piece, nor by a decently clothed abstraction like the figures
of Luxury and Poverty which speak the prologue of the
Trinummus, but by the star Arcturus, watcher and tempest-
bearer.

> *Qui gentes omnes, mariaque et terras movet,*
> *Eius sum civis civitate caelitum;*
> *Ita sum ut videtis, splendens stella candida,*
> *Signum quod semper tempore exoritur suo*
> *Hic atque in caelo; nomen Arcturo est mihi.*
> *Noctu sum in caelo clarus atque inter deos;*
> *Inter mortales ambulo interdius.*

The romantic note struck in these opening lines is continued throughout the comedy, in which, by little touches
here and there, the scene is kept constantly before us of
the rocky shore in the strong brilliant sun after the storm
of the night, the temple with its kindly priestess, and the
red-tiled country-house by the reeds of the lagoon, with the
solitary pastures behind it dotted over with fennel. Now
and again one is reminded of the *Winter's Tale,* with fisher-
men instead of shepherds for the subordinate characters;

more frequently of a play which, indeed, has borrowed a
good deal from this, *Pericles Prince of Tyre.*

The remainder of the Plautine plays may be dismissed
with scant notice. They comprise three variations on the
theme which, to modern taste, has become so excessively
tedious, of the *Fourberies de Scapin* — the *Epidicus, Mostel-
laria,* and *Persa;* the *Poenulus,* a dull play, which owes its
only interest to the passages in it written in the Carthaginian
language, which offer a tempting field for the conjectures
of the philologist; two more, the *Mercator* and *Stichus,* of
confused plot and insipid dialogue ; and a mutilated fragment of the *Cistellaria,* or *Travelling-Trunk,* which would
not have been missed had it shared the fate of the *Carpet-
Bag.*

The humour of one age is often mere weariness to the
next; and farcical comedy is, of all the forms of literature,
perhaps the least adapted for permanence. It would be
affectation to claim that Plautus is nowadays widely read
outside of the inner circle of scholars ; and there he is read
almost wholly on account of his unusual fertility and interest
as a field of linguistic study. Yet he must always remain
one of the great outstanding influences in literary history.
The strange fate which has left nothing but inconsiderable
fragments out of the immense volume of the later Athenian
Comedy, raised Plautus to a position co-ordinate with that
of Aristophanes as a model for the reviving literature of
modern Europe ; for such part of that literature (by much
the more important) as did not go beyond Latin for its
inspiration, Plautus was a source of unique and capital
value, in his own branch of literature equivalent to Cicero
or Virgil in theirs.

Plautus outlived the second Punic War, during which,
as we gather from prefaces and allusions, a number of the
extant plays were produced. Soon after the final collapse
of the Carthaginian power at Zama, a child was born
at Carthage, who, a few years later, in the course of

unexplained vicissitudes, reached Rome as a boy-slave, and
passed there into the possession of a rich and educated
senator, Terentius Lucanus. The boy showed some unusual turn for books; he was educated and manumitted
by his master, and took from him the name of Publius
Terentius the African. A small literary circle of the Roman
aristocracy — men too high in rank to need to be careful
what company they kept — admitted young Terence to their
intimate companionship; and soon he was widely known as
making a third in the friendship of Gaius Laelius with the
first citizen of the Republic, the younger Scipio Africanus.
This society, an informal academy of letters, devoted all its
energies to the purification and improvement of the Latin
language. The rough drafts of the Terentian comedies were
read out to them, and the language and style criticised in
minute detail; gossip even said that they were largely written
by Scipio's own hand, and Terence himself, as is not surprising, never took pains to deny the rumour. Six plays
had been subjected to this elaborate correction and produced on the Roman stage, when Terence undertook a
prolonged visit to Greece for the purpose of further study.
He died of fever the next year — by one account, at a village
in Arcadia; by another, when on his voyage home. The
six comedies had already taken the place which they have
ever since retained as Latin classics.

The Terentian comedy is in a way the turning-point of
Roman literature. Plautus and Ennius, however largely
they drew from Greek originals, threw into all their work
a manner and a spirit which were essentially those of a
new literature in the full tide of growth. The imitation of
Greek models was a means, not an end; in both poets the
Greek manner is continually abandoned for essays into a
new manner of their own, and they relapse upon it when
their imperfectly mastered powers of invention or expression give way under them. In the circle of Terence the
fatal doctrine was originated that the Greek manner was

an end in itself, and that the road to perfection lay, not in developing any original qualities, but in reproducing with laborious fidelity the accents of another language and civilisation. Nature took a swift and certain revenge. Correctness of sentiment and smooth elegance of diction became the standards of excellence ; and Latin literature, still mainly confined to the governing class and their dependents, was struck at the root (the word is used of Terence himself by Varro) with the fatal disease of mediocrity.

But in Terence himself (as in Addison among English writers) this mediocrity is, indeed, golden — a mediocrity full of grace and charm. The unruffled smoothness of diction, the exquisite purity of language, are qualities admirable in themselves, and are accompanied by other striking merits ; not, indeed, by dramatic force or constructive power, but by careful and delicate portraiture of character, and by an urbanity (to use a Latin word which expresses a peculiarly Latin quality) to which the world owes a deep debt for having set a fashion. In some curious lines preserved by Suetonius, Julius Caesar expresses a criticism, which we shall find it hard to improve, on the "halved Menander," to whom his own fastidious purity in the use of language, no less than his tact and courtesy as a man of the world, attracted him strongly, while not blinding him to the weakness and flaccidity of the Terentian drama. Its effect on contemporary men of letters was immediate and irresistible. A story is told, bearing all the marks of truth, of the young poet when he submitted his first play, *The Maid of Andros*, for the approval of the Commissioners of Public Works, who were responsible for the production of plays at the civic festivals. He was ordered to read it aloud to Caecilius, who, since the death of Plautus, had been supreme without a rival on the comic stage. Terence presented himself modestly while Caecilius was at supper, and was carelessly told to sit down on a stool

in the dining-room, and begin. He had not read beyond
a few verses when Caecilius stopped him, and made him
take a seat at table. After supper was over, he heard
his guest's play out with unbounded and unqualified
admiration.

But this admiration of the literary class did not make the
refined conventional art of Terence successful for its immediate purposes on the stage: he was caviare to the
general. Five of the six plays were produced at the
spring festival of the Mother of the Gods — an occasion
when the theatre had not to face the competition of the
circus; yet even then it was only by immense efforts on
the part of the management that they succeeded in attracting an audience. *The Mother-in-Law* (not, it is true, a play
which shows the author at his best) was twice produced as
a dead failure. The third time it was pulled through by
extraordinary efforts on the part of the acting-manager,
Ambivius Turpio. The prologue written by Terence for
this third performance is one of the most curious literary
documents of the time. He is too angry to extenuate the
repeated failure of his play. If we believe him, it fell dead
the first time because "that fool, the public," were all
excitement over an exhibition on the tight-rope which was
to follow the play; at the second representation only one
act had been gone through, when a rumour spread that
"there were going to be gladiators" elsewhere, and in five
minutes the theatre was empty.

The Terentian prologues (they are attached to all his
plays) are indeed all very interesting from the light they
throw on the character of the author, as well as on the ideas
and fashions of his age. In all of them there is a certain
hard and acrid purism that cloaks in modest phrases an
immense contempt for all that lies beyond the writer's own
canons of taste. *In hac est pura oratio*, a phrase of the
prologue to *The Self-Tormentor*, is the implied burden of
them all. He is a sort of literary Robespierre; one seems

to catch the premonitory echo of well-known phrases,
"degenerate condition of literary spirit, backsliding on
this hand and on that, I, Terence, alone left incorruptible."
Three times there is a reference to Plautus, and always
with a tone of chilly superiority which is too proud to
break into an open sneer. Yet among these haughty and
frigid manifestoes some felicity of phrase or of sentiment
will suddenly remind us that here, after all, we are dealing
with one of the great formative intelligences of literature;
where, for instance, in the prologue to the lively and witty
comedy of *The Eunuch*, the famous line —

Nullumst iam dictum quod non dictum sit prius —

drops with the same easy negligence as in the opening
dialogue of *The Self-Tormentor*, the immortal —

Homo sum : humani nihil a me alienum puto —

falls from the lips of the old farmer. Congreve alone of
English playwrights has this glittering smoothness, this
inimitable ease ; if we remember what Dryden, in language
too splendid to be insincere, wrote of his young friend, we
may imagine, perhaps, how Caecilius and his circle regarded
Terence. Nor is it hard to believe that, had Terence, like
Congreve, lived into an easy and honoured old age, he
would still have rested his reputation on these productions
of his early youth. Both dramatists had from the first
seen clearly and precisely what they had in view, and had
almost at the first stroke attained it : the very completeness
of the success must in both cases have precluded the dissatisfaction through which fresh advances could alone be
possible.

This, too, is one reason, though certainly not the only
one, why, with the death of Terence, the development of
Latin comedy at once ceased. His successors are mere
shadowy names. Any life that remained in the art took

the channel of the farces which, for a hundred years more, retained a genuine popularity, but which never took rank as literature of serious value. Even this, the *fabula tabernaria*, or comedy of low life, gradually melted away before the continuous competition of the shows which so moved the spleen of Terence — the pantomimists, the jugglers, the gladiators. By this time, too, the literary instinct was beginning to explore fresh channels. Not only was prose becoming year by year more copious and flexible, but the mixed mode, fluctuating between prose and verse, to which the Romans gave the name of satire, was in process of invention. Like the novel as compared with the play at the present time, it offered great and obvious advantages in ease and variety of manipulation, and in the simplicity and inexpensiveness with which, not depending on the stated performances of a public theatre, it could be produced and circulated. But before proceeding to consider this new literary invention more fully, it will be well to pause in order to gather up, as its necessary complement, the general lines on which Latin prose was now developing, whether in response to the influence of Greek models, or in the course of a more native and independent growth.

III.

LAW and government were the two great achievements of the Latin race ; and the two fountain-heads of Latin prose are, on the one hand, the texts of codes and the commentaries of jurists : on the other, the annals of the inner constitution and the external conquests and diplomacy of Rome. The beginnings of both went further back than Latin antiquaries could trace them. Out of the mists of a legendary antiquity two fixed points rise, behind which it is needless or impossible to go. The code known as that of the Twelve Tables, of which large fragments survive in later law-books, was drawn up, according to the accepted chronology, in the year 450 B.C. Sixty years later the sack of Rome by the Gauls led to the destruction of nearly all public and private records, and it was only from this date onwards that such permanent and contemporary registers — the consular *fasti*, the books of the pontifical college, the public collections of engraved laws and treaties — were extant as could afford material for the annalist. That a certain amount of work in the field both of law and history must have been going on at Rome from a very early period, is, of course, obvious ; but it was not till the time of the Punic Wars that anything was produced in either field which could very well be classed as literature.

In history as in poetry, the first steps were timidly made

with the help of Greek models. The oldest and most
important of the early historians, Quintus Fabius Pictor,
the contemporary of Naevius and Ennius, actually wrote in
Greek, though a Latin version of his work certainly existed,
whether executed by himself or some other hand is doubtful,
at an almost contemporary date. Extracts are quoted from
it by the grammarians as specimens of the language of the
period. The scope of his history was broadly the same as
that of the two great contemporary poets. It was a narrative of events starting from the legendary landing of Aeneas
in Italy, becoming more copious as it advanced, and dealing
with the events of the author's own time at great length
and from abundant actual knowledge. The work ended, so
far as can be judged, with the close of the second Punic
War. It long remained the great quarry for subsequent
historians. Polybius undertook his own great work from
dissatisfaction with Pictor's prejudice and inaccuracy ; and
he is one of the chief authorities followed in the earlier
decads of Livy. A younger contemporary of Pictor,
Lucius Cincius Alimentus, who commanded a Roman army
in the war against Hannibal, also used the Greek language
in his annals of his own life and times, and the same appears to be the case with the memoirs of other soldiers
and statesmen of the period. It is only half a century later
that we know certainly of historians who wrote in Latin.
The earliest of them, Lucius Cassius Hemina, composed
his annals in the period between the death of Terence and
the revolution of the Gracchi ; a more distinguished successor, Lucius Calpurnius Piso Frugi, is better known as
one of the leading opponents of the revolution (he was consul in the year of the tribuneship of Tiberius Gracchus)
than as the author of annals which were certainly written
with candour and simplicity, and in a style where the epithets "artless and elegant," used of them by Aulus Gellius,
need not be inconsistent with the more disparaging word
"meagre," with which they are dismissed by Cicero.

History might be written in Greek — as, indeed, throughout the Republican and Imperial times it continued to be
— by any Roman who was sufficiently conversant with that
language, in which models for every style of historical
composition were ready to his hand. In the province of
jurisprudence it was different. Here the Latin race owed
nothing to any foreign influence or example ; and the
development of Roman law pursued a straightforward and
uninterrupted course far beyond the limits of the classical
period, and after Rome itself had ceased to be the seat
even of a divided empire. The earliest juristic writings,
consisting of commentaries on collections of the semi-reli-
gious enactments in which positive law began, are attributed
to the period of the Samnite Wars, long before Rome had
become a great Mediterranean power. About 200 B.C.
two brothers, Publius and Sextus Aelius, both citizens of
consular and censorial rank, published a systematic treatise
called *Tripertita*, which was long afterwards held in reverence as containing the *cunabula iuris*, the cradle out
of which the vast systems of later ages sprang. Fifty years
later, in the circle of the younger Scipio, begins the illustrious line of the Mucii Scaevolae. Three members of this
family, each a distinguished jurist, rose to the consulate in
the stormy half-century between the Gracchi and Sulla.
The last and greatest of the three represented the ideal
Roman more nearly than any other citizen of his time.
The most eloquent of jurists and the most learned of
orators, he was at the same time a brilliant administrator
and a paragon of public and private virtue ; and his murder
at the altar of Vesta, in the Marian proscription, was universally thought the most dreadful event of an age of
horrors. His voluminous and exhaustive treatise on Civil
Law remained a text-book for centuries, and was a foundation for the writings of all later Roman jurists.

The combination of jurisconsult and orator in the younger
Scaevola was somewhat rare ; from an early period the two

professions of jurist and pleader were sharply distinguished, though both were pathways to the highest civic offices. Neither his father nor his cousin (the other two of the triad) was distinguished in oratory; nor were the two great contemporaries of the former, who both published standard works on civil law, Manius Manilius and Marcus Junius Brutus. The highest field for oratory was, of course, in the political, and not in the purely legal, sphere; and the unique Roman constitution, an oligarchy chosen almost wholly by popular suffrage, made the practice of oratory more or less of a necessity to every politician. Well-established tradition ascribed to the greatest statesman of the earlier Republic, Appius Claudius Caecus, the first institution of written oratory. His famous speech in the senate against peace with Pyrrhus was cherished in Cicero's time as one of the most precious literary treasures of Rome. From his time downwards the stream of written oratory flowed, at first in a slender stream, which gathered to a larger volume in the works of the elder Cato.

In the history of the half-century following the war with Hannibal, Cato is certainly the most striking single figure. It is only as a man of letters that he has to be noticed here; and the character of a man of letters was, perhaps, the last in which he would have wished to be remembered or praised. Yet the cynical and indomitable old man, with his rough humour, his narrow statesmanship, his obstinate ultra-conservatism, not only produced a large quantity of writings, but founded and transmitted to posterity a distinct and important body of critical dogma and literary tradition. The influence of Greece had, as we have already seen, begun to permeate the educated classes at Rome through and through. Against this Greek influence, alike in liter-ature and in manners, Cato struggled all his life with the whole force of his powerful intellect and mordant wit; yet it is most characteristic of the man that in his old age he learned Greek himself, and read deeply in the master-

pieces of that Greek literature from which he was too
honest and too intelligent to be able to withhold his
admiration. While much of contemporary literature was
launching itself on the fatal course of imitation of Greek
models, and was forcing the Latin language into the
trammels of alien forms, Cato gave it a powerful impulse
towards a purely native, if a somewhat narrow and harsh
development. The national prose literature, of which he
may fairly be called the founder, was kept up till the decay
of Rome by a large and powerful minority of Latin writers.
What results it might have produced, if allowed unchecked
scope, can only be matter for conjecture; in the main
current of Latin literature the Greek influence was, on the
whole, triumphant; Cato's was the losing side (if one may
so adapt the famous line of Lucan), and the men of genius
took the other.

The speeches of Cato, of which upwards of a hundred
and fifty were extant in Cicero's time, and which the
virtuosi of the age of Hadrian preferred, or professed to
prefer, to Cicero's own, are lost, with the exception of
inconsiderable fragments. The fragments show high oratorical gifts; shrewdness, humour, terse vigour and controlled passion; "somewhat confused and harsh," says a
late but competent Latin critic, "but strong and vivid as
it is possible for oratory to be." We have suffered a
heavier loss in his seven books of *Origines,* the work of his
old age. This may broadly be called an historical work,
but it was history treated in a style of great latitude, the
meagre, disconnected method of the annalists alternating
with digressions into all kinds of subjects — geography,
ethnography, reminiscences of his own travels and experiences, and the politics and social life of his own and
earlier times. It made no attempt to keep up either the
dignity or the continuity of history. His absence of method
made this work, however full of interest, the despair of
later historians : what were they to think, they plaintively

asked, of an author who dismissed whole campaigns without
even giving the names of the generals, while he went into
profuse detail over one of the war-elephants in the Carthaginian army?

The only work of Cato's which has been preserved in its
integrity is that variously known under the titles *De Re
Rustica* or *De Agri Cultura.* It is one of a number of treatises
of a severely didactic nature, which he published on various
subjects — agricultural, sanitary, military, and legal. This
treatise was primarily written for a friend who owned and
cultivated farms in Campania. It consists of a series of
terse and pointed directions following one on another,
with no attempt at style or literary artifice, but full of a
hard sagacity, and with occasional flashes of dry humour,
which suggest that Cato would have found a not wholly
uncongenial spirit in President Lincoln. A brief extract
from one of the earlier chapters is not without interest,
both as showing the practical Latin style, and as giving the
prose groundwork of Virgil's stately and beautiful embroidery
in the *Georgics.*

*Opera omnia mature conficias face. Nam res rustica sic
est; si unam rem sero feceris, omnia opera sero facies. Stra-
menta si deerunt frondem iligneam legito; eam substernito
ovibus bubusque. Sterquilinium magnum stude ut habeas.
Stercus sedulo conserva, cum exportabis spargito et commin-
uito; per autumnum evehito. Circum oleas autumnitate
ablaqueato et stercus addito. Frondem populneam, ulmeam,
querneam caedito, per tempus eam condito, non peraridam,
pabulum ovibus. Item foenum cordum, sicilamenta de prato;
ea arida condito. Post imbrem autumni rapinam, pabulum,
lupinumque serito.*

To the Virgilian student, every sentence here is full of
reminiscences.

In his partial yielding, towards the end of a long and
uncompromising life, to the rising tide of Greek influence,
Cato was probably moved to a large degree by his personal

admiration for the younger Scipio, whom he hailed as the single great personality among younger statesmen, and to whom he paid (strangely enough, in a line quoted from Homer) what is probably the most splendid compliment ever paid by one statesman to another. Scipio was the centre of a school which included nearly the whole literary impulse of his time. He was himself a distinguished orator and a fine scholar; after the conquest of Perseus, the royal library was the share of the spoils of Macedonia which he chose for himself, and bequeathed to his family. His celebrated friend, Gaius Laelius, known in Rome as " the Wise," was not only an orator, but a philosopher, or deeply read, at all events, in the philosophy of Greece. Another member of the circle, Lucius Furius Philus, initiated that connection of Roman law with the Stoic philosophy which continued ever after to be so intimate and so far-reaching. In this circle, too, Roman history began to be written in Latin. Cassius Hemina and Lucius Calpurnius Piso have be   already mentioned; more intimately connected with Scipio are Gaius Fannius, the son-in-law of Laelius, and Lucius Caelius Antipater, who reached, both in lucid and copious diction and in impartiality and research, a higher level than Roman history had yet attained. Literary culture became part of the ordinary equipment of a states-man; a crowd of Greek teachers, foremost among them the eminent philosopher, afterwards Master of the Portico, Panaetius of Rhodes, spread among the Roman upper classes the refining and illuminating influence of Greek ideas and Attic style.

Meanwhile, in this Scipionic circle, a new figure had appeared of great originality and force, the founder of a kind of literature which, with justifiable pride, the Romans claimed as wholly native and original. Gaius Lucilius was a member of a wealthy equestrian family, and thus could associate on equal terms with the aristocracy, while he was removed from the necessity, which members of the great senatorian houses could hardly avoid, of giving the best of their time and strength to political and administrative duties. After Terence, he is the most distinguished and the most important in his literary influence among the friends of Scipio. The form of literature which he invented and popularised, that of familiar poetry, was one which proved singularly suited to the Latin genius. He speaks of his own works under the name of *Sermones*, "talks " — a name which was retained by his great successor, Horace ; but the peculiar combination of metrical form with wide range of subject and the pedestrian style of ordinary prose, received in popular usage the name *Satura,* or " mixture." The word had, in earlier times, been used of the irregular stage performances, including songs, stories, and semi-dramatic interludes, which formed the repertory of strolling artists at popular festivals. The extension of the name to the verse of Lucilius indicates that written literature was now rising to equal importance and popularity with the spoken word.

Horace comments, not without severity, on the profuse and careless production of Lucilius. Of the thirty books of his *Satires,* few fragments of any length survive ; much, probably the greater part of them, would, if extant, long have lost its interest. But the loss of the bulk of his work is a matter of sincere regret, because it undoubtedly gave a vivid and detailed picture of the social life and the current interests of the time, such as the *Satires* of Horace give of Rome in the Augustan age. His criticisms on the public men of his day were outspoken and unsparing ; nor had he more reverence for established reputations in poetry than in public life. A great deal of his work consisted in descriptions of eating and drinking ; much, also, in lively accounts of his own travels and adventures, or those of his friends. One book of the *Satires* was occupied with an account of Scipio's famous mission to the East, in which he visited the courts of Egypt and Asia, attended by a retinue of only

five servants, but armed with the full power of the terrible
Republic. Another imitated by Horace in his story of the
journey to Brundusium, detailed the petty adventures, the
talk and laughter by roads and at inns, of an excursion of
his own through Campania and Bruttium to the Sicilian
straits. Many of the fragments deal with the literary con-
troversies of the time, going down even to the minutiae of
spelling and grammar; many more show the beginnings
of that translation into the language of common life of the
precepts of the Greek schools, which was consummated for
the world by the poets and prose-writers of the following
century. But, above all, the *Satires* of Lucilius were in the
fullest sense of the word an autobiography. The famous
description of Horace, made yet more famous for English
readers by the exquisite aptness with which Boswell placed
it on the title-page of his *Life of Johnson* —

> *Quo fit ut omnis*
> *Votiva pateat veluti descripta tabella*
> *Vita senis* —

expresses the true greatness of Lucilius. He invented a
literary method which, without being great, yields to no
other in interest and even in charm, and which, for its perfection, requires a rare and refined genius. Not Horace
only, nor all the satirists after Horace, but Montaigne and
Pepys also, belong to the school of Lucilius.

Such was the circle of the younger Scipio, formed in
the happy years — as they seemed to the backward gaze of
the succeeding generation — between the establishment of
Roman supremacy at the battle of Pydna, and the revolutionary movement of Tiberius Gracchus. Fifty years of
stormy turbulence followed, culminating in the Social War
and the reign of terror under Marius and Cinna, and finally
stilled in seas of blood by the counter-revolution of Sulla.
This is the period which separates the Scipionic from the

Ciceronian age. It was naturally, except in the single province of political oratory, not one of great literary fertility; and a brief indication of the most notable authors of the period, and of the lines on which Roman literature mainly continued to advance during it, is all that is demanded or possible here.

In oratory, this period by general consent represented the golden age of Latin achievement. The eloquence of both the Gracchi was their great political weapon; that of Gaius was the most powerful in exciting feeling that had ever been known; his death was mourned, even by fierce political opponents, as a heavy loss to Latin literature. But in the next generation, the literary perfection of oratory was carried to an even higher point by Marcus Antonius and Lucius Licinius Crassus. Both attained the highest honours that the Republic had to bestow. By a happy chance, their styles were exactly complementary to one another; to hear both in one day was the highest intellectual entertainment which Rome afforded. By this time the rules of oratory were carefully studied and reduced to scientific treatises. One of these, the work of an otherwise unknown Cornificius, is still extant. It owes its preservation to an erroneous tradition which ascribed it to the pen of Cicero, and regarded it as an earlier draft of his treatise *De Inventione.* That treatise goes over much the same ground, and is often verbally copied from the earlier work, of which it was, in fact, a new edition revised and largely rewritten.

Latin history during this period made considerable progress. It was a common practice among statesmen to write memoirs of their own life and times; among others of less note, Sulla the dictator left at his death twenty-two books of *Commentarii Rerum Gestarum*, which were afterwards published by his secretary. In regular history the most important name is that of Quintus Claudius Quadrigarius. His work differed from those of the earlier annalists

in passing over the legendary period, and beginning with
the earliest authentic documents; in research and critical
judgment it reached a point only excelled by Sallust.   His
style was formed on that of older annalists, and is therefore
somewhat archaic for the period.   Considerable fragments,
including the well-known description of the single combat
in 361 B.C. between Titus Manlius Torquatus and the
Gallic chief, survive in quotations by Aulus Gellius and the
archaists of the later Empire.   More voluminous but less
valuable than the *Annals* of Claudius were those of his
contemporary, Valerius Antias, which formed the main
groundwork for the earlier books of Livy, and were largely
used by him even for later periods, when more trustworthy authorities were available.   Other historians of this
period, Sisenna and Macer, soon fell into neglect — the
former as too archaic, the latter as too diffuse and rhetorical,
for literary permanence.

Somewhat apart from the historical writers stand the
antiquarians, who wrote during this period in large numbers,
and whose treatises filled the library from which, in the
age of Cicero, Varro compiled his monumental works.   As
numerous probably were the writers of the school of Cato,
on husbandry, domestic economy, and other practical
subjects, and the grammarians and philologists, whose
works formed two other large sections in Varro's library.
On all sides prose was full of life and growth; the complete
literary perfection of the age of Cicero, Caesar, and Sallust
might already be foreseen as within the grasp of the near
future.

Latin poetry, meanwhile, hung in the balance.   The first
great wave of the Greek impulse had exhausted itself in
Ennius and the later tragedians.   Prose had so developed
that the poetical form was no longer a necessity for the
expression of ideas, as it had been in the palmy days of
Latin tragedy.   The poetry of the future must be, so to
speak, poetry for its own sake, until some new tradition

were formed which should make certain metrical forms
once more the recognised and traditional vehicle for certain
kinds of literary expression.   In the blank of poetry we
may note a translation of the *Iliad* into hexameters by one
Gnaeus Matius, and the earliest known attempts at imitation
of the forms of Greek lyrical verse by an equally obscure
Laevius Melissus, as dim premonitions of the new growth
which Latin poetry was feeling after ; but neither these,
nor the literary tragedies which still were occasionally produced by a survival of the fashions of an earlier age, are
of any account for their own sake.   Prose and poetry stood
at the two opposite poles of their cycle ; and thus it is
that, while the poets and prose-writers of the Ciceronian
age are equally imperishable in fame, the latter but represent the culmination of a broad and harmonious development, while of the former, amidst but apart from the
beginnings of a new literary era, there shine, splendid like
stars out of the darkness, the two immortal lights of
Lucretius and Catullus.

IV.

LUCRETIUS.

THE age of Cicero, a term familiar to all readers as indi-
cating one of the culminating periods of literary history,
while its central and later years are accurately fixed, may
be dated in its commencement from varying limits.   Cicero
was born in 106 B.C., the year of the final conquest of
Jugurtha, and the year before the terrible Cimbrian disaster
at Orange : he perished in the proscription of the triumvirate in December, 43 B.C.   His first appearance in public
life was during the dictatorship of Sulla ; and either from
this date, or from one ten years later when the Sullan constitution was re-established in a modified form by Pompeius
and Crassus in their first consulate, the Ciceronian age
extends over a space which approximates in the one case
to thirty, in the other to forty years.   No period in ancient,
and few in comparatively modern history are so pregnant
with interest or so fully and intimately known.   From the
comparative obscurity of the earlier age we pass into a
full blaze of daylight.   It is hardly an exaggeration to say
that the Rome of Cicero is as familiar to modern English
readers as the London of Queen Anne, to readers in
modern France as the Paris of Louis Quatorze.   We can
still follow with unabated interest the daily fluctuations of
its politics, the current gossip and scandal of its society,
the passing fashions of domestic life as revealed in private

correspondence or the disclosures of the law courts. Yet in the very centre of this brilliantly lighted world, one of its most remarkable figures is veiled in almost complete darkness. The great poem of Lucretius, *On the Nature of Things,* though it not only revealed a profound and extraordinary genius, but marked an entirely new technical level in Latin poetry, stole into the world all but unnoticed; and of its author's life, though a pure Roman of one of the great governing families, only one or two doubtful and isolated facts could be recovered by the curiosity of later commentators. The single sentence in St. Jerome's *Chronicle* which practically sums up the whole of our information runs as follows, under the year 94 B.C. : —

Titus Lucretius poeta nascitur, postea amatorio poculo in furorem versus cum aliquot libros per intervalla insaniae conscripsisset quos postea Cicero emendavit, propria se manu interfecit anno aetatis xliiii.

Brief and straightforward as the sentence is, every clause in it has given rise to volumes of controversy. Was Lucretius born in the year named, or is another tradition correct, which, connecting his death with a particular event in the youth of Virgil, makes him either be born a few years earlier or die a few years younger? Did he ever, whether from a poisonous philtre or otherwise, lose his reason? and can a poem which ranks among the great masterpieces of genius have been built up into its stately fabric — for this is not a question of brief lyrics like those of Smart or Cowper — in the lucid intervals of insanity? Did Cicero have anything to do with the editing of the unfinished poem? If so, which Cicero — Marcus or Quintus? and why, in either case, is there no record of the fact in their correspondence, or in any writing of the period? All these questions are probably insoluble, and the notice of Jerome leaves the whole life and personality of the poet still completely hidden. Yet we have little or nothing else to go upon. There is one brief and casual allusion in one of Cicero's letters of the year 54 B.C. : yet it speaks of " poems," not the single great poem which we know ; and most editors agree that the text of the passage is corrupt, and must be amended by the insertion of a *non*, though they differ on the important detail of the particular clause in which it should be inserted. That the earlier Augustan poets should leave their great predecessor completely unnoticed is less remarkable; for it may be taken as merely a part of that curious conspiracy of silence regarding the writers of the Ciceronian age which, whether under political pressure or not, they all adopted. Even Ovid, never ungenerous though not always discriminating in his praise, dismisses him in a list of Latin poets with a single couplet of vague eulogy. In the reactionary circles of the Empire, Lucretius found recognition ; but the critics who, according to Tacitus, ranked him above Virgil may be reasonably suspected of doing so more from caprice than from rational conviction. Had the poem itself perished (and all the extant manuscripts are copies of a single original), no one would have thought that such a preference could be anything but a piece of antiquarian pedantry, like the revival, in the same period, of the plays of the early tragedians. But the fortunate and slender chance which has preserved it shows that their opinion, whether right or wrong, is one which at all events is neither absurd nor unarguable. For in the *De Rerum Natura* we are brought face to face not only with an extraordinary literary achievement, but with a mind whose profound and brilliant genius has only of late years, and with the modern advance of physical and historical science, been adequately recognised.

The earliest Greek impulse in Latin poetry had long been exhausted ; and the fashion among the new generation was to admire and study beyond all else the Greek poets of the decadence, who are generally, and without any substantial injustice, lumped together by the name of the Alexandrian school. The common quality in all this poetry was its great learning, and its remoteness from nature. It was poetry written in a library; it viewed the world through a highly coloured medium of literary and artistic tradition. The laborious perfectness of execution which the taste of the time demanded was, as a rule, lavished on little subjects, patient carvings in ivory. One branch of the Alexandrian school which was largely followed was that of the didactic poets — Aratus, Nicander, Euphorion, and a host of others less celebrated. Cicero, in mature life, speaks with some contempt of the taste for Euphorion among his contemporaries. But he had himself, as a young man, followed the fashion, and translated the *Phaenomena* of Aratus into wonderfully polished and melodious hexameter verse.

Not unaffected by this fashion of the day, but turning from it to older and nobler models,— Homer and Empedocles in Greek, Ennius in Latin — Lucretius conceived the imposing scheme of a didactic poem dealing with the whole field of life and nature as interpreted by the Epicurean philosophy. He lived to carry out his work almost to completion. It here and there wants the final touches of arrangement; one or two discussions are promised and not given; some paragraphs are repeated, and others have not been worked into their proper place; but substantially, as in the case of the *Aeneid*, we have the complete poem before us, and know perfectly within what limits it might have been altered or improved by fuller revision.

As pure literature, the *Nature of Things* has all the defects inseparable from a didactic poem, that unstable combination of discordant elements, and from a poem which is not only didactic, but argumentative, and in parts highly controversial. Nor are these difficulties in the least degree evaded or smoothed over by the poet. As a teacher, he is in deadly earnest; as a controversialist, his first object is to refute and convince. The graces of poetry are never for a moment allowed to interfere with the full development of an argument. Much of the poem is a chain of intricate

reasoning hammered into verse by sheer force of hand.   The
ardent imagination of the poet struggles through masses of
intractable material which no genius could wholly fuse into
a pure metal that could take perfect form.   His language,
in the fine prologue to the fourth book of the poem, shows
his attitude towards his art very clearly.

> *Avia Pieridum peragro loca nullius ante*
> *Trita solo ; iuvat integros accedere fontes*
> *Atque haurire, iuvatque novos decerpere flores*
> *Insignemque meo capiti petere inde coronam*
> *Unde prius nulli velarint tempora Musae :*
> *Primum quod magnis doceo de rebus, et artis*
> *Religionum animum nodis exsolvere pergo,*
> *Deinde quod obscura de re tam lucida pango*
> *Carmina, musaeo contingens cuncta lepore.*

The joy and glory of his art come second in his mind to his
passionate love of truth, and the deep moral purport of
what he believes to be the one true message for mankind.
The human race lies fettered by superstition and ignorance ;
his mission is to dispel their darkness by that light of truth
which is " clearer than the beams of the sun or the shining
shafts of day."   Spinoza has been called, in a bold figure, " a
man drunk with God ; " the contemplation of the "nature
of things," the physical structure of the universe, and the
living and all but impersonate law which forms and sustains
it, has the same intoxicating influence over Lucretius.
God and man are alike to him bubbles on the ceaseless
stream of existence ; yet they do not therefore, as they
have so often done in other philosophies, fade away to
a spectral thinness.   His contemplation of existence is no
brooding over abstractions ; Nature is not in his view the
majestic and silent figure before whose unchanging eyes
the shifting shadow-shapes go and come ; but an essential life, manifesting itself in a million workings, *creatrix,*

gubernans, daedala rerum. The universe is filled through all its illimitable spaces by the roar of her working, the ceaseless unexhausted energy with which she alternates life and death.

To our own age the Epicurean philosophy has a double interest. Not only was it a philosophy of life and conduct, but, in the effort to place life and conduct under ascertainable physical laws, it was led to frame an extremely detailed and ingenious body of natural philosophy, which, partly from being based on really sound postulates, partly from a happy instinct in connecting phenomena, still remains interesting and valuable. To the Epicureans, indeed, as to all ancient thinkers, the scientific method as it is now understood was unknown ; and a series of unverified generalisations, however brilliant and acute, is not the true way towards knowledge. But it still remains an astonishing fact that many of the most important physical discoveries of modern times are hinted at or even expressly stated by Lucretius. The general outlines of the atomic doctrine have long been accepted as in the main true ; in all important features it is superior to any other physical theory of the universe which existed up to the seventeenth century. In his theory of light Lucretius was in advance of Newton. In his theory of chemical affinities (for he describes the thing though the nomenclature was unknown to him) he was in advance of Lavoisier. In his theory of the ultimate constitution of the atom he is in striking agreement with the views of the ablest living physicists. The essential function of science — to reduce apparently disparate phenomena to the expressions of a single law — is not with him the object of a moment's doubt or uncertainty.

Towards real progress in knowledge two things are alike indispensable : a true scientific method, and imaginative insight. The former is, in the main, a creation of the modern world, nor was Lucretius here in advance of his age. But in the latter quality he is unsurpassed, if not

unequalled.   Perhaps this is even clearer in another field
of science, that which has within the last generation risen
to such immense proportions under the name of anthropology.
Thirty years ago it was the first and second books of the
De Rerum Natura which excited the greatest enthusiasm in
the scientific world.   Now that the atomic theory has passed
into the rank of received doctrines, the brilliant sketch, given
in the fifth book, of the beginnings of life upon the earth,
the evolution of man and the progress of human society, is
the portion of the poem in which his scientific imagination
is displayed most astonishingly.   A Roman aristocrat, living
among a highly cultivated society, Lucretius had been yet
endowed by nature with the primitive instincts of the savage.
He sees the ordinary processes of everyday life — weaving,
carpentry, metal-working, even such specialised forms of
manual art as the polishing of the surface of marble — with
the fresh eye of one who sees them all for the first time.
Nothing is to him indistinct through familiarity.   In virtue
of this absolute clearness of vision it costs him no effort to
throw himself back into prehistoric conditions and the
wild life of the earliest men.   Even further than this he
can pierce the strange recesses of the past.   Before his
imagination the earth rises swathed in tropical forests,
and all strange forms of life issuing and jostling one
another for existence in the steaming warmth of perpetual summer.   Among a thousand types that flowered
and fell, the feeble form of primitive man is distinguished,
without fire, without clothing, without articulate speech.
Through the midnight of the woods, shivering at the cries
of the stealthy-footed prowlers of the darkness, he crouches
huddled in fallen leaves, waiting for the rose of dawn.   Little
by little the prospect clears round him.   The branches of
great trees, grinding one against another in the windy
forest, break into a strange red flower ; he gathers it and
hoards it in his cave.   There, when wind and rain beat
without, the hearth-fire burns through the winter, and round

it gathers that other marvellous invention of which the hearth-fire became the mysterious symbol, the family. From this point the race is on the full current of progress, of which the remainder of the book gives an account as essentially true as it is incomparably brilliant. If we consider how little Lucretius had to go upon in this reconstruction of lost history, his imaginative insight seems almost miraculous. Even for the later stages of human progress he had to rely mainly on the eye which saw deep below the surface into the elementary structure of civilisation. There was no savage life within the scope of his actual observation. Books wavered between traditions of an impossible golden age and fragments of primitive legend which were then quite unintelligible, and are only now giving up their secret under a rigorous analysis. Further back, and beyond the rude civilisation of the earlier races of Greece and Italy, data wholly failed. We have supplemented, but hardly given more life to, his picture of the first beginnings, by evidence drawn from a thousand sources then unknown or unexplored — from coal-measures and mud-deposits, Pictish barrows and lacustrine midden-steads, remote tribes of hidden Africa and islands of the Pacific Sea.

Such are the characteristics which, to one or another epoch of modern times, give the poem of Lucretius so unique an interest. But for these as for all ages, its permanent value must lie mainly in more universal qualities. History and physical science alike are in all poetry ancillary to ideas. It is in his moral temper, his profound insight into life, that Lucretius rises to the greatest heights of thought and the utmost perfection of language. The Epicurean philosophy, in his hands, takes all the moral fervour, the ennobling influence of a religion. The depth of his religious instinct may be measured by the passion of his antagonism to what he regarded as superstition. Human life in his eyes was made wretched,

mean, and cruel by one great cause — the fear of death and
of what happens after it. That death is not to be feared,
that nothing happens after it, is the keystone of his whole
system. It is after an accumulation of seventeen proofs,
hurled one upon another at the reader, of the mortality of
the soul, that, letting himself loose at the highest emotional
and imaginative tension, he breaks into that wonderful
passage, which Virgil himself never equalled, and which in
its lofty passion, its piercing tenderness, the stately roll of
its cadences, is perhaps unmatched in human speech.

> " *Iam iam non domus accipiet te laeta, neque uxor*
> *Optima, nec dulces occurrent oscula nati*
> *Praeripere et tacita pectus dulcedine tangent:*
> *Non poteris factis florentibus esse, tuisque*
> *Praesidium: misero misere," aiunt, "omnia ademit*
> *Una dies infesta tibi tot praemia vitae . . ."*

" ' Now no more shall a glad home and a true wife welcome
thee, nor darling children race to snatch thy first kisses and
touch thy heart with a sweet and silent content; no more
mayest thou be prosperous in thy doings and a defence to
thine own: alas and woe ! ' say they, ' one disastrous day
has taken all these prizes of thy life away from thee ' — but
thereat they do not add this, ' and now no more does any
longing for these things beset thee.' This did their thought
but clearly see and their speech follow, they would release
themselves from great heartache and fear. ' Thou, indeed,
as thou art sunk in the sleep of death, wilt so be for the
rest of the ages, severed from all weary pains; but we,
while close by us thou didst turn ashen on the awful pyre,
made unappeasable lamentation, and everlastingly shall
time never rid our heart of anguish.' Ask we then this of
him, what there is that is so very bitter, if sleep and peace
be the conclusion of the matter, to make one fade away in
never-ending grief ?

" Thus too men often do when, set at the feast, they hold

their cups and shade their faces with garlands, saying sadly,
' Brief is this joy for wretched men ; soon will it have been,
and none may ever after recall it ! ' as if this were to be
first and foremost of the ills of death, that thirst and dry
burning should waste them miserably, or desire after anything else beset them. For not even then does any one
miss himself and his life when soul and body together are
deep asleep and at rest ; for all we care, such slumber might
go on for ever, nor does any longing after ourselves touch
us then, though then those first-beginnings through our
body swerve away but a very little from the movements that
bring back the senses when the man starts up and gathers
himself out of sleep. Far less, therefore, must we think
death concerns us, if less than nothing there can be ; for a
greater sundering in the mass of matter follows upon death,
nor does any one awake and stand, whom the cold stoppage
of death once has reached.

"Yet again, were the Nature of things suddenly to utter
a voice, and thus with her own lips upbraid one of us,
'What ails thee so, O mortal, to let thyself loose in too
feeble grievings? why weep and wail at death? for has
thy past life and overspent been sweet to thee, and not all
the good thereof, as if poured into a pierced vessel, has
run through and joylessly perished, why dost thou not retire
like a banqueter filled with life, and calmly, O fool, take thy
peaceful sleep? But if all thou hast had is perished and
spilt, and thy life is hateful, why seekest thou yet to add
more which shall once again all perish and fall joylessly
away? why not rather make an end of life and labour?
for there is nothing more that I can contrive and invent
for thy delight ; all things are the same for ever. Even
were thy body not yet withered, nor thy limbs weary and
worn, yet all things remain the same, didst thou go on to
live all the generations down, nay, even more, wert thou
never doomed to die ' — what do we answer?"

It is in passages of which the two hundred lines beginning

thus are the noblest instance, passages of profound and
majestic broodings over life and death, that the long rolling
weight of the Lucretian hexameter tells with its full force.
For the golden cadence of poesy we have to wait till Virgil ;
but the strain that Lucretius breathes through bronze is
statelier and more sonorous than any other in the stately
and sonorous Roman speech.   Like Naevius a century and
a half before, he might have left the proud and pathetic
lines on his tomb that, after he was dead, men forgot to
speak Latin in Rome.   He stands side by side with Julius
Caesar in the perfect purity of his language.   The writing
of the next age, whether prose or verse, gathered richness
and beauty from alien sources ; if the poem of Lucretius
had no other merit, it would be a priceless document as
a model of the purest Latin idiom in the precise age of its
perfection.   It follows from this that in certain points of
technique Lucretius was behind his age, or rather, deliberately
held aloof from the movement of his age towards a more
intricate and elaborate art.   The wave of Alexandrianism
only touched him distantly ; he takes up the Ennian
tradition where Ennius had left it, and puts into it the
immensely increased faculty of trained expression which
a century of continuous literary practice, and his own
admirably clear and quick intelligence, enable him to
supply.   The only Greek poets mentioned by him are
Homer and Empedocles.   His remoteness from the main
current of contemporary literature is curiously parallel to
that of Milton.   The Epicurean philosophy was at this
time, as it never was either earlier or later, the predominant
creed among the ruling class at Rome : but except in so far
as its shallower aspects gave the motive for light verse, it
was as remote from poetry as the Puritan theology of
the seventeenth century.   In both cases a single poet of
immense genius was also deeply penetrated with the spirit
of a creed.   In both cases his poetical affinity was with the
poets of an earlier day, and his poetical manner something

absolutely peculiar to himself. Both of them under this strangely mixed impulse set themselves to embody their creed in a great work of art. But the art did not appeal strongly to sectaries, nor the creed to artists. The *De Rerum Natura* and the *Paradise Lost,* while they exercised a profound influence over later poets, came silently into the world, and seem to have passed over the heads of their immediate contemporaries. There is yet another point of curious resemblance between them. Every student of Milton knows that the only English poet from whom he systematically borrowed matter and phrase was one of the third rate, who now would be almost forgotten but for the use Milton made of him. For one imitation of Spenser or Shakespeare in the *Paradise Lost* it would be easy to adduce ten — not mere coincidences of matter, but direct trans- ferences — of Sylvester's Du Bartas. While Lucretius was a boy, Cicero published the version in Latin hexameters of the *Phaenomena* and *Prognostica* of Aratus to which reference has already been made. These poems consist of only between eleven and twelve hundred lines in all, but had, in the later Alexandrian period, a reputation (like that of the *Sepmaine* of Du Bartas) far in excess of their real merit, and were among the most powerful influences in founding the new style. The many imitations in Lucretius of the extant fragments of these Ciceronian versions show that he must have studied their vocabulary and versification with minute care. The increased technical possibilities shown by them to exist in the Latin hexameter — for in them, as in nearly all his permanent work, Cicero was mastering the problem of making his own language an adequate vehicle of sustained expression — may even have been the determining influence that made Lucretius adopt this poetical form. Till then it may have been just possible that native metrical forms might still reassert themselves. Inscriptions of the last century of the Republic show that the saturnian still lingered in use side by side with the rude popular hexameters which were gradually displacing it; and the *Punic War* of Naevius was still a classic. Lucretius' choice of the hexameter, and his definite conquest of it as a medium of the richest and most varied expression, placed the matter beyond recall. The technical imperfections which remained in it were now reduced within a visible compass; its power to convey sustained argument, to express the most delicate shades of meaning, to adjust itself to the greatest heights and the subtlest tones of emotion, was already acquired when Lucretius handed it on to Virgil. And here, too, as well as in the wide field of literature with which his fame is more intimately connected, from the actual impulse given by his own early work and heightened by admiration of his brilliant maturity, even more than from the dubious tradition of his editorial care after the poet's death, the glory of the Ciceronian age is in close relation to the personal genius of Cicero.

V.

LYRIC POETRY : CATULLUS.

Contemporary with Lucretius, but, unlike him, living in the full whirl and glare of Roman life, was a group of young men who were professed followers of the Alexandrian school. In the thirty years which separate the Civil war and the Sullan restoration from the sombre period that opened with the outbreak of hostilities between Caesar and the senate, social life at Rome among the upper classes was unusually brilliant and exciting. The outward polish of Greek civilisation was for the first time fully mastered, and an intelligent interest in art and literature was the fashion of good society. The "young man about town," whom we find later fully developed in the poetry of Ovid, sprang into existence, but as the government was still in the hands of the aristocracy, fashion and politics were intimately intermingled, and the lighter literature of the day touched grave issues on every side. The poems of Catullus are full of references to his friends and his enemies among this group of writers. Two of the former, Cinna and Calvus, were poets of considerable importance. Gaius Helvius Cinna — somewhat doubtfully identified with the "Cinna the poet" who met such a tragical end at the hands of the populace after Caesar's assassination — carried the Alexandrian movement to its most uncompromising conclusions. His fame (and that fame was very great)

rested on a short poem called *Zmyrna*, over which he spent
ten years' labour, and which, by subject and treatment alike,
carried the Alexandrian method to its furthest excess. In
its recondite obscurity it outdid Lycophron himself. More
than one grammarian of the time made a reputation solely
by a commentary on it. It throws much light on the
peculiar artistic position of Catullus, to bear in mind that
this masterpiece of frigid pedantry obtained his warm and
evidently sincere praise.

The other member of the triad, Gaius Licinius Macer
Calvus, one of the most brilliant men of his time, was too
deeply plunged in politics to be more than an accomplished
amateur in poetry. Yet it must have been more than his
intimate friendship with Catullus, and their common fate
of too early a death, that made the two names so constantly coupled afterwards. By the critics of the Silver
Age, no less than by Horace and Propertius, the same idea
is frequently repeated, which has its best-known expression
in Ovid's beautiful invocation in his elegy on Tibullus —

> *Obvius huic venias, hedera iuvenilia cinctus*
> *Tempora, cum Calvo, docte Catulle, tuo.*

We must lament the total loss of a volume of lyrics which
competent judges thought worthy to be set beside that of
his wonderful friend.

Gaius Valerius Catullus of Verona, one of the greatest
names of Latin poetry, belonged, like most of this group,
to a wealthy and distinguished family, and was introduced
at an early age to the most fashionable circles of the
capital. He was just so much younger than Lucretius that
the Marian terror and the Sullan proscriptions can hardly
have left any strong traces on his memory; when he died,
Caesar was still fighting in Gaul, and the downfall of the
Republic could only be dimly foreseen. In time, no less
than in genius, he represents the fine flower of the
Ciceronian age. He was about five and twenty when the

famous liaison began between him and the lady whom he
has immortalised under the name of Lesbia. By birth a
Claudia, and wife of her cousin, a Caecilius Metellus, she
belonged by blood and marriage to the two proudest families
of the inner circle of the aristocracy. Clodia was seven
years older than Catullus ; but that only made their mutual
attraction more irresistible : and the death of her husband
in the year after his consulship, whether or not there was
foundation for the common rumour that she had poisoned
him, was an incident that seems to have passed almost
unnoticed in the first fervour of their passion. The story of
infatuation, revolt, relapse, fresh revolt and fresh entangle-
ment, lives and breathes in the verses of Catullus. It was
after their final rupture that Catullus made that journey to
Asia which gave occasion to his charming poems of travel.
In the years which followed his return to Italy, he continued to produce with great versatility and force, making
experiments in several new styles, and devoting great pains
to an elaborate metrical technique. Feats of learning and
skill alternate with political verses, into which he carries
all his violence of love and hatred. But while these later
poems compel our admiration, it is the earlier ones which
win and keep our love. Though the old liquid note ever
and again recurs, the freshness of these first lyrics, in which
life and love and poetry are all alike in their morning
glory, was never to be wholly recaptured. Nor did he
live to settle down on any matured second manner. He
was thirty-three at the utmost — perhaps not more than
thirty — when he died, leaving behind him the volume
of poems which sets him as the third beside Sappho and
Shelley.

The order of the poems in this volume seems to be an
artificial compromise between two systems — one an arrangement by metre, and the other by date of composition. In
the former view the book falls into three sections — the pure
lyrics, the idyllic pieces, and the poems in elegiac verse.

The central place is occupied by the longest and most elaborate, if not the most successful, of his poems, the epic idyl on the marriage of Peleus and Thetis. Before this are the lyrics, chiefly in the phalaecean eleven-syllabled verse which Catullus made so peculiarly his own, but in iambic, sapphic, choriambic, and other metres also, winding up with the fine epithalamium written for the marriage of his friends, Mallius and Vinia. The transition from this group of lyrics to the *Marriage of Peleus and Thetis* is made with great skill through another wedding-chant, an idyl in form, but approaching to a lyric in tone, without any personal allusions, and not apparently written for any particular occasion. Finally comes a third group of poems, extending to the end of the volume, all written in elegiac verse, but otherwise extremely varied in date, subject, and manner. The only poem thus left unaccounted for, the *Atys*, is inserted in the centre of the volume, between the two hexameter poems, as though to make its wild metre and rapid movement the more striking by contrast with their smooth and languid rhythms. Whether the arrangement of the whole book comes from the poet's own hand is very doubtful. His dedicatory verses, which stand at the head of the volume, are more probably attached to the first part only, the book of lyrics. Catullus almost certainly died in 54 B.C.; the only positive dates assignable to particular poems, in either the lyric or the elegiac section, alike lie within the three or four years previous, and, while no strict chronological order is followed, the pieces at the beginning of the book are almost certainly the earliest, and those at the end among the latest.

Among the poems of Catullus, those connected with Lesbia hold the foremost place, and, as expressions of direct personal emotion, are unsurpassed, not merely in Latin, but in any literature. There are no poems of the growth of love among them; from the first, Lesbia appears as the absolute mistress of her lover's heart:

Vivamus, mea Lesbia, atque amemus,
Rumoresque senum severiorum
Omnes unius aestimemus assis.
Soles occidere et redire possunt;
Nobis cum semel occidit brevis lux
Nox est perpetua una dormienda : —

thus he cries in the first intoxication of his happiness as
yet ignorant that the brief light of his love was to go out
before noon. Clodia soon showed that the advice not to
care for the opinion of the world was, in her case, infinitely
superfluous. That intolerable pride which was the pro-
verbial curse of the Claudian house took in her the form
of a flagrant disregard of all conventions. In the early
days of their love, Catullus only felt, or only expressed, the
beautiful side of this recklessness. His affection for Clodia
had in it, he says, something of the tenderness of parents
for their children ; and the poems themselves bear this out.
We do not need to read deeply in Catullus to be assured
that merely animal passion ran as strong in him as it ever
did in any man. But in the earlier poems to Lesbia all
this turns to air and fire ; the intensity of his love melts
its grosser elements into one white flame. There is hardly
even a word of Lesbia's bodily beauty ; her great blazing
eyes have only come down to us in the sarcastic allusions
made to them by Cicero in his speeches and letters. As
in some of the finest lyrics of Burns, with whom Catullus,
as a poet of love, has often been compared, the ardency of
passion has effected for quintessential moments the work
that long ages may work out on the whole fabric of a
human soul — *Concretam exemit labem purumque reliquit*
aetherium sensum atque auraï simplicis ignem.

But long after the rapture had passed away the enthral-
ment remained. Lesbia's first infidelities only riveted her
lover's chains —

> *Amantem iniuria talis*
> *Cogit amare magis ;*

then he hangs between love and hatred, in the poise of
soul immortalised by him in the famous verse —

> *Odi et amo : quare id faciam fortasse requiris ;*
> *Nescio, sed fieri sentio et excrucior.*

There were ruptures and reconciliations, and renewed
ruptures and repeated returns, but through them all, while
his love hardly lessens, his hatred continually grows, and
the lyrical cry becomes one of the sharpest agony : through
protestations of fidelity, through wails over ingratitude, he
sinks at last into a stupor only broken by moans of pain.
Then at last youth reasserts itself, and he is stung into new
life by the knowledge that he has simply dropped out of
Lesbia's existence. His final renunciation is no longer
addressed to her deaf ears, but flung at her in studied
insult through two of the associates of their old revels in
Rome.

> *Cum suis vivat valeatque moechis*
> *Quos simul complexa tenet trecentos*
> *Nullum amans vere, sed identidem* omnium*
>   *Ilia rumpens —*

so the hard clear verse flashes out, to melt away in the
dying fall, the long-drawn sweetness of the last words
of all —

> *Nec meum respectet ut ante amorem*
> *Qui illius culpa cecidit, velut prati*
> *Ultimi flos, praetereunte postquam*
>   *Tactus aratro est.*

Foremost among the other lyrics of Catullus which have

---

* The repetition of this word from the lovely lyric, *Ille mi par esse*,
where it occurs in the same place of the verse, is a stroke of subtle and
daring art.

a personal reference are those concerned with his journey
to Asia, and the death in the Troad of the deeply loved
brother whose tomb he visited on that journey. The
excitement of travel and the delight of return have never
been more gracefully touched than in these little lyrics, of
which every other line has become a household word, the
Iam ver egelidos refert tepores, and the lovely *Paene insularum
Sirmio insularumque,* whose cadences have gathered a fresh
sweetness in the hands of Tennyson. But a higher note is
reached in one or two of the short pieces on his brother's
death, which are lyrics in all but technical name. The
finest of these has all the delicate simplicity of an epitaph by
the best Greek artists, Leonidas or Antipater or Simonides
himself, and combines with it the Latin dignity, and a range
of tones, from the ocean-roll of its opening hexameter,
Multas per gentes et multa per aequora vectus, to the sobbing
wail of the *Atque in perpetuum frater ave atque vale* in
which it dies away, that is hardly equalled except in some
of Shakespeare's sonnets.

It is in these short lyrics of personal passion or emotion
that the genius of Catullus is most unique ; but the same
high qualities appear in the few specimens he has left of
more elaborate lyrical architecture, the *Ode to Diana,* the
marriage-song for Mallius and Vinia, and the *Atys.* The
first of these, brief as it is, has a breadth and grandeur of
manner which — as in the noble fragment of Keats' *Ode to
Maia* — lift it into the rank of great masterpieces. The
epithalamium, on the other hand, with which the book of
lyrics ends, while very simple in structure, is large in scale.
It is as much longer than the rest of the lyrics as the
marriage-song which stands at the end of *In Memoriam*
is than the other sections of that poem. In the charm
of perfect simplicity it equals the finest of his lyrics ; but
besides this, it has in its clear ringing music what is for
this period an almost unique premonition of the new world
that rose out of the darkness of the Middle Ages, the

world that had invented bells and church-organs, and had added a new romantic beauty to love and marriage. With a richness of phrase that recalls the Song of Solomon, the verses clash and swing : *Open your bars, O gates! the bride is at hand! Lo, how the torches shake out their splendid tresses!* . . . *Even so in a rich lord's garden-close might stand a hyacinth-flower. Lo, the torches shake out their golden tresses; go forth, O bride! Day wanes; go forth, O bride!* And the verse at the end, about the baby on its mother's lap —

> *Torquatus volo parvulus*
> *Matris e gremio suae*
> *Porrigens teneras manus*
> *Dulce rideat ad patrem*
> *Semihiante labello* —

is as incomparable ; not again till the Florentine art of the fifteenth century was the picture drawn with so true and tender a hand.

Over the *Atys* modern criticism has exhausted itself without any definite result. The accident of its being the only Latin poem extant in the peculiar galliambic metre has combined with the nature of the subject * to induce a tradition about it as though it were the most daring and extraordinary of Catullus' poems. The truth is quite different. It stands midway between the lyrics and the idyls in being a poem of most studied and elaborate artifice, in which Catullus has chosen, not the statelier and more familiar rhythms of the hexameter or elegiac, but one of the Greek lyric metres, of which he had already introduced several others into Latin. As a *tour de force* in metrical form it is very remarkable, and probably marks the highest point of Latin achievement in imitation of the more complex

---

* The subject was quite a usual one among the Alexandrian poets whom Catullus read and imitated. Cf. *Anthologia Palatina,* vii. 217-220.

Greek metres. As a lyric poem it preserves, even in its
highly artificial structure, much of the direct force and
simplicity which mark all Catullus' best lyrics ; that it goes
beyond this, or that — as is often repeated — it transcends
both the idyls and the briefer lyrics in sustained beauty and
passion, cannot be held by any sane judgment.

How far elaboration could lead Catullus is shown in the
long idyllic poem on the *Marriage of Peleus and Thetis.*
Here he entirely abandons the lyric manner, and adventures
on a new field, in which he does not prove very successful.
The poem is full of great beauties of detail ; but as a whole
it is cloying without being satisfying. For a few lines
together Catullus can write in hexameter more exquisitely
than any other Latin poet. The description in this piece
of the little breeze that rises at dawn, beginning *Hic qualis
flatu placidum mare matutino,* like the more famous lines in
his other idyllic poem —

> *Ut flos in septis secretum nascitur hortis,*
> *Ignotus pecori, nullo contusus aratro,*
> *Quem mulcent aurae, firmat sol, educat imber;*
> *Multi illum pueri, multae optavere puellae —*

has an intangible and inexpressible beauty such as never
recurs in the more mature art of greater masters. But
Catullus has no narrative gift ; his use of the hexameter is
confined to a limited set of rhythms which in a poem about
the length of a book of the *Georgics* become hopelessly
monotonous ; and it finally stops, rather than ends, when
the writer (as is already the case with the reader) grows tired
of it. It is remarkable that the poet who in the lightness
and speed of his other metres is unrivalled in Latin, should,
when he attempts the hexameter, be more languid and
heavy, not only than his successors, but than his contemporaries. Here, as in the elaborate imitations of
Callimachus with which he tested his command of the
Latin elegiac, he is weak because he wanders off the true

line, not from any failure in his own special gift, which was
purely and simply lyrical.   When he uses the elegiac verse
to express his own feeling, as in the attacks on political or
personal enemies, it has the same direct lucidity (as of an
extraordinarily gifted child) which is the essential charm of
his lyrics.

It is just this quality, this clear and almost terrible sim.
plicity, that puts Catullus in a place by himself among the
Latin poets.   Where others labour in the ore of thought and
gradually forge it out into sustained expression, he sees
with a single glance, and does not strike a second time.
His imperious lucidity is perfectly unhesitating in its action : whether he is using it for the daintiest flower of sentiment — *fair passions and bountiful pities and loves without
stain* — or for the expression of his vivid passions and hatreds
in some flagrant obscenity or venomous insult, it is alike
straight and reckless, with no scruple and no mincing of
words ; in Mr. Swinburne's curiously true and vivid phrase,
he " makes mouths at our speech " when we try to follow him.

With the death of Catullus and Calvus, an era in Latin
poetry definitely ends.   Only thirteen or fourteen years later
a new era begins with the appearance of Virgil ; but this
small interval of time is sufficient to mark the passage from
one age — we might almost say from one civilisation — to
another.   During these years poetry was almost silent, while
the Roman world shook with continuous civil war and the
thunder of prodigious armies.   The school of minor
Alexandrian poets still indeed continued ; the "warblers of
Euphorion" with their smooth rhythms and elaborate
finesse of workmanship are spoken of by Cicero as still
numerous and active ten years after Catullus' death.   But
their artifice had lost the gloss of novelty ; and the unexampled enthusiasm which greeted the appearance of the
Eclogues was due less perhaps to their intrinsic excellence
than to the relief with which Roman poetry shook itself free
from the fetters of so rigorous and exhausting a convention.

VI.

CICERO.

Meanwhile, in the last age of the Republic, Latin prose had reached its full splendour in the hands of the most copious and versatile master of style whom the Graeco-Roman world had yet produced. The claims of Cicero to a place among the first rank of Roman statesmen have been fiercely canvassed by modern critics; and both in oratory and philosophy some excess of veneration once paid to him has been replaced by an equally excessive depreciation. The fault in both estimates lay in the fact that they were alike based on secondary issues. Cicero's unique and imperishable glory is not, as he thought himself, that of having put down the revolutionary movement of Catiline, nor, as later ages thought, that of having rivalled Demosthenes in the *Second Philippic*, or confuted atheism in the *De Natura Deorum*. It is that he created a language which remained for sixteen centuries that of the civilised world, and used that language to create a style which nineteen centuries have not replaced, and in some respects have scarcely altered. He stands in prose, like Virgil in poetry, as the bridge between the ancient and modern world. Before his time, Latin prose was, from a wide point of view, but one among many local ancient dialects. As it left his hands, it had become a universal language, one which had definitely superseded all others, Greek included, as the type of civilised expression.

Thus the apparently obsolete criticism which ranked
Cicero together with Plato and Demosthenes, if not above
them, was based on real facts, though it may be now
apparent that it gave them a wrong interpretation. Even
scholars may admit with but slight reluctance that the
prose of the great Attic writers is, like the sculpture of
their contemporary artists, a thing remote from modern
life, requiring much training and study for its appreciation,
and confined at the best to a limited circle.   But Ciceronian
prose is practically the prose of the human race ; not only
of the Roman empire of the first and second centuries,
but of Lactantius and Augustine, of the mediaeval Church,
of the earlier and later Renaissance, and even now, when
the Renaissance is a piece of past history, of the modern
world to which the Renaissance was the prelude.

The life of Cicero as a man of letters may be divided
into four periods, which, though not of course wholly
distinct from one another, may be conveniently treated as
separate for the purpose of criticism.   The first is that of
his immature early writings — poems, treatises on rhetoric,
and forensic speeches — covering the period from his boy-
hood in the Civil wars, to the first consulship of Pompeius
and Crassus, in 70 B.C.   The second, covering his life as
an active statesman of the first prominence, begins with
the Verrine orations of that year, and goes down to the
consulship of Julius Caesar, in 59 B.C.   These ten years
mark his culmination as an orator ; and there is no trace
in them of any large literary work except in the field of
oratory.   In the next year came his exile, from which
indeed he returned within a twelvemonth, but as a broken
statesman.   From this point to the outbreak of the Civil
war in 50 B.C., the third period continues the record of his
great speeches ; but they are no longer at the old height,
nor do they occupy his full energy ; and now he breaks new
ground in two fields with works of extraordinary brilliance,
the *De Oratore* and the *De Republica*.   During the heat of

the Civil war there follows a period of comparative silence,
but for his private correspondence; then comes the fourth
and final period, perhaps the most brilliant of all, the four
years from 46 B.C. to his death in 43 B.C.   The few speeches
of the years 46 and 45 show but the ghost of former
splendours; he was turning perforce to other subjects.
The political philosophy of the *De Republica* is resumed
in the *De Legibus;* the *De Oratore* is continued by the
history of Roman oratory known as the *Brutus*.   Then, as
if realising that his true work in life was to mould his
native language into a vehicle of abstract thought, he sets
to work with amazing swiftness and copiousness to reproduce a whole series of Greek philosophical treatises,
in a style which, for flexibility and grace, recalls the Greek
of the best period — the *De Finibus*, the *Academics*, the
Tusculans, the *De Natura Deorum*, the *De Divinatione*, the
De Officiis.   Concurrently with these, he continues to throw
off further manuals of the theory and practice of oratory,
intended in the first instance for the use of the son who
proved so thankless a pupil, the *Partitiones Oratoriae*, the
Topica, the *De Optimo Genere Oratorum*.   Meanwhile, the
Roman world had again been plunged into civil war by the
assassination of Caesar.   Cicero's political influence was
no longer great, but it was still worth the while of younger
and more unscrupulous statesmen to avail themselves of
his eloquence by assumed deference and adroit flattery.
The series of fourteen speeches delivered at Rome against
Marcus Antonius, between September, 44, and April, 43
B.C., were the last outburst of free Roman oratory before
the final extinction of the Republic.   That even at the
time there was a sense of their unreality — of their being
rhetorical exercises to interest the capital while the real
issues of the period were being fought out elsewhere — is
indicated by the name that from the first they went under,
the *Philippics*.   In the epoch of the *Verrines* and the
Catilinarians it had not been necessary to find titles for

the weapons of political warfare out of old Greek history.
Yet, in spite of this unreality, and of the decline they show
in the highest oratorical qualities, the *Philippics* still remain
a noble ruin of eloquence.

Oratory at Rome had, as we have already seen, attained
a high degree of perfection when Cicero entered on public
life. Its golden age was indeed, in the estimation of
some critics, already over; old men spoke with admiring
regret of the speeches of the younger Scipio and of Gaius
Gracchus; and the death of the great pair of friendly
rivals, Crassus and Antonius, left no one at the moment
who could be called their equal. But admirable as these
great orators had been, there was still room for a higher
formal perfection, a more exhaustive and elaborate technique, without any loss of material qualities. Closer and
more careful study led the orators of the next age into
one of two opposed, or rather complementary styles, the
Attic and Asiatic; the calculated simplicity of the one
being no less artificial than the florid ornament of the
other. At an early age Cicero, with the intuition of genius,
realised that he must not attach himself to either school.
A fortunate delicacy of health led him to withdraw for two
years, at the age of seven and twenty, from the practice
at the bar, in which he was already becoming famous;
and in the schools of Athens and Rhodes he obtained
a larger view of his art, both in theory and practice, and
returned to Rome to form, not to follow, a style. Quintus
Hortensius Hortalus, the foremost representative of the
Asiatic school, was then at the height of his forensic reputation. Within a year or two Cicero was recognised as
at least his equal: it is to the honour of both, that the
eclipse of Hortensius by his younger rival brought no
jealousy or alienation; up to the death of Hortensius,
about the outbreak of the Civil war, they remained good
friends. Years afterwards Cicero inscribed with his name
the treatise, now lost, but made famous to later ages by

having been one of the great turning-points in the life of St. Augustine,* which he wrote in praise of philosophy as an introduction to the series of his philosophical works.

The years which followed Cicero's return from the East were occupied, with the single break of his quaestorship in Sicily, by hard and continuous work at the bar. His speeches of this date, being non-political, have for the most part not been preserved. The two still imperfectly extant, the *Pro Roscio Comoedo* of 76, and the *Pro Tullio* of 72 B.C., form, together with two other speeches dating from before his visit to the East, the *Pro Quinctio* and *Pro Roscio Amerino*, and, with his juvenile treatise on rhetoric known as the *De Inventione*, the body of prose composition which represents the first of his four periods. These early speeches are carefully composed according to the scholastic canons then in vogue, the hard legal style of the older courts alternating with passages of carefully executed artificial ornament. Their chief interest is one of contrast with his matured style; for they show, no doubt with much accuracy, what the general level of oratory was out of which the great Ciceronian eloquence sprang.

In 70 B.C., at the age of thirty-six, Cicero at last found his great chance, and seized it. The impeachment of Verres for maladministration in the government of Sicily was a political trial of great constitutional importance. It was undertaken at the direct encouragement of Pompeius, who had entered on his first or democratic consulate, and was indirectly a formidable attack both on the oligarchic-administration of the provinces and on the senatorian jury-panels, in whose hands the Sullan constitution had placed the only check upon misgovernment. The defence of Verres was undertaken by Hortensius; the selection of Cicero as chief counsel for the prosecution by the democratic leaders was a public recognition of him as the foremost orator on the Pompeian side. He threw himself into

* *Confess.*, III. iv.

the trial with all his energy. After his opening speech, and the evidence which followed, Verres threw up his defence and went into exile. This, of course, brought the case to an end; but the cause turned on larger issues than his particular guilt or innocence. The whole of the material prepared against him was swiftly elaborated by Cicero into five great orations, and published as a political document. These orations, the *Second Action against Verres* as they are called, were at once the most powerful attack yet made on the working of the Sullan constitution, and the high-water mark of the earlier period of Cicero's eloquence. It was not till some years later that his oratory culmi-nated; but he never excelled these speeches in richness and copiousness of style, in ease and lucidity of exposition, and in power of dealing with large masses of material. He at once became an imposing political force; perhaps it was hardly realised till later how incapable that force was of going straight or of bearing down opposition. The series of political and semi-political speeches of the next ten years, down to his exile, represent for the time the history of Rome; and together with these we now begin the series of his private letters. The year of his praetorship, 66 B.C., is marked by the two orations which are on the whole his greatest, one public and the other private. The first, the speech known as the *Pro Lege Manilia,* which should really be described as the panegyric of Pompeius and of the Roman people, does not show any profound appreciation of the problems which then confronted the Republic; but the greatness of the Republic itself never found a more august interpreter. The stately passage in which Italy and the subject provinces are called on to bear witness to the deeds of Pompeius breathes the very spirit of an imperial race. Throughout this and the other great speeches of the period "the Roman People" is a phrase that keeps perpetually recurring with an effect like that of a bourdon stop. As the eye glances down the page, *Consul populi*

Romani, Imperium Populi Romani, Fortuna Populi Romani,
glitter out of the voluminous periods with a splendour that
hardly any other words could give.

The other great speech of this year, Cicero's defence of
Aulus Cluentius Habitus of Larinum on a charge of poison-
ing, has in its own style an equal brilliance of language.
The story it unfolds of the ugly tragedies of middle-class
life in the capital and the provincial Italian towns is famous
as one of the leading documents for the social life of Rome.
According to Quintilian, Cicero confessed afterwards that
his client was not innocent, and that the elaborate and
impressive story which he unfolds with such vivid detail
was in great part an invention of his own. This may be
only bar gossip; true or false, his defence is an extraordinary masterpiece of oratorical skill.

The manner in which Cicero conducted a defence when
the cause was not so grave or so desperate is well illustrated
by a speech delivered four years later, the *Pro Archia.* The
case here was one of contested citizenship. The defendant,
one of the Greek men of letters who lived in great numbers
at Rome, had been for years intimate with the literary
circle among the Roman aristocracy. This intimacy gained
him the privilege of being defended by the first of Roman
orators, who would hardly, in any other circumstances,
have troubled himself with so trivial a case. But the
speech Cicero delivered is one of the permanent glories
of Latin literature. The matter immediately at issue is
summarily dealt with in a few pages of cursory and rather
careless argument; then the scholar lets himself go.
Among the many praises of literature which great men oi
letters have delivered, there is hardly one more perfect
than this; some of the famous sentences have remained
ever since the abiding motto and blason of literature itself.
*Haec studia adolescentiam agunt, senectutem oblectant, se-
cundas res ornant, adversis perfugium ac solatium praebent,
delectant domi, non impediunt foris, pernoctant nobiscum,*

peregrinantur, rusticantur; and again, *Nullam enim virtus aliam mercedem laborum periculorumque desiderat, praeter hanc laudis et gloriae; qua quidem detracta, iudices, quid est quod in hoc tam exiguo vitae curriculo, et tam brevi, tantis nos in laboribus exerceamus? Certe, si nihil animus praesentiret in posterum, et si quibus regionibus vitae spatium circumscriptum est, eisdem omnes cogitationes terminaret suas, nec tantis se laboribus frangeret, neque tot curis vigiliisque angeretur, neque toties de vita ipsa dimicaret.* Strange words these to fall from a pleader's lips in the dusty atmosphere of the praetor's court! *non fori, neque iudiciali consuetudine,* says Cicero himself, in the few words of graceful apology with which the speech ends. But, in truth, as he well knew, he was not speaking to the respectable gentlemen on the benches before him. He addressed a larger audience; posterity, and the civilised world.

The *Pro Archia* foreshadows already the change which was bound to take place in Cicero's life, and which was precipitated by his exile four years later. More and more he found himself forced away from the inner circle of politics, and turned to the larger field where he had an undisputed supremacy, of political and ethical philosophy clothed in the splendid prose of which he had now obtained the full mastery. The roll of his great speeches is indeed continued after his return from exile; but even in the greatest, the *Pro Sestio* and *Pro Caelio* of 56, or the *In Pisonem* of 55 B.C., something of the old tone is missing; it is as though the same voice spoke on a smaller range of notes and with less flexibility of cadence. And now alongside of the speeches begins the great series of his works on oratory and philosophy, with the *De Oratore* of 55, and the *De Republica* of 54 B.C.

The three books *De Oratore* are perhaps the most finished examples of the Ciceronian style. The subject (which cannot be said of all the subjects he deals with) was one of which, over all its breadth and in all its details, he was completely master; and, thus left unhampered by any difficulties with his material, he could give full scope to his brilliant style and diction. The arrangement of the work follows the strict scholastic divisions; but the form of dialogue into which it is thrown, and which is managed with really great skill, avoids the tediousness incident to a systematic treatise. The principal persons of the dialogue are the two great orators of the preceding age, Lucius Crassus and Marcus Antonius; this is only one sign out of many that Cicero was more and more living in a sort of dream of the past, that past of his own youth which was still full of traditions of the earlier Republic.

The *De Oratore* was so complete a masterpiece that its author probably did not care to weaken its effect by continuing at the time to bring out any of the supplementary treatises on Roman oratory for which his library, and still more his memory, had accumulated immense quantities of material. In the treatise *De Republica*, which was begun in 54 B.C., though not published till three years later, he carried the achievement of Latin prose into a larger and less technical field — that of the philosophy of politics. Again the scene of the dialogue is laid in a past age; but now he goes further back than he had done in the *De Oratore*, to the circle of the younger Scipio. The work was received, when published, with immense applause; but its loss in the Middle Ages is hardly one of those which are most seriously to be deplored, except in so far as the second and fifth books may have preserved real information on the early history of the Roman State and the development of Roman jurisprudence. Large fragments were recovered early in the present century from a palimpsest, itself incomplete, on which the work of Cicero had been expunged to make room for the commentary of St. Augustine on the Psalms. The famous *Somnium Scipionis,* with which (in imitation of the vision of Er in Plato's *Republic*) the work ended, has been independently preserved.

Though it flagrantly challenges comparison with the unequalled original, it has, nevertheless, especially in its opening
and closing passages, a grave dignity which is purely Roman,
and characteristically Ciceronian. Perhaps some of the
elaborate fantasies of De Quincey (himself naturally a
Ciceronian, and saturated in the rhythms and cadences of
the finest Latin prose) are the nearest parallel to this
piece in modern English. The opening words of Scipio's
narrative, *Cum in Africam venissem, Manio Manilio consuli
ad quartam legionem tribunus*, come on the ear like the
throb of a great organ; and here and there through the
piece come astonishing phrases of the same organ-music :
*Ostendebat autem Karthaginem de excelso et pleno stellarum
inlustri et claro quodam loco. . . . Quis in reliquis orientis
aut obeuntis solis, ultimis aut aquilonis austrive partibus,
tuum nomen audiet ? . . . Deum te igitur scito esse, siquidem
deus est, qui viget, qui sentit, qui meminit, qui providet*—
hardly from the lips of Virgil himself does the noble Latin
speech issue with a purer or a more majestic flow.

During the next few years the literary activity of Cicero
suffered a check. The course of politics at Rome filled
him with profound disappointment and disgust. Public
issues, it became more and more plain, waited for their
determination, not on the senate-house or the forum, but
on the sword. The shameful collapse of his defence of
Milo in 52 B.C. must have stung a vanity even as well-
hardened as Cicero's to the quick; and his only important
abstract work of this period, the *De Legibus*, seems to have
been undertaken with little heart and carried out without
either research or enthusiasm. His proconsulate in Cilicia
in 51 and 50 B.C. was occupied with the tedious details of
administration and petty warfare; six months after his
return the Civil war broke out, and, until permitted to
return to Rome by Caesar in the autumn of 47 B.C., he was
practically an exile, away from his beloved Rome and his
more beloved library, hating and despising the ignorant

incompetence of his colleagues, and looking forward with almost equal terror to the conclusive triumph of his own or the opposite party. When at last he returned, his mind was still agitated and unsettled. The Pompeian party held Africa and Spain with large armies; their open threats that all who had come to terms with Caesar would be proscribed as public enemies were not calculated to restore Cicero's confidence. The decisive battle of Thapsus put an end to this uncertainty; and meanwhile Cicero had resumed work on his *De Legibus*, and had once more returned to the study of oratory in one of the most interesting of his writings, the *Brutus de claris Oratoribus*, in which he gives a vivid and masterly sketch of the history of Roman oratory down to his own time, filled with historical matter and admirable sketches of character.

The spring of 45 B.C. brought with it two events of momentous importance to Cicero : the final collapse of the armed opposition to Caesar at the battle of Munda, and the loss, by the death of his daughter Tullia, of the one deep affection of his inner life. Henceforth it seemed as if politics had ceased to exist, even had he the heart to interest himself in them. He fell back more completely than ever upon philosophy; and the year that followed (45–44 B.C.) is, in mere quantity of literary production, as well as in the abiding effect on the world of letters of the work he then produced, the *annus mirabilis* of his life. Two at least of the works of this year, the *De Gloria* and the *De Virtutibus*, have perished, though the former survived long enough to be read by Petrarch; but there remain extant (besides one or two other pieces of slighter importance) the *De Finibus*, the *Academics*, the *Tusculans*, the *De Natura Deorum*, the *De Divinatione*, the *De Fato*, the *De Officiis*, and the two exquisite essays *De Senectute* and *De Amicitia*.

It is the work of this astonishing year which, on the whole, represents Cicero's permanent contribution to letters and to human thought. If his philosophy seems now to have exhausted its influence, it is because it has in great measure been absorbed into the fabric of civilised society. Ciceronianism, at the period of the Renaissance, and even in the eighteenth century, meant more than the impulse towards florid and sumptuous style. It meant all that is conveyed by the Latin word *humanitas;* the title of "the humaner letters," by which Latin was long designated in European universities, indicated that in the great Latin writers — in Cicero and Virgil pre-eminently — a higher type of human life was to be found than existed in the literature of other countries: as though at Rome, and in the first century before Christ, the political and social environment had for the first time produced men such as men would wish to be, at all events for the ideals of Western Europe. To less informed or less critical ages than our own, the absolute contribution of Cicero to ethics and metaphysics seemed comparable to that of the great Greek thinkers; the *De Natura Deorum* was taken as a workable argument against atheism, and the thin and wire-drawn discussions of the *Academics* were studied with an attention hardly given to the founder of the Academy. When a sounder historical method brought these writings into their real proportion, it was inevitable that the scale should swing violently to the other side; and for a time no language was too strong in which to attack the reputation of the "phrase-maker," the "journalist," whose name had once dominated Europe. The violence of this attack has now exhausted itself; and we may be content, without any exaggerated praise or blame, to note the actual historical effect of these writings through many ages, and the actual impression made on the world by the type of character which they embodied and, in a sense, created. In this view, Cicero represents a force that no historian can neglect, and the importance of which it is not easy to over-estimate. He did for the Empire and the Middle Ages what Lucretius, with his far greater philosophic genius, totally failed to do — created forms of thought in which the life of philosophy grew, and a body of expression which alone made its growth in the Latin-speaking world possible ; and to that world he presented a political ideal which profoundly influenced the whole course of European history even up to the French Revolution. Without Cicero, the Middle Ages would not have had Augustine or Aquinas ; but, without him, the movement which annulled the Middle Ages would have had neither Mirabeau nor Pitt.

The part of Cicero's work which the present age probably finds the most interesting, and the interest of which is, in the nature of things, perennial, has been as yet left unmentioned. It consists of the collections of his private letters from the year 68 B.C. to within a few months of his death. The first of these contains his letters to the intimate friend and adviser, Titus Pomponius Atticus, with whom, when they were not both in Rome, he kept up a constant and an extremely intimate correspondence. Atticus, whose profession, as far as he had one, was that of a banker, was not only a man of wide knowledge and great political sagacity, but a refined critic and an author of considerable merit. The publishing business, which he conducted as an adjunct to his principal profession, made him of great use to Cicero by the rapid multiplication in his workshops of copies of the speeches or other writings for which there was an immediate public demand. But the intimacy was much more than that of the politician and his confidential adviser, or the author and his publisher. Cicero found in him a friend with whom he could on all occasions be perfectly frank and at his ease, and on whose sober judgment and undemonstrative, but perfectly sincere, attachment his own excitable and emotional nature could always throw itself without reserve. About four hundred of the letters were published by Atticus several years after Cicero's death. It must always be a source of regret that

he could not, or, at all events, did not, publish the other
half of the correspondence ; many of the letters, especially
the brief confidential notes, have the tantalising interest of
a conversation where one of the speakers is inaudible.
It is the letters to Atticus that place Cicero at the head of
all epistolary stylists. We should hardly guess from the
more formal and finished writings what the real man was,
with his excitable Italian temperament, his swift power of
phrase, his sensitive affections.

The other large collection of Cicero's letters, the
Epistolae ad Familiares, was preserved and edited by his
secretary, Tiro. They are, of course, of very unequal
value and interest. Some are merely formal documents ;
others, like those to his wife and family in book xiv., are
as intimate and as valuable as any we possess. The two
smaller collections, the letters to his brother Quintus, and
those to Marcus Brutus, of which a mere fragment is
extant, are of little independent value. The *Epistolae
ad Familiares* include, besides Cicero's own letters, a
large number of letters addressed to him by various
correspondents ; a whole book, and that not the least
interesting, consists of those sent to him during his Cilician
proconsulate by the brilliant and erratic young aristocrat,
Marcus Caelius Rufus, who was the next successor of
Catullus as the favoured lover of Clodia Quadrantaria.
Full of the political and social gossip of the day, they are
written in a curiously slipshod but energetic Latin, which
brings before us even more vividly than Cicero's own the
familiar language of the upper classes at Rome at the time.
Another letter, which can hardly be passed over in silence
in any history of Latin literature, is the noble message of
condolence to Cicero on the death of his beloved Tullia,
by the statesman and jurist, Servius Sulpicius Rufus, who
carried on in this age the great tradition of the Scaevolae.

It is due to these priceless collections of letters, more
than to any other single thing, that our knowledge of the

Ciceronian age is so complete and so intimate. At every point they reinforce and vitalise the more elaborate literary productions of the period. The art of letter-writing suddenly rose in Cicero's hands to its full perfection. It fell to the lot of no later Roman to have at once such mastery over familiar style, and contemporary events of such engrossing and ever-changing interest on which to exercise it. All the great letter-writers of more modern ages have more or less, consciously or unconsciously, followed the Ciceronian model. England of the eighteenth century was peculiarly rich in them; but Horace Walpole, Cowper, Gray himself, would willingly have acknowledged Cicero as their master.

Caesar's assassination on the 15th of March, 44 B.C., plunged the political situation into a worse chaos than had ever been reached during the civil wars. For several months it was not at all plain how things were tending, or what fresh combinations were to rise out of the welter in which a vacillating and incapable senate formed the only constitutional rallying-point. In spite of all his long-cherished delusions, Cicero must have known that this way no hope lay; when at last he flung himself into the conflict, and broke away from his literary seclusion to make the fierce series of attacks upon Antonius which fill the winter of 44–43 B.C., he may have had some vague hopes from the Asiatic legions which once before, in Sulla's hands, had checked the revolution, and some from the power of his own once unequalled eloquence; but on the whole he seems to have undertaken the contest chiefly from the instinct that had become a tradition, and from his deep personal repugnance to Antonius. The fourteen *Philippics* add little to his reputation as an orator, and still less to his credit as a statesman. The old watchwords are there, but their unreality is now more obvious; the old rhetorical skill, but more coarsely and less effectively used. The last *Philippic* was delivered to advocate a public thanksgiving for the victory gained over Antonius by the consuls, Hirtius and Pansa. A month later, the consuls were both dead, and their two armies had passed into the control of the young Octavianus. In autumn the triumvirate was constituted, with an armed force of forty legions behind it. The proscription lists were issued in November. On the 7th of December, after some aimless wandering that hardly was a serious effort to escape, Cicero was overtaken near Formiae by a small party of Antonian troops. He was killed, and his head sent to Rome and displayed in the senate-house. There was nothing left for which he could have wished to live. In the five centuries of the Republic there never had been a darker time for Rome. Cicero had outlived almost all the great men of his age. The newer generation, so far as they had revealed themselves, were of a type from which those who had inherited the great traditions of the Republic shrank with horror. Caesar Octavianus, the future master of the world, was a delicate boy of twenty, already an object of dislike and distrust to nearly all his allies. Virgil, a poet still voiceless, was twenty-seven.

VII.

PROSE OF THE CICERONIAN AGE: CAESAR AND SALLUST.

FERTILE as the Ciceronian age was in authorship of many kinds, there was only one person in it whose claim to be placed in an equal rank with Cicero could ever be seriously entertained; and this was, strangely enough, one who was as it were only a man of letters by accident, and whose literary work is but among the least of his titles to fame — Julius Caesar himself. That anything written by that remarkable man must be interesting and valuable in a high degree is obvious; but the combination of literary power of the very first order with his unparalleled military and political genius is perhaps unique in history.

It is one of the most regrettable losses in Latin literature that Caesar's speeches and letters have almost completely perished. Of the latter several collections were made after his death, and were extant in the second century; but none are now preserved, except a few brief notes to Cicero, of which copies were sent by him at the time to Atticus. The fragments of his speeches are even less considerable; yet, according to the unanimous testimony both of contemporary and of later critics, they were unexcelled in that age of great oratory. He used the Latin language with a purity and distinction that no one else could equal. And along with this quality, the *mira elegantia* of Quintilian, his oratory had some kind of severe magnificence which we can partly

guess at from his extant writings — *magnifica et generosa,*
says Cicero; *facultas dicendi imperatoria* is the phrase of
a later and able critic.

Of Caesar's other lost writings little need be said. In
youth, like most of his contemporaries, he wrote poems,
including a tragedy, of which Tacitus drily observes that
they were not better than those of Cicero. A grammatical
treatise, *De Analogia,* was composed by him during one
of his long journeys between Northern Italy and the
head-quarters of his army in Gaul during his proconsulate.
A work on astronomy, apparently written in connection
with his reform of the calendar, two pamphlets attacking
Cato, and a collection of apophthegms, have also disappeared. But we possess what were by far the most
important of his writings, his famous memoirs of the Gallic
and Civil Wars.

The seven books of *Commentaries on the Gallic War*
were written in Caesar's winter-quarters in Gaul, after the
capture of Alesia and the final suppression of the Arvernian
revolt. They were primarily intended to serve an immediate
political purpose, and are indeed a defence, framed with
the most consummate skill, of the author's whole Gallic
policy and of his constitutional position. That Caesar was
able to do this without, so far as can be judged, violating, or
even to any large degree suppressing facts, does equal
credit to the clearsightedness of his policy and to his
extraordinary literary power. From first to last there is not
a word either of self-laudation or of innuendo; yet at the
end we find that, by the use of the simplest and most
lucid narration, in which hardly a fact or a detail can be
controverted, Caesar has cleared his motives and justified
his conduct with a success the more complete because his
tone is so temperate and seemingly so impartial. An officer
of his staff who was with him during that winter, and who
afterwards added an eighth book to the *Commentaries*
to complete the history of the Gallic proconsulate, has

recorded the ease and swiftness with which the work was written. Caesar issued it under the unpretending name of *Commentarii* — "notes" — on the events of his campaigns, which might be useful as materials for history; but there was no exaggeration in the splendid compliment paid it a few years later by Cicero, that no one in his senses would think of recasting a work whose succinct, perspicuous, and brilliant style — *pura et inlustris brevitas* — has been the model and the despair of later historians.

The three books of *Commentaries on the Civil War* show the same merits in a much less marked degree. They were not published in Caesar's lifetime, and do not seem to have received from him any close or careful revision. The literary incompetence of the Caesarian officers into whose hands they fell after his death, and one or more of whom must be responsible for their publication, is sufficiently evident from their own awkward attempts at continuing them in narratives of the Alexandrine, African, and Spanish campaigns; and whether from the carelessness of the original editors or from other reasons, the text is in a most deplorable condition. Yet this is not in itself sufficient to account for many positive misstatements. Either the editors used a very free hand in altering the rough manuscript, or — which is not in itself unlikely, and is borne out by other facts — Caesar's own prodigious memory and incomparable perspicuity became impaired in those five years of all but superhuman achievement, when, with the whole weight of the civilised world on his shoulders, feebly served by second-rate lieutenants and hampered at every turn by the open or passive opposition of nearly the whole of the trained governing classes, he conquered four great Roman armies, secured Egypt and Upper Asia and annexed Numidia to the Republic, carried out the unification of Italy, re-established public order and public credit, and left at his death the foundations of the Empire securely laid for his successor.

The loyal and capable officer, Aulus Hirtius (who afterwards became consul, and was killed in battle before
Mutina a year after Caesar's murder), did his best to
supplement his master's narrative. He seems to have been
a well-educated man, but without any particular literary
capacity. It was uncertain, even to the careful research of
Suetonius, whether the narrative of the campaigns in Egypt
and Pontus, known as the *Bellum Alexandrinum*, was written
by him or by another officer of Caesar's, Gaius Oppius.
The books on the campaigns of Africa and Spain which
follow are by different hands : the former evidently by
some subaltern officer who took part in the war, and very
interesting as showing the average level of intelligence and
culture among Roman officers of the period ; the latter by
another author and in very inferior Latin, full of grammatical
solecisms and popular idioms oddly mixed up with epic
phrases from Ennius, who was still, it must be remembered,
the great Latin school-book. It is these curious fragments
of history which more than anything else help us to understand the rapid decay of Latin prose after the golden
period. Under the later Republic the educated class and
the governing class had, broadly speaking, been the same.
The Civil wars, in effect, took administration away from
their hands, transferring it to the new official class, of which
these subalterns of Caesar's represent the type ; and this
change was confirmed by the Empire. The result was a
sudden and long-continued divorce between political activity
on one hand and the profession of letters on the other.
For a century after the establishment of the Empire the
aristocracy, which had produced the great literature of the
Republic, remained forcibly or sullenly silent ; and the new
hierarchy was still at the best only half educated. The
professional man of letters was at first fostered and sub-
sidised ; but even before the death of Augustus State
patronage of literature had fallen into abeyance, while the
cultured classes fell more and more back on the use of

Greek. The varying fortunes of this struggle between Greek and literary Latin as it had been formed under the Republic, belong to a later period : at present we must return to complete a general survey of the prose of the Ciceronian age.

Historical writing at Rome, as we have seen, had hitherto been in the form either of annals or memoirs. The latter were, of course, rather materials for history than history itself, even when they were not excluded from Quintilian's famous definition of history * by being composed primarily as political pamphlets. The former had so far been attempted on too large a scale, and with insufficient equipment either of research or style, to attain any permanent merit. In the ten years after Caesar's death Latin history was raised to a higher level by the works of Sallust, the first scientific historian whom Italy had produced.

Gaius Sallustius Crispus of Amiternum in Central Italy belonged to that younger generation of which Marcus Antonius and Marcus Caelius Rufus were eminent examples. Clever and dissipated, they revolted alike from the severe traditions and the narrow class prejudices of the constitutional party, and Caesar found in them enthusiastic, if somewhat imprudent and untrustworthy, supporters. Sallust was expelled from the senate just before the outbreak of the Civil war ; was reinstated by Caesar, and entrusted with high posts in Illyria and Italy ; and was afterwards sent by him to administer Africa with the rank of proconsul. There he accumulated a large fortune, and, after Caesar's death, retired to private life in his beautiful gardens on the Quirinal, and devoted himself to historical study. The largest and most important of his works, the five books of *Historiae*, covering a period of about ten years from the death of Sulla, is only extant in inconsiderable fragments ; but his two monographs on the Jugurthine war and the

* *Historia scribitur ad narrandum non ad probandum :* Inst. Or., X. i. 31.

Catilinarian conspiracy, which have been preserved, place
him beyond doubt in the first rank of Roman historians.

Sallust took Thucydides as his principal literary model.
His reputation has no doubt suffered by the comparison
which this choice makes inevitable; and though Quintilian
did not hesitate to claim for him a substantial equality with
the great Athenian, no one would now press the parallel,
except in so far as Sallust's formal treatment of his
subject affords interesting likenesses or contrasts with
the Thucydidean manner.   In his prefatory remarks, his
elaborately conceived and executed speeches, his reflections on character, and his terse method of narration,
Sallust closely follows the manner of his master.   He
even copies his faults in a sort of dryness of style and
an excessive use of antithesis.   But we cannot feel, in
reading the *Catiline* or the *Jugurtha*, that it is the work
of a writer of the very first intellectual power.   Yet
the two historians have this in common, which is not borrowed by the later from the earlier, — that they approach
and handle their subject with the mature mind, the insight
and common sense of the grown man, where their predecessors had been comparatively like children.   Both are
totally free from superstition; neither allows his own
political views to obscure his vision of facts, of men as they
were and events as they happened.   The respect for truth,
which is the first virtue of the historian, is stronger in
Sallust than in any of his more brilliant successors.   His
ideal in the matter of research and documentary evidence
was, for that age, singularly high.   In the *Catiline* he writes
very largely from direct personal knowledge of men and
events ; but the *Jugurtha*, which deals with a time two generations earlier than the date of its composition, involved
wide inquiry and much preparation.   He had translations
made from original documents in the Carthaginian language ;
and a complete synopsis of Roman history, for reference
during the progress of his work, was compiled for him by

a Greek secretary. Such pains were seldom taken by a Latin historian.

The last of the Ciceronians, Sallust is also in a sense the first of the imperial prose-writers. His style, compressed, rhetorical, and very highly polished, is in strong contrast to the graceful and fluid periods which were then, and for some time later continued to be, the predominant fashion, and foreshadows the manner of Seneca or Tacitus. His archaism in the use of pure Latin, and, alongside of it, his free adoption of Grecisms, are the first open sign of two movements which profoundly affected the prose of the earlier and later empire. The acrid critic of the Augustan age, Asinius Pollio, accused him of having had collections of obsolete words and phrases made for his use out of Cato and the older Roman writers. For a short time he was eclipsed by the brilliant and opulent style of Livy; but Livy formed no school, and Sallust on the whole remained in the first place. The line of Martial, *primus Romana Crispus in historia*, expresses the settled opinion held of him down to the final decay of letters; and even in the Middle Ages he remained widely read and highly esteemed.

Contemporary with Sallust in this period of transition between the Ciceronian and the Augustan age is Cornelius Nepos (*circ.* 99–24 B.C.). In earlier life he was one of the circle of Catullus, and after Cicero's death was one of the chief friends of Atticus, of whom a brief biography, which he wrote after Atticus' death, is still extant. Unlike Sallust, Nepos never took part in public affairs, but carried on throughout a long life the part of a man of letters, honest and kindly, but without any striking originality or ability. In him we are on the outer fringe of pure literature; and it is no doubt purposely that Quintilian wholly omits him from the list of Roman historians. Of his numerous writings on history, chronology, and grammar, we only possess a fragment of one, his collection of Roman and foreign biographies, entitled *De Viris Illustribus*. Of this work there is extant one complete section, *De Excellentibus Ducibus Exterarum Gentium*, and two lives from another section, those of Atticus and the younger Cato. The accident of their convenient length and the simplicity of their language has made them for generations a common school-book for beginners in Latin ; were it not for this, there can be little doubt that Nepos, like the later epitomators, Eutropius or Aurelius Victor, would be hardly known except to professional scholars, and perhaps only to be read in the pages of some *Corpus Scriptorum Romanorum.* The style of these little biographies is unpretentious, and the language fairly pure, though without any great command of phrase. A theory was once held that what we possess is merely a later epitome from the lost original. But for this there is no rational support. The language and treatment, such as they are (and they do not sink to the level of the histories of the African and Spanish wars), are of this, and not of a later age, and quite consonant with the good-natured contempt which Nepos met at the hands of later Roman critics. The chief interest of the work is perhaps the clearness with which it enforces the truth we are too apt to forget, that the great writers were in their own age, as now, unique, and that there is no such thing as a widely diffused level of high literary excellence.

As remote from literature in the higher sense were the innumerable writings of the Ciceronian age on science, art, antiquities, grammar, rhetoric, and a hundred miscellaneous subjects, which are, for the most part, known only from notices in the writings of later commentators and encyclopedists. Foremost among the voluminous authors of this class was the celebrated antiquarian, Marcus Terentius Varro, whose long and laborious life, reaching from two years after the death of the elder Cato till the final establishment of the Empire, covers and overlaps the entire Ciceronian age. Of the six or seven hundred volumes which issued from his pen, and which formed an inexhaustible

quarry for his successors, nearly all are lost. The most
important of them were the one hundred and fifty books
of *Saturae Menippeae*, miscellanies in prose and verse
in the manner which had been originated by Menippus of
Gadara, the master of the celebrated Meleager, and which
had at once obtained an enormous popularity throughout the
whole of the Greek-speaking world; the forty-one books of
Antiquitates Rerum Humanarum et Divinarum, the standard
work on the religious and secular antiquities of Rome down
to the time of Augustine; the fifteen books of *Imagines*,
biographical sketches, with portraits, of celebrated Greeks
and Romans, the first certain instance in history of the
publication of an illustrated book; the twenty-five books
De Lingua Latina, of which six are extant in an imperfect condition; and the treatise *De Re Rustica*, which
we possess in an almost complete state. This last work
was written at the age of eighty. It is in the form of a
dialogue, and is not without descriptive and dramatic power.
The tediousness which characterised all Varro's writing is
less felt where the subject is one of which he had a thorough
practical knowledge, and which gave ample scope for the
vein of rough but not ungenial humour which he inherited
from Cato.

Other names of this epoch have left no permanent mark
on literature. The precursors of Sallust in history seem,
like the precursors of Cicero in philosophy, to have
approached their task with little more equipment than that
of the ordinary amateur. The great orator Hortensius
wrote *Annals* (probably in the form of memoirs of his own
time), which are only known from a reference to them in
a later history written in the reign of Tiberius. Atticus,
who had an interest in literature beyond that of the mere
publisher, drew up a sort of handbook of Roman history,
which is repeatedly mentioned by Cicero. Cicero's own
brother Quintus, who passed for a man of letters, composed a work of the same kind; the tragedies with which

he relieved the tedium of winter-quarters in Gaul were, however, translations from the Greek, not originals. Cicero's private secretary, Marcus Tullius Tiro, best known by the system of shorthand which he invented or improved, and which for long remained the basis of a standard code, is also mentioned as the author of works on grammar, and, as has already been noticed, edited a collection of his master's letters after his death. Decimus Laberius, a Roman of equestrian family, and Publilius Syrus, a natural-ised native of Antioch, wrote mimes, which were performed with great applause, and gave a fugitive literary importance to this trivial form of dramatic entertainment. A collec-tion of sentences which passes under the name of the latter was formed out of his works under the Empire, and enlarged from other sources in the Middle Ages. It supplies many admirable instances of the terse vigour of the Roman popular philosophy; some of these lines, like the famous —

> *Bene vixit is qui potuit cum voluit mori,*

or —

> *Iudex damnatur ubi nocens absolvitur,*

or —

> *O vitam misero longam, felici brevem !*

or the perpetually misquoted —

> *Stultum facit fortuna, quem vult perdere,*

have sunk deeper and been more widely known than almost anything else written in Latin. Among the few poets who succeeded the circle of Catullus, the only one of interest is Publius Terentius Varro, known as Varro Atacinus from his birthplace on the banks of the Aude in Provence, the first of the long list of Transalpine writers who filled Rome at a later period. Besides the usual translations and adaptations from Alexandrian originals, and an elaborate

cosmography, he practised his considerable talent in hexameter verse both in epic and satiric poetry, and did something to clear the way in metrical technique for both Horace
and Virgil.   With these names, among a crowd of others
even more vague and shadowy, the literature of the Roman
Republic closes.   A new generation was already at the
doors.

II
THE AUGUSTAN AGE

L

VIRGIL.

PUBLIUS VERGILIUS MARO was born at the village of Andes, near Mantua, on the 15th of October, 70 B.C. The province of Cisalpine Gaul, though not formally incorporated with Italy till twenty years later, had before this become thoroughly Romanised, and was one of the principal recruiting grounds for the legions. But the population was still, by blood and sympathy, very largely Celtic; and modern theorists are fond of tracing the new element of romance, which Virgil introduced with such momentous results into Latin poetry, to the same Celtic spirit which in later ages flowered out in the Arthurian legend, and inspired the whole creative literature of mediaeval Europe. To the countrymen of Shakespeare and Keats it will not seem necessary to assume a Celtic origin, on abstract grounds, for any new birth of this romantic element. The name Maro may or may not be Celtic; any argument founded on it is of little more relevance than the fancy which once interpreted the name of Virgil's mother, Magia Polla, into a supernatural significance, and, connecting the name Virgilius itself with the word *Virgo*, metamorphosed the poet into an enchanter born of a maiden mother, the Merlin of the Roman Empire.

Virgil's father was a small freeholder in Andes, who farmed his own land, practised forestry and bee-keeping, and gradually accumulated a sufficient competence to enable him to give his son — an only child, so far as can be ascertained — the best education that the times could provide. He was sent to school at the neighbouring town of Cremona, and afterwards to Milan, the capital city of the province. At the age of seventeen he proceeded to Rome, where he studied oratory and philosophy under the best masters of the time. A tradition, which the dates make improbable, was that Gaius Octavius, afterwards the Emperor Augustus, was for a time his fellow-scholar under the rhetorician Epidius. In the class-room of the Epicurean Siro he may have made his first acquaintance with the poetry of Lucretius.

For the next ten years we know nothing of Virgil's life, which no doubt was that of a profound student. His father had died, and his mother married again, and his patrimony was sufficient to support him until a turn of the wheel of public affairs for a moment lost, and then permanently secured his fortune. After the battle of Philippi, the first task of the victorious triumvirs was to provide for the disbanding and settlement of the immense armies which had been raised for the Civil war. The lands of cities which had taken the Republican side were confiscated right and left for this purpose; among the rest, Virgil's farm, which was included in the territory of Cremona. But Virgil found in the administrator of the district, Gaius Asinius Pollio, himself a distinguished critic and man of letters, a powerful and active patron. By his influence and that of his friends, Cornelius Gallus and Alfenus Varus — the former a soldier and poet, the latter an eminent jurist, who both had been fellow-students of Virgil at Rome — Virgil was compensated by an estate in Campania, and introduced to the intimate circle of Octavianus, who, under the terms of the triumvirate, was already absolute ruler of Italy.

It was about this time that the *Eclogues* were published,

whether separately or collectively is uncertain, though the final collection and arrangement, which is Virgil's own, can hardly be later than 38 B.C. The impression they made on the world of letters was immediate and universal. To some degree no doubt a reception was secured to them by the influence of Maecenas, the Home Minister of Octavianus, who had already taken up the line which he so largely developed in later years, of a public patron of art and letters in the interest of the new government. But had Virgil made his first public appearance merely as a Court poet, it is probable that the *Eclogues* would have roused little enthusiasm and little serious criticism. Their true significance seems to have been at once realised as marking the beginning of a new era ; and amid the storm of criticism, laudatory and adverse, which has raged round them for so many ages since, this cardinal fact has always remained prominent. Alike to the humanists or the earlier Renaissance, who found in them the sunrise of a golden age of poetry and the achievement of the Latin conquest over Greece, and to the more recent critics of this century, for whom they represented the echo of an already exhausted convention and the beginning of the decadence of Roman poetry, the *Eclogues* have been the real turning-point, not only between two periods of Latin literature, but between two worlds.

The poems destined to so remarkable a significance are, in their external form, close and careful imitations of Theocritus, and have all the vices and weaknesses of imitative poetry to a degree that could not well be exceeded. Nor are these failings redeemed (as is to a certain extent true of the purely imitative work of Catullus and other poets) by any brilliant jewel-finish of workmanship. The execution is uncertain, hesitating, sometimes extraordinarily feeble. One well-known line it is impossible to explain otherwise than as a mistranslation of a phrase in Theocritus such as one would hardly expect from an average schoolboy. When

Virgil follows the convention of the Greek pastoral his copy is doubly removed from nature ; where he ventures on fresh impersonation or allegory of his own, it is generally weak in itself and always hopelessly out of tone with the rest. Even the versification is curiously unequal and imperfect. There are lines in more than one Eclogue which remind one in everything but their languor of the flattest parts of Lucretius. Contemporary critics even went so far as to say that the language here and there was simply not Latin.

Yet granted that all this and more than all this is true, it does not touch that specific Virgilian charm of which these poems first disclosed the secret. Already through their immature and tremulous cadences there pierces, from time to time, that note of brooding pity which is unique in the poetry of the world. The fourth and tenth Eclogues may be singled out especially as showing the new method, which almost amounted to a new human language, as they are also those where Virgil breaks away most decidedly from imitation of the Greek idyllists. The fourth Eclogue unfortunately has been so long and so deeply associated with purely adventitious ideas that it requires a considerable effort to read it as it ought to be read. The curious misconception which turned it into a prophecy of the birth of Christ outlasted in its effects any serious belief in its historical truth : even modern critics cite Isaiah for parallels, and are apt to decry it as a childish attempt to draw a picture of some actual golden age. But the Sibylline verses which suggested its contents and imagery were really but the accidental grain of dust round which the crystallisation of the poem began ; and the enchanted light which lingers over it is hardly distinguishable from that which saturates the *Georgics.* *Cedet et ipse mari vector, nec nautica pinus mutabit merces* — the feeling here is the same as in his mere descriptions of daily weather, like the *Omnia plenis rura natant fossis atque omnis navita ponto*

umida vela legit; not so much a vision of a golden age as
Nature herself seen through a medium of strange gold.
Or again, in the tenth Eclogue, where the masque of shepherds and gods passes before the sick lover, it is through
the same strange and golden air that they seem to move,
and the heavy lilies of Silvanus droop in the stillness of the
same unearthly day.

Seven years following on the publication of the *Eclogues*
were spent by Virgil on the composition of the *Georgics*.
They were published two years after the battle of Actium,
being thus the first, as they are the most splendid, literary
production of the Empire. They represent the art of Virgil
in its matured perfection. The subject was one in which he
was thoroughly at home and completely happy. His own
early years had been spent in the pastures of the Mincio,
among his father's cornfields and coppices and hives ; and
his newer residence, by the seashore near Naples in winter,
and in summer at his villa in the lovely hill-country of
Campania, surrounded him with all that was most beautiful
in the most beautiful of lands. His delicate health made
it easier for him to give his work the slow and arduous
elaboration that makes the *Georgics* in mere technical
finish the most perfect work of Latin, or perhaps of any
literature. There is no trace of impatience in the work.
It was in some sense a commission ; but Augustus and
Maecenas, if it be true that they suggested the subject, had,
at all events, the sense not to hurry it. The result more
than fulfilled the brilliant promise of the *Eclogues*. Virgil
was now, without doubt or dispute, the first of contemporary poets.

But his responsibilities grew with his greatness. The
scheme of a great Roman epic, which had always floated
before his own mind, was now definitely and indeed
urgently pressed upon him by authority which it was
difficult to resist. And many elements in his own mind
drew him in the same direction. Too much stress need

not be laid on the passage in the sixth Eclogue — one of the rare autobiographic touches is his work — in which he alludes to his early experiments in "singing of kings and battles." Such early exercises are the common field of young poets. But the maturing of his mind, which can be traced in the *Georgics*, was urging him towards certain methods of art for which the epic was the only literary form that gave sufficient scope. More and more he was turning from nature to man and human life, and to the contemplation of human destiny. The growth of the psychological instinct in the *Georgics* is curiously visible in the episode of Aristaeus, with which the poem now ends. According to a well-authenticated tradition, the last two hundred and fifty lines of the fourth *Georgic* were written several years after the rest of the poem, to replace the original conclusion, which had contained the praises of his early friend, Cornelius Gallus, now dead in disgrace and proscribed from court poetry. In the story of Orpheus and Eurydice, in the later version, Virgil shows a new method and a new power. It stands between the idyl and the epic, but it is the epic method towards which it tends. No return upon the earlier manner was thenceforth possible ; with many searchings of heart, with much occasional despondency and dissatisfaction, he addressed himself to the composition of the *Aeneid*.

The earlier national epics of Naevius and Ennius had framed certain lines for Roman epic poetry, which it was almost bound to follow. They had established the mythical connection of Rome with Troy and with the great cycle of Greek legend, and had originated the idea of making Rome itself — that *Fortuna Urbis* which later stood in the form of a golden statue in the imperial bedchamber — the central interest, one might almost say the central figure, of the story. To adapt the Homeric methods to this new purpose, and at the same time to make his epic the vehicle for all his own inward broodings over life and fate, for his subtle and delicate psychology, and for that philosophic passion in which all the other motives and springs of life were becoming included, was a task incapable of perfect solution. On his death-bed Virgil made it his last desire that the *Aeneid* should be destroyed, nominally on the ground that it still wanted three years' work to bring it to perfection, but one can hardly doubt from a deeper and less articulate feeling. The command of the Emperor alone prevented his wish from taking effect. With the unfinished *Aeneid,* as with the unfinished poem of Lucretius, it is easy to see within what limits any changes or improvements would have been made in it had the author lived longer: the work is, in both cases, substantially done.

The *Aeneid* was begun the year after the publication of the *Georgics,* when Virgil was forty years of age. During its progress he continued to live for the most part in his Campanian retirement. He had a house at Rome in the fashionable quarter of the Esquiline, but used it little. He was also much in Sicily, and the later books of the *Aeneid* seem to show personal observation of many parts of Central Italy. It is a debated question whether he visited Greece more than once. His last visit there was in 19 B.C. He had resolved to spend three years more on the completion of his poem, and then give himself up to philosophy for what might remain of his life. But the three years were not given him. A fever, caught while visiting Megara on a day of excessive heat, induced him to return hastily to Italy. He died a few days after landing at Brundusium, on the 26th of September. His ashes were, by his own request, buried near Naples, where his tomb was a century afterwards worshipped as a holy place.

The *Aeneid,* carefully edited from the poet's manuscript by two of his friends, was forthwith published, and had such a reception as perhaps no poem before or since has ever found. Already, while it was in progress, it had been

rumoured as "something greater than the *Iliad*," and now
that it appeared, it at once became the canon of Roman
poetry, and immediately began to exercise an unparalleled
influence over Latin literature, prose as well as verse.
Critics were not indeed wanting to point out its defects,
and there was still a school (which attained greater importance a century later) that went back to Lucretius
and the older poets, and refused to allow Virgil's pre-
eminence. But for the Roman world at large, as since
for the world of the Latin races, Virgil became what Homer
had been to Greece, "the poet." The decay of art and
letters in the third century only added a mystical and
hieratic element to his fame. Even to the Christian Church
he remained a poet sacred and apart : in his profound
tenderness and his mystical "yearning after the further
shore" as much as in the supposed prophecy of the fourth
Eclogue, they found and reverenced what seemed to them
like an unconscious inspiration. The famous passage of
St. Augustine, where he speaks of his own early love for
Virgil, shows in its half-hysterical renunciation how great
the charm of the Virgilian art had been, and still was,
to him : *Quid miserius misero*, he cries, *non miserante se
ipsum, et flente Didonis mortem quae fiebat amando Aeneam,
non flente autem mortem meam quae fiebat non amando te ?
Deus lumen cordis mei, non te amabam, et haec non flebam,
sed flebam Didonem exstinctam, ferroque extrema secutam,
sequens ipse extrema condita tua relicto te!* * To the graver
and more matured mind of Dante, Virgil was the lord and
master who, even though shut out from Paradise, was
the chosen and honoured minister of God. Up to the
beginning of the present century the supremacy of Virgil
was hardly doubted. Since then the development of
scientific criticism has passed him through all its searching
processes, and in a fair judgment his greatness has rather
gained than lost. The doubtful honour of indiscriminate

* *Confess.*, I. xii.

praise was for a brief period succeeded by the attacks
of an almost equally undiscriminating censure. An ill-
judged partiality had once spoken of the *Aeneid* as something greater than a Roman *Iliad :* it was easy to show
that in the most remarkable Homeric qualities the *Aeneid*
fell far short, and that, so far as it was an imitation of
Homer, it could no more stand beside Homer than the
imitations of Theocritus in the *Eclogues* could stand beside
Theocritus. The romantic movement, with its impatience
of established fames, damned the *Aeneid* in one word
as artificial; forgetting, or not seeing, that the *Aeneid* was
itself the fountain-head of romanticism. Long after the
theory of the noble savage had passed out of political
and social philosophy it lingered in literary criticism ; and
the distinction between " natural " and " artificial " poetry
was held to be like that between light and darkness. It
was not till a comparatively recent time that the leisurely
progress of criticism stumbled on the fact that all poetry
is artificial, and that the *Iliad* itself is artificial in a very
eminent and unusual degree.

No great work of art can be usefully judged by
comparison with any other great work of art. It may,
indeed, be interesting and fertile to compare one with
another, in order to seize more sharply and appreciate
more vividly the special beauty of each. But to press
comparison further, and to depreciate one because it has
not what is the special quality of the other, is to lose sight
of the function of criticism. We shall not find in Virgil
the bright speed, the unexhausted joyfulness, which, in
spite of a view of life as grave as Virgil's own, make the
Iliad and *Odyssey* unique in poetry ; nor, which is more
to the point as regards the *Aeneid*, the narrative power,
the genius for story-telling, which is one of the rarest of
literary gifts, and which Ovid alone among the Latin poets
possessed in any high perfection. We shall not find in
him that high and concentrated passion which in Pindar

(as afterwards in Dante) fuses the elements of thought and language into a single white heat. We shall not find in him the luminous and untroubled calm, as of a spirit in which all passion has been fused away, which makes the poetry of Sophocles so crystalline and irreproachable. Nor shall we find in him the great qualities of his own Latin predecessors, Lucretius or Catullus. All this is merely saying in amplified words that Virgil was not Lucretius or Catullus, and that still less was he Homer, or Pindar, or Sophocles; and to this may be added, that he lived in the world which the great Greek and Latin poets had created, though he looked forward out of it into another.

Yet the positive excellences of the *Aeneid* are so numerous and so splendid that the claim of its author to be the Roman Homer is not unreasonable, if it be made clear that the two poems are fundamentally disparate, and that no more is meant than that the one poet is as eminent in his own form and method as the other in his. In our haste to rest Virgil's claim to supremacy as a poet on the single quality in which he is unique and unapproachable we may seem tacitly to assent to the judgment of his detractors on other points. Yet the more one studies the *Aeneid*, the more profoundly is one impressed by its quality as a masterpiece of construction. The most adverse critic would not deny that portions of the poem are, both in dramatic and narrative quality, all but unsurpassed, and in a certain union of imaginative sympathy with their fine dramatic power and their stateliness of narration perhaps unequalled. The story of the last agony of Troy could not be told with more breadth, more richness, more brilliance than it is told in the second book: here, at least, the story neither flags nor hurries; from the moment when the Greek squadron sets sail from Tenedos and the signal-flame flashes from their flagship, the scenes of the fatal night pass before us in a smooth swift stream that gathers weight and volume as it goes, till it culminates in the

vision of awful faces which rises before Aeneas when Venus
lifts the cloud of mortality from his startled eyes. The
episode of Nisus and Euryalus in the ninth book, and that
of Camilla in the eleventh, are in their degree as admirably
vivid and· stately. The portraiture of Dido, again, in the
fourth book, is in combined breadth and subtlety one of
the dramatic masterpieces of human literature. It is idle
to urge that this touch is borrowed from Euripides or that
suggested by Sophocles, or to quote the Medea of Apollonius as the original of which Dido is an elaborate imitation. What Virgil borrowed he knew how to make his
own; and the world which, while not denying the tenderness, the grace, the charm of the heroine of the *Argonautica,* leaves the *Argonautica* unread, has thrilled and
grown pale from generation to generation over the passionate
tragedy of the Carthaginian queen.

But before a deeper and more appreciative study of the
Aeneid these great episodes cease to present themselves as
detached eminences. That the *Aeneid* is unequal is true;
that passages in it here and there are mannered, and even
flat, is true also; but to one who has had the patience to
know it thoroughly, it is in its total effect, and not in the
great passages, or even the great books, that it seems the
most consummate achievement. Virgil may seem to us to
miss some of his opportunities, to labour others beyond
their due proportion, to force himself (especially in the
later books) into material not well adapted to the distinctive
Virgilian treatment. The slight and vague portrait of the
maiden princess of Latium, in which the one vivid touch
of her "flower-like hair" is the only clear memory we carry
away with us, might, in different hands — in those of Apollonius, for instance, — have given a new grace and charm to
the scenes where she appears. The funeral games at the
tomb of Anchises, no longer described, as they had been
in early Greek poetry, from the mere pleasure in dwelling
upon their details, begin to become tedious before they

are over. In the battle-pieces of the last three books we sometimes cannot help being reminded that Virgil is rather wearily following an obsolescent literary tradition. But when we have set such passages against others which, without being as widely celebrated as the episode of the sack of Troy or the death of Dido, are equally miraculous in their workmanship — the end of the fifth book, for instance, or the muster-roll of the armies of Italy in the seventh, or, above all, the last hundred and fifty lines of the twelfth, where Virgil rises perhaps to his very greatest manner — we shall not find that the splendour of the poem depends on detached passages, but far more on the great manner and movement which, interfused with the unique Virgilian tenderness, sustains the whole structure through and through.

The merely technical quality of Virgil's art has never been disputed. The Latin hexameter, "the stateliest measure ever moulded by the lips of man," was brought by him to a perfection which made any further development impossible. Up to the last it kept taking in his hands new refinements of rhythm and movement which make the later books of the *Aeneid* (the least successful part of the poem in general estimation) an even more fascinating study to the lovers of language than the more formally perfect work of the *Georgics*, or the earlier books of the *Aeneid* itself. A brilliant modern critic has noted this in words which deserve careful study. "The innovations are individually hardly preceptible, but taken together they alter the character of the hexameter line in a way more easily felt than described. Among the more definite changes we may note that there are more full stops in the middle of lines, there are more elisions, there is a larger proportion of short words, there are more words repeated, more assonances, and a freer use of the emphasis gained by the recurrence of verbs in the same or cognate tenses. Where passages thus characterised have come down to us

still in the making, the effect is forced and fragmentary;
where they succeed, they combine in a novel manner the
rushing freedom of the old trochaics with the majesty
which is the distinguishing feature of Virgil's style.   Art
has concealed its art, and the poet's last words suggest to
us possibilities in the Latin tongue which no successor has
been able to realise."   Again, the psychological interest
and insight which keep perpetually growing throughout
Virgil's work result in an almost unequalled power of expressing in exquisite language the half-tones and delicate
shades of mental processes.   The famous simile in the
twelfth *Aeneid* —

> *Ac velut in somnis oculos ubi languida pressit*
> *Nocte quies, nequiquam avidos extendere cursus*
> *Velle videmur, et in mediis conatibus aegri*
> *Succidimus, nec lingua valet, nec corpore notae*
> *Sufficiunt vires aut vox et verba sequuntur* —

is an instance of the amazing mastery with which he makes
language have the effect of music, in expressing the subtlest
processes of feeling.

But the specific and central charm of Virgil lies deeper
than in any merely technical quality.   The word which
expresses it most nearly is that of pity.   In the most famous
of his single lines he speaks of the "tears of things;" just
this sense of tears, this voice that always, in its most sustained
splendour and in its most ordinary cadences, vibrates with
a strange pathos, is what finally places him alone among
artists.   This thrill in the voice, *come colui che piange e dice*,
is never absent from his poetry.   In the "lonely words,"
in the "pathetic half-lines" spoken of by the two great
modern masters of English prose and verse, he perpetually
touches the deepest springs of feeling;   in these it is that
he sounds, as no other poet has done, the depths of beauty
and sorrow, of patience and magnanimity, of honour in
life and hope beyond death.

A certain number of minor poems have come down to us associated more or less doubtfully with Virgil's name. Three of these are pieces in hexameter verse, belonging broadly to the class of the *epyllion*, or "little epic," which was invented as a convenient term to include short poems in the epic metre that were not definitely pastorals either in subject or treatment, and which the Alexandrian poets, headed by Theocritus, had cultivated with much assiduity and considerable success. The most important of them, the *Culex*, or *Gnat*, is a poem of about four hundred lines, in which the incident of a gnat saving the life of a sleeping shepherd from a serpent and being crushed to death in the act is made the occasion of an elaborate description of the infernal regions, from which the ghost of the insect rises to reproach his unconscious murderer. That Virgil in his youth wrote a poem with this title is established by the words of Martial and Statius; nor is there any certain argument against the Virgilian authorship of the extant poem, but various delicate metrical considerations incline recent critics to the belief that it is from the hand of an almost contemporary imitator who had caught the Virgilian manner with great accuracy. The *Ciris*, another piece of somewhat greater length, on the story of Scylla and Nisus, is more certainly the production of some forgotten poet belonging to the circle of Marcus Valerius Messalla, and is of interest as showing the immense pains taken in the later Augustan age to continue the Virgilian tradition. The third poem, the *Moretum*, is at once briefer and slighter in structure and more masterly in form. It is said to be a close copy of a Greek original by Parthenius of Nicaea, a distinguished man of letters of this period who taught Virgil Greek; nor is there any grave improbability in supposing that the *Moretum* is really one of the early exercises in verse over which Virgil must have spent years of his laborious apprenticeship, saved by some accident from the fate to which his own rigorous judgment condemned the rest.

So far the whole of the poetry attributed to Virgil is in the single form of hexameter verse, to the perfecting of which his whole life was devoted. The other little pieces in elegiac and lyric metres require but slight notice. Some are obviously spurious; others are so slight and juvenile that it matters little whether they are spurious or not. One elegiac piece, the *Copa*, is of admirable vivacity and grace, and the touch in it is so singularly unlike the Virgilian manner as to tempt one into the paradox of its authenticity. That Virgil wrote much which he deliberately destroyed is obviously certain; his fastidiousness and his melancholy alike drove him towards the search after perfection, and his mercilessness towards his own work may be measured by his intention to burn the *Aeneid*. Not less by this passionate desire of unattainable perfection than by the sustained glory of his actual achievement, — his haunting and liquid rhythms, his majestic sadness, his grace and pity, — he embodies for all ages that secret which makes art the life of life itself.

II.

HORACE.

In that great turning-point of the world's history marked by the establishment of the Roman Empire, the position of Virgil is so unique because he looks almost equally forwards and backwards. His attitude towards his own age is that of one who was in it rather than of it. On the one hand is his intense feeling for antiquity, based on and reinforced by that immense antiquarian knowledge which made him so dear to commentators, and which renders some of his work so difficult to appreciate from our mere want of information; on the other, is that perpetual brooding over futurity which made him, within a comparatively short time after his death, regarded as a prophet and his works as in some sense oracular. The *Sortes Vergilianae*, if we may believe the confused gossip of the Augustan History, were almost a State institution, while rationalism was still the State creed in ordinary matters. Thus, while, in a way, he represented and, as it were, gave voice to the Rome of Augustus, he did so in a transcendental manner; the Rome which he represents, whether as city or empire, being less a fact than an idea, and already strongly tinged with that mysticism which we regard as essentially mediaeval, and which culminated later without any violent breach of continuity in the conception of a spiritual Rome which was a kingdom of God on earth, and of which the Empire and the Papacy were only two imperfect and mutually complementary phases ; *quella Roma onde Cristo è Romano,* as it was expressed by Dante with his characteristic width and precision.

To this mystical temper the whole mind and art of Virgil's great contemporary stands in the most pointed contrast. More than almost any other poet of equal eminence, Horace lived in the present and actual world ; it is only when he turns aside from it that he loses himself. Certain external similarities of method there are between them — above all, in that mastery of verbal technique which made the Latin language something new in the hands of both. Both were laborious and indefatigable artists, and in their earlier acquaintanceship, at all events, were close personal friends. But the five years' difference in their ages represents a much more important interval in their poetical development. The earlier work of Horace, in the years when he was intimate with Virgil, is that which least shows the real man or the real poet ; it was not till Virgil, sunk in his *Aeneid,* and living in a somewhat melancholy retirement far away from Rome, was within a few years of his death, that Horace, amid the gaiety and vivid life of the capital, found his true scope, and produced the work that has made him immortal.

Yet the earlier circumstances of the two poets' lives had been not unlike. Like Virgil, Horace sprang from the ranks of the provincial lower middle class, in whom the virtues of industry, frugality, and sense were generally accompanied by little grace or geniality. But he was exceptionally fortunate in his father. This excellent man, who is always spoken of by his son with a deep respect and affection, was a freedman of Venusia in Southern Italy, who had acquired a small estate by his economies as a collector of taxes in the neighbourhood. Horace must have shown some unusual promise as a boy ; yet, according to his own account, it was less from this motive than from a disinterested belief in the value of education that his father resolved to give him, at whatever personal sacrifice, every advantage that was enjoyed by the children of the highest social class. The boy was taken to Rome about the age of twelve — Virgil, a youth of seventeen, came there from Milan about the same time — and given the best education that the capital could provide. Nor did he stop there ; at eighteen he proceeded to Athens, the most celebrated university then existing, to spend several years in completing his studies in literature and philosophy. While he was there the assassination of Caesar took place, and the Civil war broke out. Marcus Brutus occupied Macedonia, and swept Greece for recruits. The scarcity of Roman officers was so great in the newly levied legions that the young student, a boy of barely twenty-one, with no birth or connection, no experience, and no military or organising ability, was not only accepted with eagerness, but at once given a high commission. He served in the Republican army till Philippi, apparently without any flagrant discredit ; after the defeat, like many of his companions, he gave up the idea of further resistance, and made the best of his way back to Italy. He found his little estate forfeited, but he was not so important a person that he had to fear proscription, and with the strong common sense which he had already developed, he bought or begged himself a small post in the civil service which just enabled him to live. Three years later he was introduced by Virgil to Maecenas, and his uninterrupted prosperity began.

Did we know more of the history of Horace's life in the interval between his leaving the university and his becoming one of the circle of recognised Augustan poets, much in his poetical development might be less perplexing to us. The effect of these years was apparently to throw him back, to arrest or thwart what would have been his natural growth. No doubt he was one of the men who (like Caesar or Cromwell in other fields of action) develop late ; but

something more than this seems needed to account for the
extraordinary weakness and badness of his first volume of
lyrical pieces, published by him when he was thirty-five.
In the first book of the *Satires*, produced about five years
earlier, he had shown much of his admirable later qualities,
— humour, sense, urbanity, perception, — but all strangely
mingled with a vein of artistic vulgarity (the worst perhaps
of all vulgarities) which is totally absent from his matured
writing. It is not merely that in this earlier work he is
often deliberately coarse — that was a literary tradition,
from which it would require more than ordinary originality
to break free, — but that he again and again allows himself
to fall into such absolute flatness as can only be excused
on the theory that his artistic sense had been checked or
crippled in its growth, and here and there disappeared in
his nature altogether. How elaborate and severe the self-
education must have been which he undertook and carried
through may be guessed from the vast interval that separates the spirit and workmanship of the *Odes* from that of
the *Epodes*, and can partly be traced step by step in the
autobiographic passages of the second book of *Satires* and
the later *Epistles*. We are ignorant in what circumstances
or under what pressure the *Epodes* were published; it is
a plausible conjecture that their faults were just such as
would meet the approbation of Maecenas, on whose favour
Horace was at the time almost wholly dependent; and
Horace may himself have been glad to get rid, as it were,
of his own bad immature work by committing it to publicity.
The celebrated passage in Keats' preface to *Endymion*,
where he gives his reasons for publishing a poem of whose
weakness and faultiness he was himself acutely conscious,
is of very wide application; and it is easy to believe that,
after the publication of the *Epodes*, Horace could turn with
an easier and less embarrassed mind to the composition of
the *Odes*.

Meanwhile he was content to be known as a writer of

satire, one whose wish it was to bring up to an Augustan polish the literary form already carried to a high degree of success by Lucilius. The second book of *Satires* was published not long after the *Epodes*. It shows in every way an enormous advance over the first. He has shaken himself free from the imitation of Lucilius, which alternates in the earliest satires with a rather bitter and self-conscious depreciation of the work of the older poet and his successors. The prosperous turn Horace's own life had taken was ripening him fast, and undoing the bad effects of earlier years. We have passed for good out of the society of Rupilius Rex and Canidia. At one time Horace must have run the risk of turning out a sort of ineffectual François Villon; this, too, is over, and his earlier education bears fruit in a temper of remarkable and delicate gifts.

This second book of *Satires* marks in one way the culmination of Horace's powers. The brilliance of the first years of the Empire stimulated the social aptitude and dramatic perception of a poet who lived in the heart of Rome, already free from fear or ambition, but as yet untouched by the melancholy temper which grew on him in later years. He employs the semi-dramatic form of easy dialogue throughout the book with extraordinary lightness and skill. The familiar hexameter, which Lucilius had left still cumbrous and verbose, is like wax in his hands; his perfection in this use of the metre is as complete as that of Virgil in the stately and serious manner. And behind this accomplished literary method lies an unequalled perception of common human nature, a rich vein of serious and quiet humour, and a power of language the more remarkable that it is so unassuming, and always seems as it were to say the right thing by accident. With the free growth of his natural humour he has attained a power of self-appreciation which is unerring. The *Satires* are full from end to end of himself and his own affairs; but the name of egoism cannot be applied to any self-revelation or self-criticism

which is so just and so certain. From the opening lines
of the first satire, where he notes the faults of his own
earlier work, to the last line of the book, with its Parthian
shot at Canidia and the *jeunesse orageuse* that he had so
long left behind, there is not a page which is not full of
that self-reference which, in its truth and tact, constantly
passes beyond itself and holds up the mirror to universal
human nature. In reading the *Satires* we all read our own
minds and hearts.

Nearly ten years elapsed between the publication of the
second book of the *Satires* and that of the first book of
the *Epistles.* Horace had passed meanwhile into later
middle life. He had in great measure retired from society,
and lived more and more in the quietness of his little estate
among the Sabine hills. Life was still full of vivid interest ;
but books were more than ever a second world to him,
and, like Virgil, he was returning with a perpetually increasing absorption to the Greek philosophies, which had
been the earliest passion of his youth. Years had brought
the philosophic mind ; the more so that these years had
been filled with the labour of the *Odes,* a work of the
highest and most intricate effort, and involving the constant
study of the masterpieces of Greek thought and art. The
" monument more imperishable than bronze " had now
been completed ; its results are marked in the *Epistles* by
a new and admirable maturity and refinement. Good
sense, good feeling, good taste, — these qualities, latent from
the first in Horace, had obtained a final mastery over the
coarser strain with which they had at first been mingled ;
and in their shadow now appear glimpses of an inner
nature even more rare, from which only now and then he
lifts the veil with a sort of delicate self-depreciation, in an
occasional line of sonorous rhythm, or in some light touch
by which he gives a glimpse into a more magical view of
life and nature : the earliest swallow of spring on the coast,
the mellow autumn sunshine on a Sabine coppice, the

everlasting sound of a talking brook ; or, again, the unforgettable phrases, the *fallentis semita vitae,* or *quod petis hic
est,* or *ire tamen restat,* that have, to so many minds in so
many ages, been key-words to the whole of life.

It is in the *Epistles* that Horace reveals himself most
intimately, and perhaps with the most subtle charm. But
the great work of his life, for posterity as well as for his
own age, was the three books of *Odes* which were published
by him in 23 B.C., at the age of forty-two, and represent
the sustained effort of about ten years. This collection
of eighty-eight lyrics was at once taken to the heart of
the world. Before a volume of which every other line
is as familiar as a proverb, which embodies in a quintessential form that imperishable delight of literature to which
the great words of Cicero already quoted * give such
beautiful expression, whose phrases are on all men's lips
as those of hardly any other ancient author have been,
criticism is almost silenced. In the brief and graceful
epilogue, Horace claims for himself, with no uncertainty and
with no arrogance, such eternity as earth can give. The
claim was completely just. The school-book of the
European world, the *Odes* have been no less for nineteen
centuries the companions of mature years and the delight
of age — *adolescentiam agunt, senectutem oblectant,* may be
said of them with as much truth as ever now. Yet no
analysis will explain their indefinable charm. If the so-
called " lyrical cry " be of the essence of a true lyric, they
are not true lyrics at all. Few of them are free from a
marked artificiality, an almost rigid adherence to canon.
Their range of thought is not great ; their range of feeling
is studiously narrow. Beside the air and fire of a lyric of
Catullus, an ode of Horace for the moment grows pale
and heavy, *cineris specie decoloratur.* Beside one of the
pathetic half-lines of Virgil, with their broken gleams and
murmurs as of another world, a Horatian phrase loses lustre

* *Supra,* p. 68.

and sound.   Yet Horace appeals to a tenfold larger audience
than Catullus — to a larger audience, it may even be said,
than Virgil.   Nor is he a poets' poet : the refined and
exquisite technique of the *Odes* may be only appreciable
by a trained artist in language ; but it is the untrained mind,
on whom other art falls flat, that the art of Horace, by
some unique penetrative power, kindles and quickens.
His own phrase of " golden mediocrity " expresses with
some truth the paradox of his poetry ; in no other poet,
ancient or modern, has such studied and unintermitted
mediocrity been wrought in pure gold.   By some tact or
instinct — the " felicity," which is half of the famous phrase
in which he is characterised by Petronius — he realised that,
limited as his own range of emotion was, that of mankind
at large was still more so, and that the cardinal matter was
to strike in the centre.   Wherever he finds himself on the
edge of the range in which his touch is certain, he draws
back with a smile ; and so his concentrated effect, within
his limited but central field, is unsurpassed, and perhaps
unequalled.

This may partly explain how it was that with Horace
the Latin lyric stops dead.   His success was so immediate
and so immense that it fixed the limit, so to speak, for
future poets within the confined range which he had chosen
to adopt ; and that range he had filled so perfectly that no
room was left for anything but imitation on the one hand,
or, on the other, such a painful avoidance of imitation as
would be equally disastrous in its results.   With the
principal lyric metres, too, the sapphic and alcaic, he had
done what Virgil had done with the dactylic hexameter,
carried them to the highest point of which the foreign Latin
tongue was capable.   They were naturalised, but remained
sterile.   When at last Latin lyric poetry took a new development, it was by starting afresh from a wholly different point,
and by a reversion to types which, for the culture of the
early imperial age, were obsolete and almost non-existent.

The phrase, *verbis felicissime audax*, used of Horace as
a lyric poet by Quintilian, expresses, with something less
than that fine critic's usual accuracy, another quality which
goes far to make the merit of the *Odes*. Horace's use of
words is, indeed, remarkably dexterous; but less so from
happy daring than from the tact which perpetually poises
and balances words, and counts no pains lost to find the
word that is exactly right. His audacities — if one cares to
call them so,— in the use of epithet, in Greek constructions
(which he uses rather more freely than any other Latin
poet), and in allusive turns of phrase, are all carefully
calculated and precisely measured. His unique power of
compression is not that of the poet who suddenly flashes
out in a golden phrase, but more akin to the art of the
distiller who imprisons an essence, or the gem-engraver
working by minute touches on a fragment of translucent
stone. With very great resources of language at his disposal,
he uses them with singular and scrupulous frugality; in his
measured epithets, his curious fondness for a number of
very simple and abstract words, and the studious simplicity
of effect in his most elaborately designed lyrics, he reminds
one of the method of Greek bas-reliefs, or, still more (after
allowing for all the difference made by religious feeling),
of the sculptured work of Mino of Fiesole, with its pale
colours and carefully ordered outlines. Phrases of ordinary
prose, which he uses freely, do not, as in Virgil's hands,
turn into poetry by his mere use of them; they give rather
than receive dignity in his verses, and only in a few rare
instances, like the stately *Motum ex Metello consule civicum*,
are they completely fused into the structure of the poem.
So, too, his vivid and clearly-cut descriptions of nature in
single lines and phrases stand out by themselves like golden
tesserae in a mosaic, each distinct in a glittering atmosphere
— *qua tumidus rigat arva Nilus; opacam porticus excipiebat
Arcton; nec prata canis albicant pruinis* — a hundred phrases
like these, all exquisitely turned, and all with the same

effect of detachment, which makes them akin to sculpture, rather than painting or music. Virgil, as we learn from an interesting fragment of biography, wrote his first drafts swiftly and copiously, and wrought them down by long labour into their final structure; with Horace we may rather imagine that words came to the surface slowly and one by one, and that the *Odes* grew like the deposit, cell by cell, of the honeycomb to which, in a later poem, he compares his own workmanship. In some passages where the *Odes* flag, it seems as though material had failed him before the poem was finished, and he had filled in the gaps, not as he wished, but as he could, yet always with the same deliberate gravity of workmanship.

Horatii curiosa felicitas — this, one of the earliest criticisms made on the *Odes*, remains the phrase which most completely describes their value. Such minute elaboration, on so narrow a range of subject, and within such confined limits of thought and feeling, could only be redeemed from dulness by the perpetual felicity — something between luck and skill — that was Horace's secret. How far it was happy chance, how far deliberately aimed at and attained, is a question which brings us before one of the insoluble problems of art; we may remind ourselves that, in the words of the Greek dramatist Agathon, which Aristotle was so fond of quoting, skill and chance in all art cling close to one another. "Safe in his golden mediocrity," to use the words of his own counsel to Licinius, Horace has somehow or another taken deep hold of the mind, and even the imagination, of mankind. This very mediocrity, so fine, so chastened, so certain, is in truth as inimitable as any other great artistic quality; we must fall back on the word genius, and remember that genius does not confine itself within the borders of any theory, but works its own will.

With the publication of the three books of the *Odes*, and the first book of the *Epistles*, Horace's finest and maturest work was complete. In the twelve years of his life which

were still to run he published but little, nor is there any
reason to suppose that he wrote more than he published.
In 17 B.C., he composed, by special command, an ode to
be sung at the celebration of the Secular Games. The task
was one in which he was much hampered by a stringent
religious convention, and the result is interesting, but not
very happy. We may admire the skill with which formu-
laries of the national worship are moulded into the sapphic
stanza, and prescribed language, hardly, if at all, removed
from prose, made to run in stately, though stiff and monotonous, verse ; but our admiration is of the ingenuity, not of
the poetry. The *Jubilee Ode* written by Lord Tennyson
is curiously like the *Carmen Seculare* in its metrical in-
genuities, and in the way in which the unmistakeable
personal note of style sounds through its heavy and formal
movement.

Four years later a fourth book of *Odes* was published, the
greater part of which consists of poems less distinctly official
than the *Secular Hymn*, but written with reference to public
affairs by the direct command of the Emperor, some in
celebration of the victories of Drusus and Tiberius on the
north-eastern frontier, and others in more general praise of
the peace and external prosperity established throughout
Italy under the new government. Together with these
official pieces he included some others : an early sketch for
the *Carmen Seculare,* a curious fragment of literary criticism
in the form of an ode addressed to one of the young aris-
tocrats who followed the fashion of the Augustan age in
studying and writing poetry, and eight pieces of the same
kind as his earlier odes, written at various times within the
ten years which had now passed since the publication of
the first three books. An introductory poem, of graceful
but half-ironical lamentation over the passing of youth,
seems placed at the head of the little collection in studious
depreciation of its importance. Had it not been for the
necessity of publishing the official odes, it is probable

enough that Horace would have left these few later lyrics ungathered. They show the same care and finish in workmanship as the rest, but there is a certain loss of brilliance; except one ode of mellow and refined beauty, the famous *Diffugere nives,* they hardly reach the old level. The creative impulse in Horace had never been very powerful or copious; with growing years he became less interested in the achievement of literary artifice, and turned more completely to his other great field, the criticism of life and literature. To the concluding years of his life belong the three delightful essays in verse which complete the list of his works. Two of these, which are placed together as a second book of *Epistles,* seem to have been published at about the same time as the fourth book of the *Odes.* The first, addressed to the Emperor, contains the most matured and complete expression of his views on Latin poetry, and is in great measure a vindication of the poetry of his own age against the school which, partly from literary and partly from political motives, persisted in giving a preference to that of the earlier Republic. In the second, inscribed to one of his younger friends belonging to the circle of Tiberius, he reviews his own life as one who was now done with literature and literary fame, and was giving himself up to the pursuit of wisdom. The melancholy of temperament and advancing age is subtly interwoven in his final words with the urbane humour and strong sense that had been his companions through life : —

> *Lusisti satis, edisti satis atque bibisti,*
> *Tempus abire tibi est, ne potum largius aequo*
> *Rideat et pulset lasciva decentius aetas.*

A new generation, clever, audacious, and corrupt, had silently been growing up under the Empire. Ovid was thirty, and had published his *Amores.* The death of Virgil had left the field of serious poetry to little men. The younger race had learned only too well the lesson of minute care and formal polish so elaborately taught them by the earlier Augustan poets, and had caught the ear of the town with work of superficial but, for the time, captivating brilliance. Gloom was already beginning to gather round the Imperial household; the influence of Maecenas, the great support of letters for the last twenty years, was fast on the wane. In the words just quoted, with their half-sad and half-mocking echo of the famous passage of Lucretius,* Horace bids farewell to poetry.

But literary criticism, in which he had so fine a taste, and on which he was a recognised authority, continued to interest him ; and the more seriously minded of the younger poets turned to him for advice, which he was always willing to give. The *Epistle to the Pisos*, known more generally under the name of the *Art of Poetry*, seems to have been composed at intervals during these later years, and was, perhaps, not published till after his death in the year 8 B.C. It is a discussion of dramatic poetry, largely based on Greek text-books, but full of Horace's own experience and of his own good sense. Young aspirants to poetical fame regularly began with tragedies ; and Horace, accepting this as an actual fact, discusses the rules of tragedy with as much gravity as if he were dealing with some really living and national form of poetry. This discursive and fragmentary essay was taken in later ages as an authoritative treatise ; and the views expressed by Horace on a form of poetical art with which he had little practical acquaintance had, at the revival of literature, and even down to last century, an immense influence over the structure and development of the drama. Just as modern comedy based itself on imitation of Plautus and Terence, and as the earliest attempts at tragedy followed haltingly in the steps of Seneca, so as regards the theory of both, Horace, and not the Greeks, was the guiding influence.

Among the many amazing achievements of the Greek

* *Supra*, p. 48.

genius in the field of human thought were a lyrical poetry
of unexampled beauty, a refined critical faculty, and, later
than the great thinkers and outside of the strict schools, a
temperate philosophy of life such as we see afterwards in the
beautiful personality of Plutarch.   In all these three Horace
interpreted Greece to the world, while adding that peculiarly
Roman urbanity — the spirit at once of the grown man as
distinguished from children, of the man of the world, and
of the gentleman — which up till now has been a dominant
ideal over the thought and life of Europe.

III.

THOSE years of the early Empire in which the names of Virgil and Horace stand out above all the rest were a period of great fertility in Latin poetry. Great poets naturally bring small poets after them; and there was no age at Rome in which the art was more assiduously practised or more fashionable in society. The Court set a tone which was followed in other circles, and more especially among the younger men of the old aristocracy, now largely excluded from the public life which had engrossed their parents under the Republic. The influence of the Alexandrian poets, so potent in the age of Catullus, was not yet exhausted; and a wider culture had now made the educated classes familiar with the whole range of earlier Greek poetry as well. Rome was full of highly educated Greek scholars, some of whom were themselves poets of considerable merit. It was the fashion to form libraries; the public collection, formed by Augustus, and housed in a sumptuous building on the Palatine, was only the largest among many others in the great houses of Rome. The earlier Latin poets had known only a small part of Greek literature, and that very imperfectly; their successors had been trammelled by too exclusive an admiration of the Greek of the decadence. Virgil and Horace, though professed students of the Alexandrians, had gone back themselves, and had recalled the attention of the public, to the poets of free Greece, and had stimulated the widely felt longing to conquer the whole field of poetry for the Latin tongue.

For this attempt, tradition and circumstance finally proved too strong; and Augustan poetry, outside of these two great names, is largely a chronicle of failure. This was most eminently so in the drama. Augustan tragedy seems never to have risen for a moment beyond mere academic exercises. Of the many poets who attempted it, nothing survives beyond a string of names. Lucius Varius Rufus, the intimate friend of both Virgil and Horace, and one of the two joint-editors of the *Aeneid* after the death of the former, wrote one tragedy, on the story of Thyestes, which was acted with applause at the games held to celebrate the victory of Actium, and obtained high praise from later critics. But he does not appear to have repeated the experiment; like so many other Latin poets, he turned to the common path of annalistic epic. Augustus himself began a tragedy of *Ajax*, but never finished it. Gaius Asinius Pollio, the first orator and critic of the period, and a magnificent patron of art and science, also composed tragedies more on the antique model of Accius and Pacuvius, in a dry and severe manner. But neither in these, nor in the work of the young men for whose benefit Horace wrote the *Epistle to the Pisos*, was there any real vitality; the precepts of Horace could no more create a school of tragedians than his example could create a school of lyric poets.

The poetic forms, on the other hand, used by Virgil were so much more on the main line of tendency that he stands among a large number of others, some of whom might have had a high reputation but for his overwhelming superiority. Of the other essays made in this period in bucolic poetry we know too little to speak with any confidence. But both didactic poetry and the little epic were largely culti-vated, and the greater epic itself was not without followers.

The extant poems of the *Culex* and *Ciris* have already been noted as showing with what skill and grace unknown poets, almost if not absolutely contemporary with Virgil, could use the slighter epic forms. Varius, when he abandoned tragedy, wrote epics on the death of Julius Caesar, and on the achievements of Agrippa. The few fragments of the former which survive show a remarkable power and refinement; Virgil paid them the sincerest of all compliments by conveying, not once only but again and again, whole lines of Varius into his own work. Another intimate friend of Virgil, Aemilius Macer of Verona, wrote didactic poems in the Alexandrian manner on several branches of natural history, which were soon eclipsed by the fame of the *Georgics*, but remained a model for later imitators of Nicander. One of these, a younger contemporary of Virgil called Gratius, or Grattius, was the author of a poem on hunting, still extant in an imperfect form. In its tame and laboured correctness it is only interesting as showing the early decay of the Virgilian manner in the hands of inferior men.

A more interesting figure, and one the loss of whose works is deeply to be regretted, is that of Gaius Cornelius Gallus, the earliest and one of the most brilliant of the Augustan poets. Like Varro Atacinus, he was born in Narbonese Gaul, and brought into Roman poetry a new touch of Gallic vivacity and sentiment. The year of his birth was the same as that of Virgil's, but his genius matured much earlier, and before the composition of the *Eclogues* he was already a celebrated poet, as well as a distinguished man of action. The history of his life, with its swift rise from the lowest fortune to the splendid viceroyalty of Egypt, and his sudden disgrace and death at the age of forty-three, is one of the most dramatic in Roman history. The translations from Euphorion, by which he first made his reputation, followed the current fashion; but about the same time he introduced a new kind of poetry, the erotic elegy, which had a swift and far-reaching success. To Gallus, more than to any other single poet, is due the naturalisation in Latin of the elegiac couplet, which, together with the lyrics of Horace and the Virgilian hexameter, makes up the threefold poetical achievement of the Augustan period, and which, after the Latin lyric had died out with Horace himself, halved the field with the hexameter. For the remaining literature of the Empire, for that of the Middle Ages so far as it followed classical models, and even for that of the Renaissance, which carries us down to within a measurable distance of the present day, the hexameter as fixed by Virgil, and the elegiac as popularised by Gallus and rapidly brought to perfection by his immediate followers, are the only two poetical forms of real importance.

The elegiac couplet had, of course, been in use at Rome long before; Ennius himself had employed it, and in the Ciceronian age Catullus had written in it largely, and not without success. But its successful use had been hitherto mainly confined to short pieces, such as would fall within the definition of the Greek epigram. The four books of poems in which Gallus told the story of his passion for the courtesan Cytheris (the Lycoris of the tenth Eclogue) showed the capacities of the metre in a new light. The fashion they set was at once followed by a crowd of poets. The literary circles of Maecenas and Messalla had each their elegiac poet of the first eminence; and the early death of both Propertius and Tibullus was followed, amid the decline of the other forms of the earlier Augustan poetry, by the consummate brilliance of Ovid.

Of the Augustan elegiac poets, Sextus Propertius, a native of Assisi in Umbria, and introduced at a very early age to the circle of Maecenas, is much the most striking and interesting figure, not only from the formal merit of his poetry, but as representing a type till then almost unknown in ancient literature. Of his life little is known. Like Virgil, he lost his patrimonial property in the confiscations which followed the Civil war, but he was then a mere child. He seems to have been introduced to imperial patronage by the publication of the first book of his *Elegies* at the age of about twenty. He died young, before he was thirty-five, if we may draw an inference from the latest allusions in his extant poems; he had then written four other books of elegiac pieces, which were probably published separately at intervals of a few years. In the last book there is a noticeable widening of range of subject, which foreshadows the further development that elegiac verse took in the hands of Ovid soon after his death.

In striking contrast to Virgil or Horace, Propertius is a genius of great and, indeed, phenomenal precocity. His first book of *Elegies*, the *Cynthia monobiblos* of the grammarians, was a literary feat comparable to the early achievements of Keats or Byron. The boy of twenty had already mastered the secret of elegiac verse, which even Catullus had used stiffly and awkwardly, and writes it with an ease, a colour, a sumptuousness of rhythm which no later poet ever equalled. The splendid cadence of the opening couplet —

> *Cynthia prima suis miserum me cepit ocellis*
> *Contactum nullis ante cupidinibus —*

must have come on its readers with the shock of a new revelation. Nothing like it had ever been written in Latin before: itself and alone it assures a great future to the Latin elegiac. His instinct for richness of sound is equally conspicuous where it is found in purely Latin phrases, as in the opening of the sixteenth elegy —

> *Quae fueram magnis olim patefacta triumphis*
> *Ianua Tarpeiae nota pudicitiae*
> *Cuius inaurati celebrarunt limina currus*
> *Captorum lacrimis umida supplicibus,*

and where it depends on a lavish use of Greek ornament, as in the opening of the third —

Qualis Thesea iacuit cedente carina
  Languida desertis Gnosia litoribus,
Qualis et accubuit primo Cepheïa somno
  Libera iam duris cotibus Andromede.

Even when one comes to them fresh from Virgil, lines like these open a new world of sound. The Greek elegiac, as it is known to us by the finest work of the epigrammatists, had an almost unequalled flexibility and elasticity of rhythm; this quality Propertius from the first seized, and all but made his own. By what course of reasoning he was led in his later work to suppress this large and elastic treatment, and approximate more and more closely to the fine but somewhat limited and metallic rhythm which has been perpetuated by the usage of Ovid, we cannot guess. In this first book he ends the pentameter freely with words of three, four, and five syllables; the monotony of the perpetual dissyllabic termination, which afterwards became the normal usage, is hardly compensated by the increased smoothness which it gives the verse.

But this new power of versification accompanied a new spirit even more remarkable, which is of profound import as the precursor of a whole school of modern European poetry. The *Cynthia* is the first appearance in literature of the neurotic young man, who reappeared last century in Rousseau's *Confessions* and Goethe's *Werther,* and who has dominated a whole side of French literature since Alfred de Musset. The way had been shown half a century before by that remarkable poet, Meleager of Gadara, whom Propertius had obviously studied with keen appreciation. Phrases in the *Cynthia,* like —

Tum mihi constantis deiecit lumina fastus
  Et caput impositis pressit Amor pedibus,

or —

Qui non ante patet donec manus attigit ossa,

are in the essential spirit of Meleager, and, though not

verbally copied from him, have the precise quality of his rhythms and turns of phrase. But the abandonment to sensibility, the absorption in self-pity and the sentiment of passion, are carried by Propertius to a far greater length. The self-abasement of a line like —

> *Sis quodcumque voles, non aliena tamen,*

is in the strongest possible contrast to that powerful passion which fills the poetry of Catullus, or to the romantic tenderness of the *Eclogues;* and in the extraordinary couplet —

> *Me sine, quem semper voluit fortuna iacere,*
> *Hanc animam extremae reddere nequitiae,*

"the expense of spirit in a waste of shame" reaches its culminating point. This tremulous self-absorption, rather than any defect of eye or imagination, is the reason of the extraordinary lapses which now and then he makes both in description and in sentiment. The vivid and picturesque sketches he gives of fashionable life at watering-places and country-houses in the eleventh and fourteenth elegies, or single touches, like that in the remarkable couplet —

> *Me mediae noctes, me sidera prona iacentem,*
> *Frigidaque Eoo me dolet aura gelu,*

show that where he was interested neither his eye nor his language had any weakness ; but, as a rule, he is not interested either in nature or, if the truth be told, in Cynthia, but wholly in himself. He ranks among the most learned of the Augustan poets ; but, for want of the rigorous training and self-criticism in which Virgil and Horace spent their lives, he made on the whole but a weak and ineffective use of a natural gift perhaps equal to either of theirs. Thus it is that his earliest work is at the same time his most fascinating and brilliant. After the *Cynthia* he rapidly became, in the mordant phrase

used by Heine of De Musset, *un jeune homme d'un bien
beau passé.* Some premonition of early death seems to
have haunted him ; and the want of self-control in his
poetry may reflect actual physical weakness united with
his vivid imagination.

The second and third books of the *Elegies,** though
they show some technical advance, and are without the
puerilities which here and there occur in the *Cynthia,*
are on the whole immensely inferior to it in interest and
charm.   There is still an occasional line of splendid
beauty, like the wonderful—

Sunt apud infernos tot milia formosarum;

an occasional passage of stately rhythm, like the lines
beginning—

Quandocunque igitur nostros mors clausit ocellos;

but the smooth versification has now few surprises ; the
learning is becoming more mechanical ; there is a tendency
to say over again what he had said before, and not to say
it quite so well.

Through these two books Cynthia is still the main
subject.   But with the advance of years, and his own
growing fame as a poet, his passion — if that can be called
a passion which was so self-conscious and so sentimental —
fell away from him, and left his desire for literary reputation the really controlling motive of his work.   In the
introductory poem to the fourth book there is a new and
almost aggressive tone with regard to his own position
among the Roman poets, which is in strong contrast to
the modesty of the epilogue to the third book.   The
inflated invocation of the ghost of Callimachus laid him
fatally open to the quietly disdainful reference by which,
without even mentioning Propertius by name, Horace met

* These are the two parts of what is printed as book ii. in the older
editions.

it a year or two later in the second book of the *Epistles*
But even Horace is not infallible; and Propertius was, at
all events, justified in regarding himself as the head of a
new school of poetry, and one which struck its roots wide
and deep.

In the fourth and fifth books of the *Elegies* there is a
wide range of subject; the verse is being tested for various
purposes, and its flexibility answers to almost every demand.   But already we feel its fatal facility.   The passage
beginning *Atque ubi iam Venerem*, in the poem where he
contrasts his own life with those of the followers of riches
and ambition, is a dilution into twelve couplets of eight
noble lines of the *Georgics*, with an effect almost as feeble,
if not so grotesque, as that of the later metaphrasts, who
occupied themselves in turning heroic into elegiac poems
by inserting a pentameter between each two lines.   The
sixth elegy of the same book is nothing but a cento of
translations from the *Anthology*, strung together and fastened
up at the end by an original couplet in the worst and
most puerile manner of his early writing.   On the other
hand, these books include fresh work of great merit, and
some of great beauty.   The use of the elegiac metre to
tell stories from Graeco-Roman mythology and legendary
Roman history is begun in several poems which, though
Propertius has not the story-telling gift of Ovid, showed
the way to the delightful narratives of the *Fasti*.   A few
of the more personal elegies have a new and not very
agreeable kind of realism, as though De Musset had been
touched with the spirit of Flaubert.   In one, the ninth
of the fourth book, the realism is in a different and
pleasanter vein; only Herrick among English poets has
given such imaginative charm to straightforward descriptions of the ordinary private life of the middle classes.
The fifth book ends with the noble elegy on Cornelia,
the wife of Paulus Aemilius Lepidus, in which all that
is best in Propertius' nature at last finds splendid and

memorable expression. It has some of his common failings, — passages of inappropriate learning, and a little falling
off towards the end. But where it rises to its height, in
the lines familiar to all who know Latin, it is unsurpassed
in any poetry for grace and tenderness.

> *Nunc tibi commendo communia pignora natos;*
>   *Haec cura et cineri spirat inusta meo.*
> *Fungere maternis vicibus pater : illa meorum*
>   *Omnis erit collo turba fovenda tuo.*
> *Oscula cum dederis tua flentibus, adice matris;*
>   *Tota domus coepit nunc onus esse tuum.*
> *Et siquid doliturus eris, sine testibus illis !*
>   *Cum venient, siccis oscula falle genis :*
> *Sat tibi sint noctes quas de me, Paule, fatiges,*
>   *Somniaque in faciem reddita saepe meam.*

In these lines, hardly to be read without tears, Propertius
for once rises into that clear air in which art passes beyond
the reach of criticism. What he might have done in
this new manner had he lived longer can only be conjectured; at the same age neither Virgil nor Horace had
developed their full genius. But the perpetual recurrence
in the later poems of that brooding over death, which had
already marked his juvenile work, indicates increasing
exhaustion of power. Even the sparkling elegy on the
perils of a lover's rapid night journey from Rome to Tibur
passes at the end into a sombre imagination of his own
grave ; and the fine and remarkable poem (beginning with
the famous *Sunt aliquid Manes*) in which the ghost of
Cynthia visits him, is full of the same morbid dwelling
on the world of shadows, where the "golden girl" awaits
her forgetful lover. *Atque hoc sollicitum vince sopore caput*
had become the sum of his prayers. But a little while
afterwards the restless brain of the poet found the sleep
that it had so long desired.

At a time when literary criticism was so powerful at

Rome, and poetry was ruled by somewhat rigid canons of taste, it is not surprising that more stress was laid on the defects than on the merits of Propertius' poetry. It evidently annoyed Horace; and in later times Propertius remained the favourite of a minority, while general taste preferred the more faultless, if less powerfully original, elegiacs of his contemporary, Albius Tibullus. This pleasing and graceful poet was a few years older than Propertius, and, like him, died at the age of about thirty-five. He did not belong to the group of court poets who formed the circle of Maecenas, but to a smaller school under the patronage of Marcus Valerius Messalla, a distinguished member of the old aristocracy, who, though accepting the new government and loyal in his service to the Emperor, held somewhat aloof from the court, and lived in a small literary world of his own. Tibullus published in his lifetime two books of elegiac poems; after his death a third volume was published, containing a few of his posthumous pieces, together with poems by other members of the same circle. Of these, six are elegies by a young poet of the upper class, writing under the name of Lygdamus, and plausibly conjectured to have been a near relative of Tibullus. One, a panegyric on Messalla, by an unknown author, is without any poetical merit, and only interesting as an average specimen of the amateur poetry of the time when, in the phrase of Horace —

> *Populus calet uno*
> *Scribendi studio; pueri patresque severi*
> *Fronde comas vincti cenant et carmina dictant.*

The curious set of little poems going under the name of Sulpicia, and included in the volume, will be noticed later.

Tibullus might be succinctly and perhaps not unjustly described as a Virgil without the genius. The two poets died in the same year, and a contemporary epigram speaks

of them as the recognised masters of heroic and elegiac
verse ; while the famous tribute of Ovid, in the third book
of the *Amores*, shows that the death of Tibullus was regarded
as an overwhelming loss by the general world of letters.
" Pure and fine," the well-chosen epithets of Quintilian,
are in themselves no slight praise ; and the poems reveal
a gentleness of nature and sincerity of feeling which make
us think of their author less with admiration than with a
sort of quiet affection.   No two poets could be more
strongly contrasted than Tibullus and Propertius, even
when their subject and manner of treatment approximate
most closely.   In Tibullus the eagerness, the audacity, the
irregular brilliance of Propertius are wholly absent ; as are
the feverish self-consciousness and the want of good taste
and good sense which are equally characteristic of the latter.
Poetry is with him, not the outburst of passion, or the
fruit of high imagination, but the natural and refined
expression of sincere feeling in equable and melodious
verse.   The delightful epistle addressed to him by Horace
shows how high he stood in the esteem and affection of
a severe critic, and a man whose friendship was not lightly
won or lavishly expressed.   He stands easily at the head
of Latin poets of the second order.   In delicacy, in refinement, in grace of rhythm and diction, he cannot be easily
surpassed ; he only wants the final and incommunicable
touch of genius which separates really great artists from the
rest of the world.

IV.

OVID.

THE Peace of the Empire, secured by the victory of Actium, and fully established during the years which followed by Augustus and his lieutenants, inaugurated a new era of social life in the capital. The saying of Augustus, that he found Rome brick and left it marble, may be applied beyond the sphere of mere architectural decoration. A French critic has well observed that now, for the first time, the Court and the City existed in their full meaning. Both had an organised life and a glittering external ease such as was hardly known again in Europe till the reign of the Grand Monarque. The enormous accumulated wealth of the aristocracy was in the mass hardly touched by all the waste and confiscations of the civil wars; and, in spite of a more rigorous administration, fresh accumulations were continually made by the new official hierarchy, and flowed in from all parts of the Empire to feed the luxury and splendour of the capital. Wealth and peace, the increasing influence of Greek culture, and the absence of political excitement, induced a period of brilliant laxity among the upper classes. The severe and frugal morals of the Republic still survived in great families, as well as among that middle class, from which the Empire drew its solid support; but in fashionable society there was a marked and rapid relaxation of morals which was vainly combated by stringent social and sumptuary legislation.

The part taken by women in social and political life is among the most powerful factors in determining the general aspect of an age. This, which had already been great under the later Republic, was now greater than ever. The Empress Livia was throughout the reign of Augustus, and even after his death, one of the most important persons in Rome. Partly under her influence, partly from the temperament and policy of Augustus himself, a sort of court Puritanism grew up, like that of the later years of Louis Quatorze. The aristocracy on the whole disliked and despised it; but the monarchy was stronger than they. The same gloom overshadows the end of these two long reigns. Sentences of death or banishment fell thick among the leaders of that gay and profligate society; to later historians it seemed that all the result of the imperial policy had been to add hypocrisy to profligacy, and incidentally to cripple and silence literature.

Of this later Augustan period Ovid is the representative poet. The world in which he lived may be illustrated by a reference to two ladies of his acquaintance, both in different ways singularly typical of the time. Julia, the only daughter of Augustus, still a mere child when her father became master of the world, was brought up with a strictness which excited remark even among those who were familiar with the strict traditions of earlier times. Married, when a girl of fourteen, to her cousin, Marcus Claudius Marcellus; after his death, two years later, to the Emperor's chief lieutenant, Marcus Agrippa; and a third time, when he also died, to the son of the Empress Livia, afterwards the Emperor Tiberius, — she was throughout treated as a part of the State machinery, and as something more or less than a woman. But she turned out to be, in fact, a woman whose beauty, wit, and recklessness were alike extraordinary, and who rose in disastrous revolt against the system in which she was forced to be a pivot. Alike by birth and genius she easily took the first place in Roman society ; and under the very eyes of the Emperor she multiplied her lovers right and left, and launched out into a career that for years was the scandal of all Rome. When she had reached the age of thirty-seven, in the same year when Ovid's *Art of Love* was published, the axe suddenly fell ; she was banished, disinherited, and kept till her death in rigorous imprisonment, almost without the necessaries of life. Such were the firstfruits of the social reform inaugurated by Augustus and sung by Horace.

In the volume of poems which includes the posthumous elegies of Tibullus, there is also contained a group of short pieces by another lady of high birth and social standing, a niece of Messalla and a daughter of Servius Sulpicius, and so belonging by both parents to the inner circle of the aristocracy. Nothing is known of her life beyond what can be gathered from the poems. But that they should have been published at all, still more that they should have been published, as they almost certainly were, with the sanction of Messalla, is a striking instance of the unique freedom enjoyed by Roman women of the upper classes, and of their disregard of the ordinary moral conventions. The only ancient parallel is in the period of the Aeolic Greek civilisation which produced Sappho. The poems are addressed to her lover, who (according to the fashion of the time — like Catullus' Lesbia or Propertius' Cynthia) is spoken of by a Greek name, but was most probably a young Roman of her own circle. The writer, a young, and apparently an unmarried woman, addresses him with a frankness of passion that has no idea of concealment. She does not even take the pains to seal her letters to him, though they contain what most women would hesitate to put on paper. They have all the same directness, which sometimes becomes a splendid simplicity. One note, reproaching him for a supposed infidelity —

> *Si tibi cura togae potior pressumque quasillo*
> *Scortum quam Servi filia Sulpicia —*

has all the noble pride of Shakespeare's Imogen. Of the world and its ways she has no girlish ignorance; but the talk of the world, as a motive for reticence, simply does not exist for her.

Where young ladies of the upper classes had such freedom as is shown in these poems, and used it, the ordinary lines of demarcation between respectable women and women who are not respectable must have largely disappeared. It has been much and inconclusively debated whether the Hostia and Plania, to whom, under assumed names, the amatory poems of Propertius and Tibullus were addressed, were more or less married women (for at Rome there were degrees of marriage), or women for whom marriage was a remote and immaterial event. The same controversy has raged over Ovid's Corinna, who is variously identified as Julia the daughter of the Emperor herself, as a figment of the imagination, or as an ordinary courtesan. The truth is, that in the society so brilliantly drawn in the *Art of Love*, such distinctions were for the time suspended, and we are in a world which, though for the time it was living and actual, is as unreal to us as that of the Restoration dramatists.

The young lawyer and man of fashion, Publius Ovidius Naso, who was the laureate of this gay society, was a few years younger than Propertius, with whom he was in close and friendly intimacy. The early death of both Propertius and Tibullus occurred before Ovid published his first volume; and Horace, the last survivor of the older Augustans, had died some years before that volume was followed by any important work. The period of Ovid's greatest fertility was the decad immediately following the opening of the Christian era; he outlived Augustus by three years, and so laps over into the sombre period of the Julio-Claudian dynasty, which culminated in the reign of Nero.

As the eldest surviving son of an opulent equestrian family of Upper Italy, Ovid was trained for the usual

career of civil and judicial office. He studied for the bar
at Rome, and, though he never worked hard at law, filled
several judicial offices of importance. But his interest was
almost wholly in the rhetorical side of his profession; he
" hated argument ; " and from the rhetoric of the schools to
the highly rhetorical poetry which was coming into fashion
there was no violent transition. An easy fortune, a brilliant
wit, an inexhaustible memory, and an unfailing social tact,
soon made him a prominent figure in society; and his
genuine love of literature and admiration for genius —
unmingled in his case with the slightest trace of literary
jealousy or self-consciousness — made him the friend of the
whole contemporary world of letters. He did not begin to
publish poetry very early ; not because he had any delicacy
about doing so, nor because his genius took long to ripen,
but from the good-humoured laziness which never allowed
him to take his own poetry too seriously. When he was
about thirty he published, to be in the fashion, a volume
of amatory elegiacs, which was afterwards re-edited and
enlarged into the existing three books of *Amores.* Probably
about the same time he formally graduated in serious poetry
with his tragedy of *Medea.* For ten or twelve years afterwards he continued to throw off elegiac poems, some light,
others serious, but all alike in their easy polish, and written
from the very first with complete and effortless mastery of
the metre. To this period belong the *Heroides,* the later
pieces in the *Amores,* the elaborate poem on the feminine
toilet called *De Medicamine Faciei,* and other poems now
lost. Finally, in 2 or 1 B.C., he published what is perhaps
on the whole his most remarkable work, the three books
De Arte Amatoria.

Just about the time of the publication of the *Art of Love,*
the exile of the elder Julia fell like a thunderbolt on Roman
society. Staggered for a little under the sudden blow, it
soon gathered itself together again, and a perpetual influx
of younger men and women gathered round her daughter

and namesake, the wife of Lucius Aemilius Paulus, into a circle as corrupt, if not so accomplished, as that of which Ovid had been a chief ornament. He was himself now forty; though singularly free from literary ambition, he could not but be conscious of his extraordinary powers, and willing to employ them on larger work. He had already incidentally proved that he possessed an instinct for narrative such as no Roman poet had hitherto had — such, indeed, as it would be difficult to match even in Greek poetry outside Homer. A born story-teller, and an accomplished master of easy and melodious verse, he naturally turned for subjects to the inexhaustible stores of the Graeco-Roman mythology, and formed the scheme of his *Metamorphoses* and *Fasti*. Both poems were all but complete, but only the first half of the latter had been published, when, at the end of the year 8, his life and work were suddenly shattered by a mysterious catastrophe. An imperial edict ordered him to leave Rome on a named day, and take up his residence at the small barbarous town of Tomi, on the Black Sea, at the extreme outposts of civilisation. No reason was assigned, and no appeal allowed. The cause of this sudden action on the part of the Emperor remains insoluble. The only reason ever officially given, that the publication of the *Art of Love* (which was already ten years old) was an offence against public morals, is too flimsy to have been ever meant seriously. The allusions Ovid himself makes to his own " error " or " crime " are not meant to be intelligible, and none of the many theories which have been advanced fully satisfies the facts. But, whatever may have been the cause — whether Ovid had become implicated in one of those aristocratic conspiracies against which Augustus had to exercise constant vigilance, or in the intrigues of the younger Julia, or in some domestic scandal that touched the Emperor even more personally — it brought his literary career irretrievably to the ground. The elegies which he continued to pour forth from his place of exile, though not without their grace and pathos, struggle almost from the first under the crowning unhappiness of un- happiness, that it ceases to be interesting. The five books of the *Tristia*, written during the earlier years of his banish- ment, still retain, through the monotony of their subject, and the abject humility of their attitude to Augustus, much of the old dexterity. In the four books of *Epistles from Pontus*, which continue the lamentation over his calamities, the failure of power is evident. He went on writing pro- fusely, because there was nothing else to do; panegyrics on Augustus and Tiberius alternated with a natural history of fish — the *Halieutica* — and with abusive poems on his real or fancied enemies at Rome. While Augustus lived he did not give up hopes of a remission, or at least an alleviation, of his sentence; but the accession of Tiberius, who never forgot or forgave anything, must have extinguished them finally; and he died some three years later, still a heart- broken exile.

Apart from his single tragedy, from a few didactic or mock-didactic pieces, imitated from Alexandrian originals, and from his great poem of the *Metamorphoses*, the whole of Ovid's work was executed in the elegiac couplet. His earliest poems closely approximate in their management of this metre to the later work of Propertius. The narrower range of cadence allowed by the rule which makes every couplet regularly end in a dissyllable, involves a monotony which only Ovid's immense dexterity enabled him to overcome. In the *Fasti* this dexterity becomes almost portentous : when his genius began to fail him, the essential vice of the metre is soon evident. But the usage was stereotyped by his example; all through the Empire and through the Middle Ages, and even down to the present day, the Ovidian metre has been the single dominant type : and though no one ever managed it with such ingenuity again, he taught enough of the secret to make its use possible for almost every kind of subject. His own elegiac poetry covers an ample range. In the impassioned rhetoric of the *Heroides*, the brilliant pictures of life and manners in the *De Arte Amatoria,* or the sparkling narratives of the *Fasti,* the same sure and swift touch is applied to widely diverse forms and moods. Ovid was a trained rhetorician and an accomplished man of the world before he began to write poetry; that, in spite of his worldliness and his glittering rhetoric, he has so much of feeling and charm, is the highest proof of his real greatness as a poet.

But this feeling and charm are the growth of more mature years. In his early poetry there is no passion and little sentiment. He writes of love, but never as a lover; nor, with all his quickness of insight and adroitness of impersonation, does he ever catch the lover's tone. From the amatory poems written in his own person one might judge him to be quite heartless, the mere hard and polished mirror of a corrupt society; and in the *Art of Love* he is the keen observer of men and women whose wit and lucid common sense are the more insolently triumphant because untouched by any sentiment or sympathy. We know him from other sources to have been a man of really warm and tender feeling; in the poetry which he wrote as laureate of the world of fashion he keeps this out of sight, and outdoes them all in cynical worldliness. It is only when writing in the person of a woman — as in the Phyllis or Laodamia of the *Heroides* — that he allows himself any approach to tenderness. The *Ars Amatoria,* full as it is of a not unkindly humour, of worldly wisdom and fine insight, is perhaps the most immoral poem ever written. The most immoral, not the most demoralizing : he writes for an audience for whom morality, apart from the code of good manners which society required, did not exist; and wholly free as it is from morbid sentiment, the one great demoralizing influence over men and women, it may be doubted whether the poem is one which ever did any reader serious harm, while few works are more intellectually stimulating within a certain limited range. To readers for whom its qualities have exhausted or have not acquired their stimulating force, it merely is tiresome; and this, indeed, is the fate which in the present age, when wit is not in vogue, has very largely overtaken it.

Interspersed in the *Art of Love* are a number of stories from the old mythology, introduced to illustrate the argument, but set out at greater length than was necessary for that purpose, from the active pleasure it always gives Ovid to tell a story. When he conceived the plan of his *Metamorphoses*, he had recognised this narrative instinct as his special gift. His tragedy of *Medea* had remained a single effort in dramatic form, unless the *Heroides* can be classed as dramatic monologues. The *Medea*, but for two fine single lines, is lost; but all the evidence is clear that Ovid had no natural turn for dramatic writing, and that it was merely a clever *tour de force*. In the idea of the *Metamorphoses* he found a subject, already treated in more than one Alexandrian poem, that gave full scope for his narrative gift and his fertile ingenuity. The result was a poem as long, and almost as unflagging, as the *Odyssey*. A vast mass of multifarious stories, whose only connection is the casual fact of their involving or alluding to some transformation of human beings into stones, trees, plants, beasts, birds, and the like, is cast into a continuous narrative. The adroitness with which this is done makes the poem rank as a masterpiece of construction. The atmosphere of romantic fable in which it is enveloped even gives it a certain plausibility of effect almost amounting to epic unity. In the fabulous superhuman element that appears in all the stories, and in their natural surroundings of wood, or mountain, or sea — always realised with fresh enjoyment and vivid form and colour — there is something which gives the same sort of unity of effect as we feel in reading the *Arabian Nights*. It is not a real world; it is hardly even a world conceived as real; but it is a world so plausible, so directly appealing to simple instincts and unclouded senses, above all so completely taken for granted, that the illusion is, for the time, all but complete. For later ages, the *Metamorphoses* became the great text-book of classical mythology ; the legends were understood as Ovid had told them, and were reproduced (as, for instance, throughout the whole of the painting of the Renaissance) in the spirit and colour of this Italian story-teller.

For the metre of the *Metamorphoses* Ovid chose the heroic hexameter, but used it in a strikingly new and original way. He makes no attempt, as later poets unsuccessfully did, at reproducing the richness of tone and intricacy of modulation which it had in the hands of Virgil. Ovid's hexameter is a thing of his own. It becomes with him almost a new metre — light, brilliant, and rapid, but with some monotony of cadence, and without the deep swell that it had, not in Virgil only, but in his predecessors. The swift, equable movement is admirably adapted to the matter of the poem, smoothing over the transitions from story to story, and never allowing a story to pause or flag halfway. Within its limits, the workmanship is faultless. The style neither rises nor sinks with the variation of subject. One might almost say that it was without moral quality. Ovid narrates the treachery of Scylla or the incestuous passion of Myrrha with the same light and secure touch as he applies to the charming idyl of Baucis and Philemon or the love-tale of Pyramus and Thisbe ; his interest is in what happened, in the story for the story's sake. So, likewise, in the rhetorical evolution of his thought, and the management of his metre, he writes simply as the artist, with the artistic conscience as his only rule. The rhetorician is as strong in him as it had been in the *Amores ;* but it is under better control, and seldom leads him into excesses of bad taste, nor is it so overmastering as not to allow free play to his better qualities, his kindliness, his good-humour, his ungrudging appreciation of excellence. In his evolution of thought — or his play of fancy, if the expression be preferred — he has an alertness and precision akin to great intellectual qualities; and it is this, perhaps, which has made him a favourite with so many great men of letters. Shakespeare himself, in his earlier work, alike the plays and the poems, writes in the Ovidian manner, and often in what might be direct imitation of Ovid; the motto from the *Amores* prefixed to the *Venus and Adonis* is not idly chosen. Still more remarkable, because less superficially evident, is the affinity between Ovid and Milton. At first sight no two poets, perhaps, could seem less alike. But it is known that Ovid was one of Milton's favourite poets; and if one reads the *Meta-morphoses* with an eye kept on *Paradise Lost,* the intellectual resemblance, in the manner of treatment of thought and language, is abundantly evident, as well in the general structure of their rhetoric as in the lapses of taste and obstinate puerilities (*non ignoravit vitia sua sed amavit* might be said of Milton also), which come from time to time in their maturest work.

The *Metamorphoses* was regarded by Ovid himself as his masterpiece. In the first impulse of his despair at leaving Rome, he burned his own copy of the still incomplete poem. But other copies were in existence; and though he writes afterwards as though it had been published without his correction and without his consent, we may suspect that it was neither without his knowledge nor against his will; when he speaks of the *manus ultima* as wanting, it is probably a mere piece of harmless affectation to make himself seem liker the author of the *Aeneid.* The case was different with the *Fasti,* the other long poem which he worked at side by side with the *Metamorphoses.* The twelve books of this work, dealing with the calendar of the twelve months, were also all but complete when he was banished, and the first six, if not actually published had, at all events, got into private circulation. At Tomi he began a revision of the poem which, apparently, he never completed. The first half of the poem, prefaced by a fresh dedication to Germanicus, was published, or republished, after the death of Augustus, to whom, in its earlier form, it had been inscribed; the second half never reached the public. It cannot be said that Latin poetry would be much poorer had the first six books been suppressed also. The student of metrical forms would, indeed, have lost what is metrically the most dexterous of all Latin poems, and the archaeologist some curious information as to Roman customs; but, for other readers, little would be missed but a few of the exquisitely told stories, like that of Tarquin and Lucretia, or of the Rape of Proserpine, which vary the somewhat tedious chronicle of astronomical changes and national festivals.

The poems of the years of Ovid's exile, the *Tristia* and the *Letters from Pontus*, are a melancholy record of flagging vitality and failing powers. His adulation of the Emperor and the imperial family passes all bounds; it exhausts what would otherwise seem the inexhaustible copiousness of his vocabulary. The long supplication to Augustus, which stands by itself as book ii. of the *Tristia*, is the most elaborate and skilful of these pieces; but those which may be read with the most pleasure are the letters to his wife, for whom he had a deep affection, and whom he addresses with a pathos that is quite sincere. As hope of recall grew fainter, his work failed more and more; the incorrect language and slovenly versification of some of the *Letters from Pontus* are in sad contrast to the Ovid of ten years before, and if he went on writing till the end, it was only because writing had long been a second nature to him.

Of the extraordinary force and fineness of Ovid's natural genius, there never have been two opinions; had he but been capable of controlling it, instead of indulging it, he might have, in Quintilian's opinion, been second to no Roman poet. In his *Medea*, the critic adds, he did show some of this self-control; its loss is the more to be lamented. But the easy good-nature of his own disposition, no less than the whole impulse of the literary fashion then prevalent, was fatal to the continuous exercise of such severe self-education: and the man who was so keen and shrewd in his appreciation of the follies of lovers had all the weakness of a lover for the faults of his own poetry. The delightful story of the three lines which his critical friends urged him to erase proves, if proof were needed, that this weakness was not blindness, and that he was perfectly aware of the vices of his own work. The child of his time, he threw all his brilliant gifts unhesitatingly into the scale of new ideas and new fashions; his "modernity," to use a current phrase of the present day, is greater than that of any other ancient author of anything like his eminence.

> *Prisca iuvent alios, ego me nunc denique natum*
> *Gratulor: haec aetas moribus apta meis —*

this is his deliberate attitude throughout his life.

Such a spirit has more than once in the history of the arts marked the point from which their downward course began. *I do not sing the old things, for the new are far better,* the famous Greek musician Timotheus had said four centuries earlier, and the decay of Greek music was dated from that period. But to make any artist, however eminent, responsible for the decadence of art, is to confuse cause with effect; and the note of ignominy affixed by Augustus to the *Art of Love* was as futile as the action of the Spartan ephor when he cut the strings away from the cithara of Timotheus. The actual achievement of Ovid was to perfect and popularise a poetical form of unusual scope and flexibility; to throw a vivid and lasting life into the world of Graeco-Roman mythology; and, above all, to complete the work of Cicero and Horace in fixing a certain ideal of civilised manners for the Latin Empire and for modern Europe. He was not a poet of the first order; yet few poets of the first order have done a work of such wide importance.

V.

THE Ciceronian age represents on the whole the culmination of Latin prose, as the Augustan does the culmination
of Latin poetry. In the former field, the purity of the
language as it had been used by Caesar and Cicero could
hardly be retained in a period of more diffused culture ; and
the influence of the schools of rhetoric, themselves based
on inferior Greek models, became more and more marked.
Poetry, too, was for the time more important than prose,
and one result was that prose became infected with certain
qualities of poetical style. The reign of Augustus includes
only one prose writer of the first rank, the historian Titus
Livius.

Though not living like Virgil or Horace in the immediate
circle of Augustus and under direct court patronage, Livy
was in friendly relations with the Emperor and his family,
and accepted the new rule with cordiality, if without much
enthusiasm. Of his life, which seems to have been wholly
spent in literary pursuits, little is known. He was born at
Padua in the year of Julius Caesar's first consulship, and
had survived Augustus by three years when he died at the
age of seventy-five. In earlier life he wrote some philosophical dialogues and treatises on rhetoric which have not
been preserved. An allusion in the first book of his history
shows that it was written, or at all events published, after
the first and before the second closing of the temple of

Janus by Augustus, in the years 29 and 25 B.C. For forty years thereafter he continued this colossal task, which, like the *Decline and Fall,* was published in parts from time to time. He lived to bring it down as far as the death of Drusus, the younger son of the Empress Livia, in the year 9 B.C. The division into books, of which there were one hundred and forty-two in the whole work, is his own; these again were arranged in *volumina,* or sections issued as separate volumes, and containing a varying number of books. The division of the work into decads was made by copyists at a much later period, and was no part of the author's own plan. Only one-fourth of the whole history has survived the Middle Ages. This consists of the first, the third, the fourth, and half of the fifth decad, or books i.–x. and xxi.–xlv. of the work; of the rest we only possess brief tables of contents, drawn up in the fourth century, not from the original work but from an abridgment, itself now lost, which was then in use. The scale of the history is very different in the two surviving portions. The first decad carries it from the foundation of the city through the Regal and early Republican periods down to the third Samnite war, a period of four centuries and a half. The twenty-five extant books of the third, fourth, and fifth decads cover a period of fifty years, from the beginning of the second Punic to the conclusion of the third Macedonian war. This half century, it is true, was second in importance to none in Roman history. But the scale of the work had a constant tendency to expand as it approached more modern times, and more abundant documents; and when he reached his own time, nearly a book was occupied with the events of each year.

Founded as it was, at least for the earlier periods, upon the works of preceding annalists, the history of Livy adopted from them the arrangement by years marked by successive consulates, which was familiar to all his readers. He even speaks of his own work as *annales,* though its formal title seems to have been *Historiae* (or *Libri Historiarum*) *ab Urbe Condita*. There is no reason to suppose that he intended to conclude it at any fixed point. In a preface to one of the later volumes, he observed with justifiable pride that he had already satisfied the desire of fame, and only went on writing because the task of composition had become a fixed habit, which he could not discontinue without uneasiness. His fame even in his lifetime was unbounded. He seems to have made no enemies. The acrid criticism of Asinius Pollio, a purist by profession, on certain provincialities of his style, was an insignificant exception to the general chorus of praise. In treading the delicate ground of the Civil wars his candour towards the Republican party led Augustus to tax him half jestingly as a Pompeian; yet Livy lost no favour either with him or with his more jealous successor. The younger Pliny relates how a citizen of Cadiz was so fired by his fame that he travelled the whole way to Rome merely to see him, and as soon as he had seen him returned home, as though Rome had no other spectacles to offer.

Roman history had hitherto been divided between the annalists and the writers of personal and contemporary memoirs. Sallust was almost the only example of the definite historical treatment of a single epoch or episode of the past. As a rule each annalist set himself the same task, of compiling, from the work of his predecessors, and such additional information as he found accessible to him, a general history of the Roman people from its beginnings, carried down as far towards his own day as he found time or patience to continue it. Each successive annalist tried to improve upon previous writers, either in elegance of style or in copiousness of matter, and so far as he succeeded in the double task his work replaced those already written. It was not considered unfair to transcribe whole passages from former annalists, or even to copy their works with additions and improvements, and bring them out as new and original histories.   The idea of literary property seems, in truth, to be very much a creation of positive law.   When no copyright existed, and when the circulation of any book was confined within very small limits by the cost and labour of transcription, the vaguest ideas prevailed, not at Rome alone, on what we should now regard as the elementary morality of plagiarism.   Virgil himself transferred whole lines and passages, not merely from earlier, but even from contemporary poets ;   and in prose writing, one annalist cut up and reshaped the work of another with as little hesitation as a mediaeval romance-writer.

In this matter Livy allowed himself full liberty ; and his work absorbed, and in a great measure blotted out, those of his predecessors.   In his general preface he speaks of the two motives which animate new historians, as the hope that they will throw further light on events, or the belief that their own art will excel that of a ruder age.   The former he hardly professes to do, at least as regards times anterior to his own ; his hope is that by his pen the great story of the Republic will be told more impressively, more vividly, in a manner more stimulating to the reader and more worthy of the subject than had hitherto been done.   This purpose at least he amply and nobly carried out ; nor can it be said to be a low ideal of the function of history.

So far, however, as the office of the historian is to investigate facts, to get at the exact truth of what physically happened, or to appreciate the varying degrees of probability with which that truth can be attained, Livy falls far short of any respectable ideal.   His romantic temper and the ethical bent of his mind alike indisposed him to set any very great value on facts as such.   His history bears little trace of any independent investigation.   Sources for history lay round him in immense profusion.   The enormous collections made by Varro in every field of antiquarian research were at his hand, but he does not seem to have used them, still less to have undertaken any similar labour

on his own account. While he never wilfully distorts the
truth, he takes comparatively little pains to disengage it
from fables and inaccuracies. In his account of a battle
in Greece he finds that Valerius Antias puts the number of
the enemy killed as inside ten thousand, while Claudius
Quadrigarius says forty thousand. The discrepancy does
not ruffle him, nor even seem to him very important; he
contents himself with an expression of mild surprise that
Valerius for once allows himself to be outstripped in exaggerating numbers. Yet where Valerius is his only authority
or is not contradicted by others, he accepts his statements,
figures and all, without uneasiness.   This instance is typical
of his method as a critical — or rather an uncritical — historian.
When his authorities do not disagree, he accepts what they
say without much question.   When they do disagree, he
has several courses open to him, and takes one or another
according to his fancy at the moment.   Sometimes he
counts heads and follows the majority of his authors;
sometimes he adopts the account of the earliest; often he
tries to combine or mediate between discordant stories;
when this is not easy, he chooses the account which is
most superficially probable or most dramatically impressive.
He even bases a choice on the ground that the story he
adopts shows Roman statesmanship or virtue in a more
favourable light, though he finds some of the inventions of
Roman vanity too much for him to swallow.   Throughout
he tends to let his own preferences decide whether or not
a story is true. *In rebus tam antiquis si quae similia veri
sint pro veris accipiantur* is the easy canon which he lays
down for early and uncertain events. Even when original
documents of great value were extant, he refrains from
citing them if they do not satisfy his taste. During the
second Punic war a hymn to Juno had been written by
Livius Andronicus for a propitiatory festival. It was one
of the most celebrated documents of early Latin; but he
refuses to insert it, on the ground that to the taste of his

own day it seemed rude and harsh. Yet as a historian, and not a collector of materials for history, he may plead the privilege of the artist. The modern compromise by which documents are cited in notes without being inserted in the text of histories had not then been invented ; and notes, even when as in the case of Gibbon's they have a substantive value as literature, are an adjunct to the history itself, rather than any essential part of it. A more serious charge is, that when he had trustworthy authorities to follow, he did not appreciate their value. In his account of the Macedonian wars, he often follows Polybius all but word for word, but without apparently realising the Greek historian's admirable accuracy and judgment. Such appreciation only comes of knowledge ; and Livy lacked the vast learning and the keen critical insight of Gibbon, to whom in many respects he has a strong affinity. His imperfect knowledge of the military art and of Roman law often confuses his narrative of campaigns and constitutional struggles, and gives too much reason to the charge of negligence brought against him by that clever and impudent critic, the Emperor Caligula.

Yet, in spite of all his inaccuracies of detail, and in spite of the graver defect of insufficient historical perspective, which makes him colour the whole political development of the Roman state with the ideas of his own time, the history of Rome as narrated by Livy is essentially true and vital, because based on a large insight into the permanent qualities of human nature. The spirit in which he writes history is well illustrated by the speeches. These, in a way, set the tone of the whole work. He does not affect in them to reproduce the substance of words actually spoken, or even to imitate the tone of the time in which the speech is laid. He uses them as a vivid and dramatic method of portraying character and motive. The method, in its brilliance and its truth to permanent facts, is like that of Shakespeare's *Coriolanus.* Such truth, according to

the celebrated aphorism in Aristotle's *Poetics*, is the truth of
poetry rather than of history : and the history of Livy, in
this, as in his opulent and coloured diction, has some affinity
to poetry. Yet, when such insight into motive and such
vivid creative imagination are based on really large knowledge and perfect sincerity, a higher historical truth may
be reached than by the most laborious accumulation of
documents and sifting of evidence.

Livy's humane and romantic temper prevented him from
being a political partisan, even if political partisanship had
been consistent with the view he took of his own art.
In common with most educated Romans of his time, he
idealised the earlier Republic, and spoke of his own age
as fatally degenerate. But this is a tendency common to
writers of all periods. He frequently pauses to deplore the
loss of the ancient qualities by which Rome had grown
great — simplicity, equity, piety, orderliness. In his remarkable preface he speaks of himself as turning to historical
study in order to withdraw his mind from the evils of his
own age, and the spectacle of an empire tottering to the
fall under the weight of its own greatness and the vices
of its citizens. " Into no State," he continues, " were greed
and luxury so long in entering ; in these late days avarice
has grown with wealth, and the frantic pursuit of pleasure
leads fast towards a collapse of the whole social fabric ; in
our ever-accelerating downward course we have already
reached a point where our vices and their remedies are
alike intolerable." But his idealisation of earlier ages was
that of the romantic student rather than the reactionary
politician. He is always on the side of order, moderation,
conciliation ; there was nothing politically dangerous to
the imperial government in his mild republicanism. He
shrinks instinctively from violence wherever he meets it,
whether on the side of the populace or of the governing
class ; he cannot conceive why people should not be
reasonable, and live in peace under a moderate and settled

government. This was the temper which was welcome at court, even in men of Pompeian sympathies.

So, too, Livy's attitude towards the established religion and towards the beliefs of former times has the same sentimental tinge. The moral reform attempted by Augustus had gone hand in hand with an elaborate revival and amplification of religious ceremony. Outward conformity at least was required of all citizens. *Expedit esse deos, et ut expedit esse putemus;* "the existence of the gods is a matter of public policy, and we must believe it accordingly," Ovid had said, in the most daring and cynical of his poems. The old associations, the antiquarian charm, that lingered round this faded ancestral belief, appealed strongly to the romantic patriotism of the historian. His own religion was a sort of mild fatalism; he pauses now and then to draw rather commonplace reflections on the blindness of men destined to misfortune, or the helplessness of human wisdom and foresight against destiny. But at the same time he gravely chronicles miracles and portents, not so much from any belief in their truth as because they are part of the story. The fact that they had ceased to be regarded seriously in his own time, and were accordingly in a great measure ceasing to happen, he laments as one among many declensions from older and purer fashions.

As a master of style, Livy is supreme among historians. He marks the highest point which the enlarged and enriched prose of the Augustan age reached just before it began to fall into decadence. It is no longer the famous *urbanus sermo* of the later Republic, the pure and somewhat austere language of a governing class. The influence of Virgil is already traceable in Livy, in actual phrases whose use had hitherto been confined to poetry, and also in a certain warmth of colouring unknown to earlier prose. To Augustan purists this relaxation of the language seemed provincial and unworthy of the severe tradition of the best Latin; and it was this probably, rather than any definite novelties in

grammar or vocabulary, that made Asinius Pollio accuse
Livy of " Patavinity." But in the hands of Livy the new
style, by its increased volume and flexibility, is as admirably
suited to a work of great length and scope as the older
had been for the purposes of Caesar or Sallust. It is drawn,
so to speak, with a larger pattern; and the added richness
of tone enables him to advance without flagging through
the long and intricate narrative where a simpler diction
must necessarily have grown monotonous, as one more
florid would be cloying. In the earlier books we seem to
find the manner still a little uncertain and tentative, and
a little trammelled by the traditional manner of the older
annalists; as he proceeds in his work he falls into his
stride, and advances with a movement as certain as that
of Gibbon, and claimed by Roman critics as comparable
in ease and grace to that of Herodotus. The periodic
structure of Latin prose which had been developed by
Cicero is carried by him to an even greater complexity,
and used with a greater daring and freedom; a sort of
fine carelessness in detail enhancing the large and continuous excellence of his broad effect. Even where he
copies Polybius most closely he invariably puts life and
grace into his cumbrous Greek. For the facts of the war
with Hannibal we can rely more safely on the latter; but
it is in the picture of Livy that we see it live before us.
His imagination never fails to kindle at great actions; it
is he, more than any other author, who has impressed
the great soldiers and statesmen of the Republic on the
imagination of the world.

> *Quin Decios Drusosque procul, saevumque securi*
> *Aspice Torquatum, et referentem signa Camillum . . .*
> *Quis te, magne Cato, tacitum, aut te, Cosse, relinquat?*
> *Quis Gracchi genus, aut geminos, duo fulmina belli,*
> *Scipiadas, cladem Libyae, parvoque potentem*
> *Fabricium, vel te sulco, Serrane, serentem ? —*

his whole work is a splendid expansion of that vision of Rome which passes before the eyes of Aeneas in the Fortunate Fields of the underworld. In the description of great events, no less than of great characters and actions, he rises and kindles with his subject. His eye for dramatic effect is extraordinary. The picture of the siege and storming of Saguntum, with which he opens the stately narrative of the war between Rome and Hannibal, is an instance of his instinctive skill; together with the masterly sketch of the character of Hannibal and the description of the scene in the Carthaginian senate-house at the reception of the Roman ambassadors, it forms a complete prelude to the whole drama of the war. His great battle-pieces, too, in spite of his imperfect mastery of military science, are admirable as works of art. Among others may be specially instanced, as masterpieces of execution, the account of the victory over Antiochus at Magnesia in the thirty-seventh book, and, still more that in the forty-fourth of the fiercely contested battle of Pydna, the desperate heroism of the Pelignian cohort, and the final and terrible destruction of the Macedonian phalanx.

Yet, with all his admiration for great men and deeds, what most of all kindles Livy's imagination and sustains his enthusiasm is a subject larger, and to him hardly more abstract, the Roman Commonwealth itself, almost personified as a continuous living force. This is almost the only matter in which patriotism leads him to marked partiality. The epithet "Roman" signifies to him all that is high and noble. That Rome can do no wrong is a sort of article of faith with him, and he has always a tendency to do less than justice to her enemies. The two qualities of eloquence and candour are justly ascribed to him by Tacitus, but from the latter some deduction must be made when he is dealing with foreign relations and external diplomacy. Without any intention to falsify history, he is sometimes completely carried away by his romantic enthusiasm for Roman statesmanship.

This canonisation of Rome is Livy's largest and most abiding achievement. The elder Seneca, one of his ablest literary contemporaries, observes, in a fine passage, that when historians reach in their narrative the death of some great man, they give a summing-up of his whole life as though it were an eulogy pronounced over his grave. Livy, he adds, the most candid of all historians in his appreciation of genius, does this with unusual grace and sympathy. The remark may bear a wider scope ; for the whole of his work is animated by a similar spirit towards the idealised Commonwealth, to the story of whose life he devoted his splendid literary gifts. As the title of *Gesta Populi Romani* was given to the *Aeneid* on its appearance, so the *Historiae ab Urbe Condita* might be called, with no less truth, a funeral eulogy — *consummatio totius vitae et quasi funebris laudatio* — delivered, by the most loving and most eloquent of her children, over the grave of the great Republic.

VI.

THE LESSER AUGUSTANS.

THE impulse given to Latin literature by the great poets and prose writers of the first century before Christ ebbed slowly away. The end of the so-called Golden Age may be conveniently fixed in the year which saw the death of Livy and Ovid; but the smaller literature of the period suffered no violent breach of continuity, and one can hardly name any definite date at which the Silver Age begins. Until the appearance of a new school of writers in the reign of Nero, the history of Roman literature is a continuation of the Augustan tradition. But it is continued by feeble hands, and dwindles away more and more under several unfavourable influences. Among these influences may be specially noted the growing despotism of the Empire, which had already become grave in the later years of Augustus, and under his successors reached a point which made free writing, like free speech, impossible; the perpetually increasing importance of the schools of declamation, which forced a fashion of overstrained and unnatural rhetoric on both prose and verse; and the paralysing effect of the great Augustan writers themselves, which led poetry at all events to lose itself in imitations of imitations within an arbitrary and rigid limit of subjects and methods.

In mere amount of production, however, literature remained active during the first half-century of the Christian era. That far the greater part of it has perished is probably a matter for congratulation rather than regret; even of what survives there is a good deal that we could well do without, and such of it as is valuable is so rather from incidental than essential reasons. *Scribimus indocti doctique poemata passim,* Horace had written in half-humorous bitterness; the crowd of names that flit like autumn leaves through the pages of Ovid represent probably but a small part of the immense production. Among the works of Ovid himself were included at various times poems by other contemporary hands — some, like the *Consolatio ad Liviam,* and the elegy on the *Nut-tree,* without any author's name; others of known authorship, like the continuation by Sabinus of Ovid's *Heroides,* in the form of replies addressed to them by their lovers. Heroic poetry, too, both on mythological and historical subjects, continued to be largely written; but few of the writers are more than names. Cornelius Severus, author of an epic on the civil wars, gave in his earlier work promise of great excellence, which was but poorly fulfilled. The fine and stately passage on the death of Cicero, quoted by Seneca, fully reaches the higher level of post-Virgilian style. Two other poets of considerable note at the time, but soon forgotten after their death, were Albinovanus Pedo and Rabirius. The former, besides a *Theseid,* wrote a narrative and descriptive poem in the epic manner, on the northern campaigns of Germanicus; the latter was the author of an epic on the conflict with Antonius, which was kept alive for a short time by court favour; the stupid and amiable aide-de-camp of Tiberius, Velleius Paterculus, no doubt repeating what he heard in official circles, speaks of him and Virgil as the two most eminent poets of the age! Tiberius himself, though he chiefly wrote in Greek, occasionally turned off a copy of Latin verses; and his nephew Germanicus, a man of much learning and culture, composed a Latin version of the famous *Phaenomena* of Aratus, which shows uncommon skill and talent. Another, and a more important work of the same type, but with more original power, and less a mere adaptation of Greek originals, is the *Astronomica*, ascribed on doubtful manuscript evidence to an otherwise unknown Gaius or Marcus Manilius. This poem, from the allusions in it to the destruction of the three legions under Varus, and the retirement of Tiberius in Rhodes, must have been begun in the later years of Augustus, though probably not completed till after his death. As extant it consists of five books, the last being incomplete; the full plan seems to have included a sixth, and would have extended the work to about five thousand lines, or two-thirds of the length of the *De Rerum Natura*. Next to the poem of Lucretius it is, therefore, much the largest in bulk of extant Latin didactic poems. The oblivion into which it has fallen is, perhaps, a little hard if one considers how much Latin poetry of no greater merit continues to have a certain reputation, and even now and then to be read. The author is not a great poet; but he is a writer of real power both in thought and style. The versification of his *Astronomica* shows a high mastery of technique. The matter is often prosaically handled, and often seeks relief from prosaic handling in ill-judged flights of rhetoric; but throughout we feel a strong and original mind, with a large power over lucid and forcible expression. In the prologue to the third book he rejects for himself the common material for hexameter poems, subjects from the Greek heroic cycle, or from Roman history. His total want of narrative gift, as shown by the languor and flatness of the elaborate episode in which he attempts to tell the story of Perseus and Andromeda, would have been sufficient reason for this decision; but he justifies it, in lines of much grace and feeling, as due to his desire to take a line of his own, and make a fresh if a small conquest for Latin poetry.

> *Omnis ad accessus Heliconis semita trita est,*
> *Et iam confusi manant de fontibus amnes*

Nec capiunt haustum, turbamque ad nota ruentem :
Integra quaeramus rorantes prata per herbas
Undamque occultis meditantem murmur in antris.

In a passage of nobler and more sincere feeling, he breaks
off his catalogue of the signs of the Zodiac to vindicate
the arduous study of abstract science —

" Multum " inquis " tenuemque iubes me ferre laborem
Cernere cum facili lucem ratione viderer."
Quod quaeris, Deus est.   Coneris scandere caelum
Fataque fatali genitus cognoscere lege
Et transire tuum pectus, mundoque potiri :
Pro pretio labor est, nec sunt immunia tanta.

Wherever one found this language used, in prose or verse,
it would be memorable.   The thought is not a mere text
of the schools ; it is strongly and finely conceived, and put
in a form that anticipates the ardent and lofty manner of
Lucan, without his perpetual overstrain of expression.
Other passages, showing the same mental force, occur in
the *Astronomica :* one might instance the fine passage on the
power of the human eye to take in, within its tiny compass,
the whole immensity of the heavens ; or another, suggested
by the mention of the constellation Argo, on the influence
of sea-power on history, where the inevitable and well-
worn instances of Salamis and Actium receive a fresh
life from the citation of the destruction of the Athenian
fleet in the bay of Syracuse, and the great naval battles of
the first Punic war.   Or again, the lines with which he opens
the fourth book, weakened as their effect is by what follows
them, a tedious enumeration of events showing the power
of destiny over human fortunes, are worthy of a great
poet : —

Quid tam sollicitis vitam consumimus annis,
Torquemurque metu caecaque cupidine rerum ?

Aeternisque senes curis, dum quaerimus aevum
Perdimus, et nullo votorum fine beati
Victuros agimus semper, nec vivimus unquam ?

These passages have been cited from the *Astronomica* because, to all but a few professional students of Latin, the poem is practically unknown. The only other poet who survives from the reign of Tiberius is in a very different position, being so well known and so slight in literary quality as to make any quotations superfluous. Phaedrus, a Thracian freedman belonging to the household of Augustus, published at this time the well-known collection of *Fables* which, like the lyrics of the pseudo-Anacreon, have obtained from their use as a school-book a circulation much out of proportion to their merit. Their chief interest is as the last survival of the *urbanus sermo* in Latin poetry. They are written in iambic senarii, in the fluent and studiously simple Latin of an earlier period, not without occasional vulgarisms, but with a total absence of the turgid rhetoric which was coming into fashion. The *Fables* are the last utterance made by the speech of Terence : it is singular that this intimately Roman style should have begun and ended with two authors of servile birth and foreign blood. But the patronage of literature was now passing out of the hands of statesmen. Terence had moved in the circle of the younger Scipio ; one book of the *Fables* of Phaedrus is dedicated to Eutychus, the famous chariot-driver of the Greens in the reign of Caligula. It was not long before Phaedrus was in use as a school-book ; but his volume was apparently regarded as hardly coming within the province of serious literature. It is ignored by Seneca and not mentioned by Quintilian. But we must remind ourselves that the most celebrated works, whether in prose or verse, do not of necessity have the widest circulation or the largest influence. Among the poems produced in the first ten years of this century the *Original Poems* of Jane

and Ann Taylor are hardly if at all mentioned in handbooks
of English literature; but to thousands of readers they
were more familiar than the contemporary poems of
Wordsworth or Coleridge or even of Scott. In their
terse and pure English, the language which is transmitted from one generation to another through the continuous tradition of the nursery, they may remind us of the
Fables of Phaedrus.

The collection consists of nearly a hundred pieces. Of
these three-fourths are fables proper; being not so much
translations from the Greek of Aesop as versions of the
traditional stories, written and unwritten, which were the
common inheritance of the Aryan peoples. Mixed up with
these are a number of stories which are not strictly fables;
five of them are about Aesop himself, and there are also
stories told of Simonides, Socrates, and Menander. Two
are from the history of his own time, one relating a grim
jest of the Emperor Tiberius, and the other a domestic
tragedy which had been for a while the talk of the town in
the previous reign. There are also, besides the prologues
and epilogues of the several books, a few pieces in which
Phaedrus speaks in his own person,* defending himself
against detractors with an acrid tone which recalls the
Terentian prologues. The collection formed the basis for
others; but the body of fables current in the Middle Ages
seems to descend more directly from translations of a larger
Greek collection, made by Babrius in choliambic verse,
about the same time as that of Phaedrus, but probably
independently of his.

Though Livy is the single great historian of the
Augustan age, there was throughout this period a profuse production of memoirs and commentaries, as well as

---

* It is one of these which opens with the two sonorous lines —

> *Aesopi statuam ingentem posuere Attici*
> *Servumque aeterna collocarunt in basi,*

which so powerfully affected the imagination of De Quincey.

of regular histories. Augustus wrote thirteen books of memoirs of his own life down to the pacification of the Empire at the close of the Cantabrian war. These are lost ; but the *Index Rerum a se Gestarum*, a brief epitome of his career, which he composed as a sort of epitaph on himself, is extant. This document was engraved on plates of bronze affixed to the imperial mausoleum by the Tiber, and copies of it were inscribed on the various temples dedicated to him in many provincial cities after his death. It is one of these copies, engraved on the vestibule wall of the temple of Augustus and Rome at Ancyra in Galatia, which still exists with inconsiderable gaps. His two great ministers, Maecenas and Agrippa, also composed memoirs. The most important work of the latter hardly, however, falls within the province of literature ; it was a commentary on the great geographical survey of the Empire carried out under his supervision.

Gaius Asinius Pollio, already mentioned as a critic and tragedian, was also the author of the most important historical work of the Augustan age after Livy's. His *History of the Civil Wars*, in seventeen books, from the formation of the first triumvirate in 60 B.C. to the battle of Philippi, was undoubtedly a work of great ability and value. Though Pollio was a practised rhetorician, his narrative style was simple and austere. The fine ode addressed to him by Horace during the composition of this history seems to hint that in Horace's opinion — or perhaps, rather, in that of Horace's masters — Pollio would find a truer field for his great literary ability in tragedy. But apart from its artistic quality, the work of Pollio was of the utmost value as giving the view held of the Civil wars by a trained administrator of the highest rank. It was one of the main sources used by Appian and Plutarch, and its almost total loss is matter of deep regret.

An author of less eminence, and belonging rather to the class of encyclopedists than of historians, is Pompeius

Trogus, the descendant of a family of Narbonese Gaul, which had for two generations enjoyed the Roman citizen-ship. Besides works on zoology and botany, translated or adapted from the Greek of Aristotle and Theophrastus, Trogus wrote an important *History of the World*, exclusive of the Roman Empire, which served as, and may have been designed to be, a complement to that of Livy. The original work, which extended to forty-four books, is not extant; but an abridgment, which was executed in the age of the Antonines by one Marcus Junianus Justinus, and has fortunately escaped the fate which overtook the abridgment of Livy made about the same time, preserves the main outlines and much of the actual form of the original. Justin, whose individual talent was but small, had the good sense to leave the diction of his original as far as possible unaltered. The pure and vivacious style, and the evident care and research which Trogus himself, or the Greek historians whom he follows, had bestowed on the material, make the work one of very considerable value. Its title, *Historiae Philippicae*, is borrowed from that of a history conceived on a somewhat similar plan by Theopompus, the pupil of Isocrates, in or after the reign of Alexander the Great; and it followed Theopompus in making the Macedonian Empire the core round which the history of the various countries included in or bordering upon it was arranged.

Gaius Velleius Paterculus, a Roman officer, who after passing with credit through high military appointments, entered the general administrative service of the Empire, and rose to the praetorship, wrote, in the reign of Tiberius, an abridgment of Roman history in two books, which hardly rises beyond the mark of the military man who dabbles in letters. The pretentiousness of his style is partly due to the declining taste of the period, partly to an idea of his own that he could write in the manner of Sallust. It alternates between a sort of laboured sprightliness and a careless conversational manner full of endless parentheses. Yet Velleius had two real merits; the eye of the trained soldier for character, and an unaffected, if not a very intelligent, interest in literature. Where he approaches his own times, his servile attitude towards all the members of the imperial family, and towards Sejanus, who was still first minister to Tiberius when the book was published, makes him almost valueless as a historian; but in the earlier periods his observations are often just and pointed, and he seems to have been almost the first historian who included as an essential part of his work some account of the more eminent writers of his country. A still lower level of aim and attainment is shown in another work of the same date as that of Velleius, the nine books of historical anecdotes, *Facta et Dicta Memorabilia,* by Valerius Maximus, whose turgid and involved style is not redeemed by any originality of thought or treatment.

The study of archaeology, both on its linguistic and material sides, was carried on in the Augustan age with great vigour, though no single name is comparable to that of Varro for extent and variety of research. One of the most eminent and copious writers on these subjects was Gaius Julius Hyginus, a Spanish freedman of Augustus, who made him principal keeper of tbe Palatine library. He was a pupil of the Greek grammarian, Cornelius Alexander (called Polyhistor, from his immense learning), and an intimate acquaintance of Ovid. Of his voluminous works on geography, history, astrology, agriculture, and poetry, all are lost but two treatises on mythology, which in their present form are of a much later date, and are at best only abridged and corrupted versions, if (as many modern critics are inclined to think) they are not wholly the work of some author of the second or third century. Hyginus was also one of the earliest commentators on Virgil; he possessed among his treasures a manuscript

of the *Georgics,* which came from Virgil's own house,
though it was not actually written by his hand ; and many
of his annotations and criticisms on the *Aeneid* are preserved by Aulus Gellius and later commentators. A little
later, in the reigns of Tiberius and Claudius, Virgilian
criticism was carried on by Quintus Remmius Palaemon
of Vicenza, the most fashionable teacher in the capital,
and the author of a famous Latin grammar on which all
subsequent ones were more or less based. Perhaps the
most distinguished of Augustan grammarians was another
celebrated teacher, Marcus Verrius Flaccus, who was
chosen by Augustus as tutor for his two grandsons, and
thenceforward held his school in the imperial residence
on the Palatine. His lexicon, entitled *De Verborum
Significatu,* was a rich treasury of antiquarian research :
such parts of it as survive in the abridgments made from
it in the second and eighth centuries, by Sextus Pompeius
Festus and Paulus Diaconus, are still among our most
valuable sources for the study of early Latin language
and institutions. The more practical side of science in
the same period was ably represented by Aulus Cornelius
Celsus, the compiler of an encyclopedia which included
comprehensive treatises not only on oratory, jurisprudence,
and philosophy, but on the arts of war, agriculture, and
medicine. The eight books dealing with this last subject
are the only part of the work that has been preserved.
This treatise, which is written in a pure, simple, and
elegant Latin, became a standard work. It was one of
the earliest books printed in the fifteenth century, and
remained a text-book for medical students till within living
memory. Medical science had then reached, in the hands
of its leading professors, a greater perfection than it
regained till the eighteenth century. Celsus, though not,
so far as is known, the author of any important discovery
or improvement, had fully mastered a branch of knowledge which even then was highly complicated, and takes

rank by his extensive and accurate knowledge, as well
as by his rare literary skill, with the highest names in his
profession. That with his eminent medical acquirement
he should have been able to write at length on so many
other subjects as well, has long been a subject of perplexity.
The cold censure of Quintilian, who refers to him slightly
as "a man of moderate ability," may be principally aimed
at the treatise on rhetoric, which formed a section of his
encyclopedia. Columella, writing in the next age, speaks
of him as one of the two leading authorities on agriculture; and he is also quoted as an authority of some
value on military tactics. Yet we cannot suppose that
the encyclopedist, however great his excellence in one
or even more subjects, would not lay himself open in
others to the censure of the specialist. It seems most
reasonable to suppose that Celsus was one of a class which
is not, after all, very uncommon — doctors of eminent knowledge and skill in their own art, who at the same time
are men of wide literary culture and far-ranging practical
interests.

In striking contrast to Celsus as regards width of knowledge and literary skill, though no less famous in the
history of his own art, is his contemporary, the celebrated
architect Vitruvius Pollio. The ten books *De Architectura*,
dedicated to Augustus about the year 14 B.C., are the
single important work on classical architecture which has
come down from the ancient world, and, as such, have
been the object of continuous professional study from
the Renaissance down to the present day. But their
reputation is not due to any literary merit. Vitruvius,
however able as an architect, was a man of little general
knowledge, and far from handy with his pen. His style
varies between immoderate diffuseness and obscure brevity;
sometimes he is barely intelligible, and he never writes
with grace. Where in his introductory chapters or elsewhere he ventures beyond his strict province, his writing

is that of a half-educated man who has lost simplicity without acquiring skill.

Among the innumerable rhetoricians of this age one only requires formal notice, Lucius Annaeus Seneca of Cordova, the father of the famous philosopher, and the grandfather of the poet Lucan. His long life reached from before the outbreak of war betweem Caesar and Pompeius till after the death of Tiberius. His only extant work, a collection of themes treated in the schools of rhetoric, was written in his old age, after the fall of Sejanus, and bears witness to the amazing power of memory which he tells us himself was, when in its prime, absolutely unique. How much of his life was spent at Rome is uncertain. As a young man he had heard all the greatest orators of the time except Cicero; and up to the end of his life he could repeat word for word and without effort whole passages, if not whole speeches, to which he had listened many years before. His ten books of *Controversiae* are only extant in a mutilated form, which comprises thirty-five out of seventy-four themes; to these is prefixed a single book of *Suasoriae*, which is also imperfect. The work is a mine of information for the history of rhetoric under Augustus and Tiberius, and incidentally includes many interesting quotations, anecdotes, and criticisms. But we feel in reading it that we have passed definitely away from the Golden Age. Yet once more " they have forgotten to speak the Latin tongue at Rome." The Latinity of the later Empire is as distinct from that of the Augustan age as this last is from the Latinity of the Republic. Seneca, it is true, was not an Italian by birth; but it is just this influx of the provinces into literature, which went on under the early Empire with continually accelerating force, that determined what type the new Latinity should take. Gaul, Spain, and Africa are henceforth side by side with Italy, and Italy herself sinks towards the level of a province. Within thirty

years of the death of the elder Seneca " the fatal secret
of empire, that Emperors could be made elsewhere than
at Rome," was discovered by the Spanish and German
legions ; of hardly less moment was the other discovery,
that Latin could be written in another than the Roman
manner.   In literature no less than in politics the discovery
meant the final breaking up of the old world, and the
slow birth of a new one through alternate torpors and
agonies.   It might already have been said of Rome, in
the words of a poet of four hundred years later, that she
had made a city of what had been a world.   But in this
absorption of the world into a single citizenship, the city
itself was ceasing to be a world of its own ; and with
the self-centred *urbs* passed away the *urbanus sermo*, that
austere and noble language which was the finest flower
of her civilisation.

III
THE EMPIRE

L.

THE ROME OF NERO : SENECA, LUCAN, PETRONIUS.

THE later years of the Julio-Claudian dynasty, while they brought about the complete transformation of the government into an absolute monarchy, also laid the foundations for that reign of the philosophers which had been dreamed of by Plato, and which had never been so nearly realised as it was in Rome during the second century after Christ. The Stoical philosophy, passing beyond the limits of the schools to become at once a religious creed and a practical code of morals for everyday use, penetrated deeply into the life of Rome. At first associated with the aristocratic opposition to the imperial government, it passed through a period of persecution which only strengthened and consolidated its growth. The final struggle took place under Domitian, whose edict of the year 94, expelling all philosophers from Rome, was followed two years afterwards by his assassination and the establishment, for upwards of eighty years, of a government deeply imbued with the principles of Stoicism.

Of the men who set this revolution in motion by their writings, the earliest and the most distinguished was Lucius Annaeus Seneca, the son of the rhetorician. Though only of the second rank as a classic, he is a figure of very great importance in the history of human thought from the work he did in the exposition of the new creed. As a practical exponent of morals, he stands, with Plutarch, at the head of all Greek and Roman writers.

The life of Seneca was one of singularly dramatic contrasts and vicissitudes. He was born in the year 4 B.C., at Cordova, where, at a somewhat advanced age, his father had married Helvia, a lady of high birth, and brought up in the strictest family traditions. Through the influence of his mother's family (her sister had married Vitrasius Pollio, who for sixteen years was viceroy of Egypt), the way was easy to him for advancement in the public service. But delicate health, which continued throughout his life, kept him as a young man from taking more than a nominal share in administrative work. He passed into the senate through the quaestorship, and became a well-known figure at court during the reign of Caligula. On the accession of Claudius, he was banished to Corsica at the instance of the Empress Messalina, on the charge of being the favoured lover of Julia Livilla, Caligula's youngest sister. Whether the scandal which connected his name with hers, or with that of her sister Agrippina, had any other foundation than the prurient gossip which raged round all the members of the imperial family may well be doubted; but when Agrippina married Claudius, after the downfall and execution of Messalina seven years later, she recalled him from exile, obtained his nomination to the quaestorship, and appointed him tutor to her son Domitius Nero, then a boy of ten. The influence gained by Seneca, an accomplished courtier and a clever man of the world, as well as a brilliant scholar, over his young pupil was for a long time almost unbounded; and when Nero became Emperor at the age of seventeen, Seneca, in conjunction with his close friend, Afranius Burrus, commander of the imperial guards, became practically the administrator of the Empire. His philosophy was not one which rejected wealth or power; a fortune of three million pounds may have been amassed without absolute dishonesty, or even forced upon him, as he pleads himself, by the lavish generosity of his pupil; but there can be no doubt that in indulging the weaknesses and passions of Nero, Seneca went far beyond the limits, not only of honour, but of ordinary prudence. The mild and enlightened administration of the earlier years of the new reign, the famous *quinquennium Neronis*, which was looked back to afterwards as a sort of brief golden age, may indeed be ascribed largely to Seneca's influence; but this influence was based on an excessive indulgence of Nero's caprices, which soon worked out its own punishment. His consent to the murder of Agrippina was the death-blow to his influence for good, or to any self-respect that he may till then have retained; the death of Burrus left him without support; and, by retiring into private life and formally offering to make over his whole fortune to the Emperor, he did not long delay his fate. In the year 65, on the pretext of complicity in the conspiracy of Piso, he was commanded to commit suicide, and obeyed with that strange mixture of helplessness and heroism with which the orders of the master of the world were then accepted as a sort of inevitable law of nature.

The philosophical writings of Seneca were extremely voluminous; and though a large number of them are lost, he is still one of the bulkiest of ancient authors. They fall into three main groups: formal treatises on ethics; moral letters (*epistolae morales*), dealing in a less continuous way with the same general range of subjects; and writings on natural philosophy, from the point of view of the Stoical system. The whole of these are, however, animated by the same spirit; to the Stoical philosophy, physics were merely a branch of ethics, and a study to be pursued for the sake of moral edification, not of reaching truth by accurate observation or research. The discussions of natural phenomena are mere texts for religious meditations; and though the eight books of *Naturales Quaestiones* were used as a text-book of physical science in the Middle Ages, they are totally without any scientific value. So, too, the twenty books of moral letters, nominally addressed to Lucilius, the procurator of Sicily, merely represent a slight variation of method from the more formal treatises, *On Anger, On Clemency, On Consolation, On Peace of Mind, On the Shortness of Life, On Giving and Receiving Favours,* which are the main substance of Seneca's writings.

As a moral writer, Seneca stands deservedly high. Though infected with the rhetorical vices of the age, his treatises are full of striking and often gorgeous eloquence, and in their combination of high thought with deep feeling, have rarely, if at all, been surpassed. The rhetorical manner was so essentially part of Seneca's nature, that the warm colouring and perpetual mannerism of his language does not imply any insincerity or want of earnestness. In spite of the laboured style, there is no failure either in lucidity or in force, and even where the rhetoric is most profuse, it seldom is without a solid basis of thought. " It would not be easy," says a modern scholar, who was himself averse to all ornament of diction, and deeply penetrated with the spirit of Stoicism, " to name any modern writer who has treated on morality and has said so much that is practically good and true, or has treated the matter in so attractive a way."

In the moral writings we have the picture of Seneca the philosopher ; Seneca the courtier is less attractively presented in the curious pamphlet called the *Apocolocyntosis,* a silly and spiteful attack on the memory of the Emperor Claudius, written to make the laughter of an afternoon at the court of Nero. The gross bad taste of this satire is hardly relieved by any great wit in the treatment, and the reputation of the author would stand higher if it had not survived the occasion for which it was written.

Among Seneca's extant works are also included nine tragedies, written in imitation of the Greek, upon the well-worn subjects of the epic cycle. At what period of his life

they were written cannot be ascertained. As a rule, only
young authors had courage enough to attempt the dis-
credited task of flogging this dead horse; but it is not
improbable that these dramas were written by Seneca in
mature life, in deference to his imperial pupil's craze for
the stage. All the rhetorical vices of his prose are here
exaggerated. The tragedies are totally without dramatic
life, consisting merely of a series of declamatory speeches,
in correct but monotonous versification, interspersed with
choruses, which only differ from the speeches by being
written in lyric metres instead of the iambic. To say that
the tragedies are without merit would be an overstatement,
for Seneca, though no poet, remained even in his poetry
an extremely able man of letters and an accomplished
rhetorician. His declamation comes in the same tones
from all his puppets; but it is often grandiose, and sometimes really fine. The lines with which the curtain falls in
his *Medea* remind one, by their startling audacity, of Victor
Hugo in his most Titanic vein. As the only extant Latin
tragedies, these pieces had a great effect upon the early
drama of the sixteenth century in England and elsewhere.
In the well-known verses prefixed to the first folio Shakespeare, Jonson calls on " him of Cordova dead," in the same
breath with Aeschylus and Euripides; and long after the
Jacobean period the false tradition remained which, by
putting these lifeless copies on the same footing as their
great originals, perplexed and stultified literary criticism,
much as the criticism of classical art was confused by an
age which drew no distinction between late Graeco-Roman
sculpture and the finest work of Praxiteles or Pheidias.

  By far the most brilliant poet of the Neronian age was
Seneca's nephew, Marcus Annaeus Lucanus. His father,
Annaeus Mela, the younger brother of the philosopher, is
known chiefly through his more distinguished son; an
interesting but puzzling notice in a life of Lucan speaks
of him as famous at Rome " from his pursuit of the quiet

life." This may imply refusal of some great office when his elder brother was practically ruler of the Empire ; whatever stirrings of ambition he suppressed broke out with accumulated force in his son. Lucan's short life was one of feverish activity. At twenty-one he made his first public sensation by the recitation, in the theatre of Pompeius, of a panegyric on Nero, who had already murdered his own mother, but had not yet broken with the poet's uncle. Soon afterwards, he was advanced to the quaestorship, and a seat in the college of Augurs : but his brilliant poetical reputation seems to have excited the jealousy of the artist-emperor ; a violent quarrel broke out between them, and Lucan, already in theory an ardent republican, became one of the principal movers in the conspiracy of Piso. The plan discussed among the conspirators of assassinating Nero while in the act of singing on the stage would, no doubt, commend itself specially to the young poet whom the Emperor had forbidden to recite in public. When the conspiracy was detected, Lucan's fortitude soon gave way ; he betrayed one accomplice after another, one of the first names he surrendered being that of his mother, Açilia. The promise of pardon, under which his confessions were obtained, was not kept after they were completed ; and the execution of Lucan, at the age of twenty-six, while it cut short a remarkable poetical career, rid the world of a very poor creature. The final effort of bravado with which he died, declaiming a passage from his own epic, was small ground for Shelley to name him in the same verse with Sydney and Chatterton.

Yet the *Pharsalia*, the only large work which Lucan left complete, or all but complete, among a number of essays in different styles of poetry, and the only work of his which has been preserved, is a poem which, in spite of its immaturity and bad taste, compels admiration by its elevation of thought and sustained brilliance of execution. Pure rhetoric has, perhaps, never come quite so near being

poetry; and if the perpetual overstraining of both thought
and expression inevitably ends by fatiguing the reader,
there are at least few instances of a large work throughout
which so lofty and grandiose a style is carried with such
elasticity and force. The *Pharsalia* is full of quotations,
and this itself is no small praise. Lines like *Nil actum
credens dum quid superesset agendum,* or *Nec sibi, sed toti
genitum se credere mundo,* or *Iupiter est quodcunque vides
quocunque moveris,* or the sad and noble

> *Victurosque dei celant, ut vivere durent,*
> *Felix esse mori* —

are as well known and have sunk as deep as the great lines
of Virgil himself; and not only in single lines, but in longer
passages of lofty thought or sustained imagination, as in
his description of the dream of Pompeius, at the beginning
of the seventh book ; or the passage on the extension of the
Roman Empire, later in the same book ; or the magnificent
speech of Cato when he refuses to seek counsel of the
oracle of Ammon, Lucan sometimes touches a point
where he challenges comparison with his master. In these
passages, without any delicacy of modulation, with a limited
range of rhythm, his verse has a metallic clangour that stirs
the blood like a trumpet-note. But his range of ideas is
as limited as that of his rhythms ; and the thought is not
sustained by any basis of character. His fierce republicanism sits side by side with flattery of the reigning Emperor
more gross and servile than had till then been known as
Rome. He makes no attempt to realise his persons or to
grasp the significance of events. Caesar, Pompeius, Cato
himself — the hero of the epic — are not human beings, but
mere lay-figures round which he drapes his gorgeous rhetoric.
The Civil wars are alternately regarded as the death-agony
of freedom and as the destined channel through which the
world was led to the blessings of an uncontrolled despotism.
His ideas are borrowed indifferently from the Epicurean

and Stoical philosophies according to the convenience of
the moment. Great events and actions do not kindle in
him any imaginative sympathy; they are greedily seized as
opportunities for more and more immoderate flights of
extravagant embellishment. He "prates of mountains;"
his "phrase conjures the wandering stars, and makes them
stand like wonder-wounded hearers;" freedom, virtue, fate,
the sea and the sun, gods and men before whom the gods
themselves stand abased, hurtle through the poem in a confused thunder of sonorous phrase. Such brilliance, in the
exact manner that was then most admired, dazzled his
contemporaries and retained a permanent influence over
later poets. Statius, himself an author of far higher poetical
gifts, speaks of him in terms of almost extravagant admiration; with a more balanced judgment Quintilian sums him
up in words which may be taken as on the whole the final
criticism adopted by the world; *ardens et concitatus et
sententiis clarissimus, et, ut dicam quod sentio, magis oratoribus quam poetis imitandus.*

One of Lucan's intimate friends was a young man of
high family, Aulus Persius Flaccus of Volaterrae in Etruria,
a near relation of the celebrated Arria, wife of Paetus.
Through his kinswoman he was early introduced to the
circle of earnest thinkers and moralists among whom the
higher life was kept up at Rome amid the corruption of
the Neronian age. The gentle and delicate boy won the
hearts of all who knew him. When he died, at the age of
twenty-eight, a little book of six satires, which he had
written with much effort and at long intervals, was retouched
by his master, the Stoic philosopher Cornutus, and published
by another friend, Caesius Bassus, himself a poet of some
reputation. Several other writings which Persius left were
destroyed by the advice of Cornutus. The six pieces —
only between six and seven hundred lines in all — were at
once recognised as showing a refined and uncommon
literary gift. Persius, we are informed, had no admiration

for the genius of Seneca; and, indeed, no two styles, though
both are deeply artificial, could be more unlike one another.
With all his moral elevation, Seneca was a courtier, an
opportunist, a man of the world: Stoicism took a very
different colour in the boy "of maidenly modesty," as his
biographer tells us, who lived in a household of devoted
female relations, and only knew the world as a remote
spectator. Though within the narrow field of his own
experience he shows keen observation and delicate power
of portraiture, the world that he knows is mainly one of
books; his perpetual imitations of Horace are not so much
plagiarisms as the unaffected outcome of the mind of a
very young student, to whom the *Satires* of Horace were
more familiar than the Rome of his own day. So, too,
the involved and obscure style which has made him the
paradise of commentators is less a deliberate literary
artifice than the natural effect of looking at everything
through a literary medium, and choosing phrases, not for
their own fitness, but for the associations they recall. His
deep moral earnestness, his gentleness of nature, and, it
must be added, his want of humour, made him a favourite
author beyond the circles which were merely attracted by
his verbal obscurities and the way in which he locks up
his meaning in hints and allusions. His unquestionable
dramatic power might, in later life, have ripened into really
great achievement; as it is, he lives to us chiefly in the few
beautiful passages where he slips into being natural, and
draws, with a grace and charm that are strikingly absent
from the rest of his writing, the picture of his own quiet
life as a student, and of the awakening of his moral and
intellectual nature at the touch of philosophy.

Lucan and Persius represent the effect which Roman
Stoicism had on two natures of equal sensibility but widely
different quality and taste. Among the many other professors or adherents of the Stoic school in the age of Nero,
a considerable number were also authors, but the habit of

writing in Greek, which a hundred years later grew to such proportions as to threaten the continued existence of Latin literature, had already taken root. The three most distinguished representatives of the stricter Stoicism, Cornutus, Quintus Sextius, and Gaius Musonius Rufus (the first and last of whom were exiled by Nero) wrote on philosophy in Greek, though they seem to have written in Latin on other subjects. Musonius was, indeed, hardly more Roman than his own most illustrious pupil, the Phrygian Epictetus. Stoicism, as they understood it, left no room for nationality, and little for writing as a fine art.

This growing prevalence of Greek at Rome combined with political reasons to check the production of important prose works. History more especially languished under the jealous censorship of the government. The only important historical work of the period is one of which the subject could hardly excite suspicion, the *Life of Alexander the Great*, by Quintus Curtius Rufus. The precise date is uncertain, and different theories have assigned it to an earlier or later period in the reign of Augustus or of Vespasian. The subject is one which hardly any degree of dulness in the writer could make wholly uninteresting. But the clear and orderly narrative of Curtius, written in a style studied from that of Livy, but kept within simpler limits, has real merit of its own; and against his imperfect technical knowledge of campaigns and battles must be set the pains he took to consult the best Greek authorities.

Memoirs were written in the Neronian age by numbers both of men and women. Those of the Empress Agrippina were used by Tacitus; and we have references to others by the two great Roman generals of the period, Suetonius Paulinus and Domitius Corbulo. The production of scientific or technical treatises, which had been so profuse in the preceding generation, still went on. Only two of any importance are extant; one of these, the *Chorographia* of Pomponius Mela, a geographical manual based on the best authorities and embellished with descriptions of places, peoples, and customs, is valuable as the earliest and one of the most complete systems of ancient geography which we possess ; but in literary merit it falls far short of the other, the elaborate work on agriculture by Lucius Junius Moderatus Columella.   Both Mela and Columella were natives of Spain, and thus belong to the Spanish school of Latin authors, which begins with the Senecas and is continued later by Martial and Quintilian.   But while Mela, in his style, followed the new fashion, Columella, an enthusiast for antiquity and a warm admirer of the Augustan writers, reverts to the more classical manner, which a little later became once more predominant in the writers of the Flavian period.   His simple and dignified style is much above the level of a mere technical treatise.   His prose, indeed, may be read with more pleasure than the verse in which, by a singular caprice, one of the twelve books is composed. In one of the most beautiful episodes of the *Georgics*, Virgil had briefly touched on the subject of gardening, and left it to be treated by others who might come after him : *praetereo atque aliis post me memoranda relinquo.*   At the instance, he says, of friends, Columella attempts to fill up the gap by a fifth Georgic on horticulture.   He approaches the task so modestly, and carries it out so simply, that critics are not inclined to be very severe ; but he was no poet, and the book is little more than a cento from Virgil, carefully and smoothly written, and hardly if at all disfigured by pretentiousness or rhetorical conceits.

The same return upon the Virgilian manner is shown in the seven *Eclogues*, composed in the early years of Nero's reign, by Titus Calpurnius Siculus.   These are remarkable rather as the only specimens for nearly three hundred years of a direct attempt to continue the manner of Virgil's *Bucolics* than for any substantive merit of their own.   That manner, indeed, is so exceptionally unmanageable that it is hardly surprising that it should have been passed over

by later poets of high original gift; but that even poets
of the second and third rate should hardly ever have
attempted to imitate poems which stood in the very first
rank of fame bears striking testimony to Virgil's singular
quality of unapproachableness. The *Eclogues* of Calpurnius
(six of them are Eclogues within the ordinary meaning, the
seventh rather a brief Georgic on the care of sheep and
goats, made formally a pastoral by being put into the mouth
of an old shepherd sitting in the shade at midday) are,
notwithstanding their almost servile imitation of Virgil,
written in such graceful verse, and with so few serious lapses
of taste, that they may be read with considerable pleasure.
The picture, in the sixth Eclogue, of the fawn lying among
the white lilies, will recall to English readers one of the
prettiest fancies of Marvell; that in the second, of Flora
scattering her tresses over the spring meadow, and Pomona
playing under the orchard boughs, is at least a vivid
pictorial presentment of a sufficiently well-worn theme. A
more normal specimen of Calpurnius' manner may be
instanced in the lines (v. 52–62) where one of the most
beautiful passages in the third *Georgic*, the description of
a long summer day among the Italian hill-pastures, is
simply copied in different words.

The didactic poem on volcanoes, called *Aetna*, probably
written by the Lucilius to whom Seneca addressed his
writings on natural philosophy, belongs to the same period
and shows the same influences. Of the other minor poetical
works of the time the only one which requires special
mention is the tragedy of *Octavia*, which is written in
the same style as those of Seneca, and was long included
among his works. Its only interest is as the single extant
specimen of the *fabula praetexta*, or drama with a Roman
subject and characters. The characters here include Nero
and Seneca himself. But the treatment is as conventional
and declamatory as that of the mythological tragedies
among which it has been preserved, and the result, if
possible, even flatter and more tedious.

One other work of extreme and unique interest survives from the reign of Nero, the fragments of a novel by Petronius Arbiter, one of the Emperor's intimate circle in the excesses of his later years. In the year 66 he fell a victim to the jealousy of the infamous and all but omnipotent Tigellinus; and on this occasion Tacitus sketches his life and character in a few of his strong masterly touches. " His days were passed," says Tacitus, " in sleep, his nights in the duties or pleasures of life; where others toiled for fame he had lounged into it, and he had the reputation not, like most members of that profligate society, of a dissolute wanton, but of a trained master in luxury. A sort of careless ease, an entire absence of self-consciousness, added the charm of complete simplicity to all he said and did. Yet, as governor of Bithynia, and afterwards as consul, he showed himself a vigorous and capable administrator; then relapsing into the habit of assuming the mask of vice, he was adopted as Arbiter of Elegance into the small circle of Nero's intimate companions; no luxury was charming or refined till Petronius had given it his approval, and the jealousy of Tigellinus was roused against a rival and master in the science of debauchery."

The novel written by this remarkable man was in the form of an autobiography narrating the adventures, in various Italian towns, of a Greek freedman. The fragments hardly enable us to trace any regular plot; its interest probably lay chiefly in the series of vivid pictures which it presented of life among all orders of society from the highest to the lowest, and its accurate reproduction of popular language and manners. The hero of the story uses the ordinary Latin speech of educated persons, though, from the nature of the work, the style is much more colloquial than that of the formal prose used for serious writing. But the conversation of many of the characters is in the *plebeius sermo,* the actual speech of the lower orders, of which so little survives in literature. It is full of solecisms and popular slang ; and where the scene lies, as it mostly does in the extant fragments, in the semi-Greek seaports of Southern Italy, it passes into what was almost a dialect of its own, the *lingua franca* of the Mediterranean under the Empire, a dialect of mixed Latin and Greek. The longest and most important fragment is the well-known *Supper of Trimalchio.* It is the description, full of brilliant wit, of a dinner-party given by a sort of Golden Dustman and his wife, people of low birth and little education, who had come into an enormous fortune. Trimalchio, a figure drawn with extraordinary life, is constantly making himself ridiculous by his blunders and affectations, while he almost wins our liking by his childlike simplicity and good nature. The dinner itself, and the conversation on literature and art that goes on at the dinner-table, are conceived in a spirit of the wildest humour. Trimalchio, who has two libraries, besides everything else handsome about him, is anxious to air his erudition. " Can you tell us a story," he asks a guest, " of the twelve sorrows of Hercules, or how the Cyclops pulled Ulysses' leg ? I used to read them in Homer when I was a boy." After an interruption, caused by the entrance of a boar, roasted whole and stuffed with sausages, he goes on to talk of his collection of plate ; his unique cups of Corinthian bronze (so called from a dealer named Corinthus ; the metal was invented by Hannibal at the capture of Troy), and his huge silver vases, " a hundred of them, more or less," chased with the story of Daedalus shutting Niobe into the Trojan horse, and Cassandra killing her sons — " the dead children so good, you would think they were alive ; for I sell my knowledge in matters of art for no money." Presently there follow the two wonderful ghost stories — that of the wer-wolf, told by one of the guests, and that of the witches by Trimalchio himself in return — both masterpieces of vivid realism. As the evening advances the fun becomes more fast and furious. The cook, who had excelled himself in the ingenuity of his dishes, is called

up to take a seat at table, and after favouring the company
with an imitation of a popular tragedian, begins to make
a book with Trimalchio over the next chariot races.
Fortunata, Trimalchio's wife, is a little in liquor, and gets
up to dance.   Just at this point Trimalchio suddenly turns
sentimental, and, after giving elaborate directions for his
own obsequies, begins to cry.   The whole company are in
tears round him when he suddenly rallies, and proposes
that, as death is certain, they shall all go and have a hot
bath.   In the little confusion that follows, the narrator and
his friend slip quietly away.   This scene of exquisite fooling
is quite unique in Greek or Latin literature : the breadth
and sureness of touch are almost Shakespearian.   Another
fragment relates the famous story of the *Matron of Ephesus*,
one of the popular tales which can be traced back to India,
but which appears here for the first time in the Western
world.   Others deal with literary criticism, and include
passages in verse ; the longest of these, part of an epic on
the civil wars in the manner of Lucan, is recited by one
of the principal characters, the professional poet Eumolpus,
to exemplify the rules he has laid down for epic poetry in
a most curious discussion that precedes it.   That so small
a part of the novel has been preserved is deeply to be
regretted ; it must have been comparable, in dramatic
power and (notwithstanding the gross indecency of many
passages) in a certain large sanity, to the great work of
Fielding.   In all the refined writing of the next age we
never again come on anything at once so masterly and
so human.

II.

THE SILVER AGE: STATIUS, THE ELDER PLINY, MARTIAL,
QUINTILIAN.

To the age of the rhetoricians succeeded the age of the
scholars. Quintilian, Pliny, and Statius, the three foremost
authors of the Flavian dynasty, have common qualities of
great learning and sober judgment which give them a
certain mutual affinity, and divide them sharply from their
immediate predecessors. The effort to outdo the Augustan
writers had exhausted itself; the new school rather aimed
at reproducing their manner. In the hands of inferior
writers this attempt only issued in tame imitations; but
with those of really original power it carried the Latin of
the Silver Age to a point higher in quality than it ever
reached, except in the single case of Tacitus, a writer of
unique genius who stands in a class of his own.

The reigns of the three Flavian emperors nearly occupy
the last thirty years of the first century after Christ. The
"year of four Emperors" which passed between the downfall of Nero and the accession of Vespasian had shaken
the whole Empire to its foundations. The recovery from
that shock left the Roman world established on a new
footing. In literature, no less than in government and
finance, a feverish period of inflated credit had brought it
to the verge of ruin. At the beginning of his reign
Vespasian announced a deficit of four hundred million
pounds (a sum the like of which had never been heard of

186

before) in the public exchequer; some similar estimate
might have been formed by a fanciful analogy of the
collapse that had to be made good in literature, when style
could no longer bear the tremendous overdrafts made on
it by Seneca and Lucan. And in the literary as in the
political world there was no complete recovery : throughout
the second century we have to trace the gradual decline of
letters going on alongside of that mysterious decay of the
Empire itself before which a continuously admirable government was all but helpless.

Publius Papinius Statius, the most eminent of the poets
of this age, was born towards the end of the reign of
Tiberius, and seems to have died before the accession of
Nerva. His poetry can all be assigned to the reign of Domitian, or the few years immediately preceding it. As to his
life little is known, probably because it passed without
much incident. He was born at Naples, and returned to
it in advanced age after the completion of his *Thebaid;*
but the greater part of his life was spent at Rome, where
his father was a grammarian of some distinction who had
acted for a time as tutor to Domitian. He had thus access
to the court, where he improved his opportunities by un-
stinted adulation of the Emperor and his favourite eunuch
Earinus. The curious mediaeval tradition of his conversion
to Christianity, which is so finely used by Dante in the
Purgatorio, cannot be traced to its origin, and does not
appear to have any historical foundation.

Twelve years were spent by Statius over his epic poem
on the War of Thebes, which was published about the year
92, with a florid dedication to Domitian. After its completion he began another epic, on an even more imposing
scale, on the life of Achilles and the whole of the Trojan
war. Of this *Achilleid* only the first and part of the
second book were ever completed ; had it continued on
the same scale it would have been the longest of Greek or
Latin epics. At various times after the publication of the

Thebaid appeared the five books of *Silvae*, miscellaneous and occasional poems on different subjects, often of a personal nature. Another epic, on the campaign of Domitian in Germany, has not been preserved.

The *Thebaid* became very famous; later poets, like Ausonius or Claudian, constantly imitate it. Its smooth versification, copious diction, and sustained elegance made it a sort of canon of poetical technique. But, itself, it rises beyond the merely mechanical level. Without any quality that can quite be called genius, Statius had real poetical feeling. His taste preserves him from any great extravagances; and among much tedious rhetoric and cumbrous mythology, there is enough of imagination and pathos to make the poem interesting and even charming. At a time when Guercino and the Caracci were counted great masters in the sister art, the *Thebaid* was also held to be a masterpiece. Besides complete versions by inferior hands, both Pope and Gray took the pains to translate portions of it into English verse, and it is perpetually quoted in the literature of the eighteenth century. It is, indeed, perhaps its severest condemnation that it reads best in quotations. Not only the more highly elaborated passages, but almost any passage taken at random, may be read with pleasure and admiration; those who have had the patience to read it through, however much they may respect the continuous excellence of its workmanship, will (as with the *Gierusalemme Liberata* of Tasso) feel nearly as much respect for their own achievement as for that of the poet.

The *Silvae*, consisting as they do of comparatively short pieces, display the excellences of Statius to greater advantage. Of the thirty-two poems, six are in lyric metres, the rest being all written in the smooth graceful hexameters of which the author of the *Thebaid* was so accomplished a master. The subjects, for the most part of a familiar nature, are very various. A touching and affectionate poem to his wife Claudia is one of the best known. Several

are on the death of friends; one of very great beauty is
on the marriage of his brother poet, Arruntius Stella, to a
lady with the beautiful name of Violantilla.   The descriptive
pieces on the villas of acquaintances at Tivoli and Sorrento,
and on the garden of another in Rome, are full of a genuine
feeling for natural beauty.   The poem on the death of
his father, though it has passages of romantic fancy, is
deformed by an excess of literary allusions; but that on
the death of his adopted son (he had no children of his
own), which ends the collection, is very touching in the
sincerity of its grief and its reminiscences of the dead boy's
infancy.   Perhaps the finest, certainly the most remarkable
of all these pieces is the short poem (one might almost call
it a sonnet) addressed to Sleep.   This, though included in
the last book of the *Silvae*, must have been written in
earlier life; it shows that had Statius not been entangled
in the composition of epics by the conventional taste of his
age, he might have struck out a new manner in ancient
poetry.   The poem is so brief that it may be quoted in
full : —

> *Crimine quo merui iuvenis, placidissime divom,*
> *Quove errore miser, donis ut solus egerem,*
> *Somne, tuis ?   Tacet omne pecus, volucresque, feraeque,*
> *Et simulant fessos curvata cacumina somnos ;*
> *Nec trucibus fluviis idem sonus ; occidit horror*
> *Aequoris, et terris maria inclinata quiescunt.*
> *Septima iam rediens Phoebe mihi respicit aegras*
> *Stare genas, totidem Oeteae Paphiaeque revisunt*
> *Lampades, et toties nostros Tithonia questus*
> *Praeterit et gelido spargit miserata flagello.*
> *Unde ego sufficiam ?   Non si mihi lumina mille*
> *Quae sacer alterna tantum statione tenebat*
> *Argus, et haud unquam vigilabat corpore toto.*
> *At nunc, heu, aliquis longa sub nocte puellae*
> *Brachia nexa tenens, ultro te, Somne, repellit:*

Inde veni : nec te totas infundere pennas
Luminibus compello meis : hoc turba precatur
Laetior ; extremae me tange cacumine virgae,
Sufficit, aut leviter suspenso poplite transi.

Were the three lines beginning *Unde ego sufficiam* struck
out — and one might almost fancy them to have been inserted later by an unhappy second thought — the remainder
of this poem would be as perfect as it is unique. The
famous sonnet of Wordsworth on the same subject must
at once occur to an English reader; but the poem in its
manner, especially in the dying cadence of the last two
lines, recalls even more strongly some of the finest sonnets
of Keats. " Had Statius written often thus," in the words
Johnson uses of Gray, " it had been vain to blame, and
useless to praise him."

The two other epic poets contemporary with Statius
whose works are extant, Valerius Flaccus and Silius Italicus,
belong generally to the same school, but stand on a much
lower level of excellence. The former is only known as
the author of the *Argonautica*. An allusion in the proem
of his epic to the recent destruction of Jerusalem by Titus
in the year 70, and another in a later book to the great
eruption of Vesuvius in 79, fix the date of the poem ; and
Quintilian, writing in the later years of Domitian, refers to
the poet's recent death. From another passage in the
Argonautica it has been inferred that Flaccus was one of
the college of quindecemvirs, and therefore of high family.
The *Argonautica* follows the well-known poem of Apollonius
Rhodius, but by his diffuse rhetorical treatment the author
expands the story to such a length that in between five and
six thousand lines he has only got as far as the escape of
Jason and Medea from Colchos. Here the poem breaks
off abruptly in the eighth book ; it was probably meant to
consist of twelve, and to end with the return of the Argo-
nauts to Greece. In all respects, except the choice of

subject, Valerius Flaccus is far inferior to Statius. He cannot indeed wholly destroy the perennial charm of the story of the Golden Fleece, but he comes as near doing so as is reasonably possible. His versification is correct, but without freedom or variety; and incidents and persons are alike presented through a cloud of monotonous and mechanical rhetoric.

If Valerius Flaccus to some degree redeemed his imaginative poverty by the choice of his subject, the other epic poet of the Flavian era, Tiberius Catius Silius Italicus, chose a subject which no ingenuity could have adapted to epic treatment. His *Punic War* may fairly contend for the distinction of being the worst epic ever written; and its author is the most striking example in Latin literature of the incorrigible amateur. He had, in earlier life, passed through a distinguished official career; he was consul the year before the fall of Nero, and in the political revolutions which followed conducted himself with such prudence that, through an intimate friend of Vitellius, he remained in favour under Vespasian. After a term of further service as proconsul of Asia, he retired to a dignified and easy leisure. His love of literature was sincere; he prided himself on owning one of Cicero's villas, and the land which held Virgil's grave, and he was a generous patron to men of letters. The fulsome compliments paid to him by Martial (who has the effrontery to speak of him as a combined Virgil and Cicero) are, no doubt, only an average specimen of the atmosphere which surrounded so munificent a patron; but the admiration which he openly expressed for the slave Epictetus does him a truer honour. The *Bellum Punicum*, in seventeen books, is longer than the *Odyssey*. It closely follows the history as told by Livy; but the elements of almost epic grandeur in the contest between Rome and Hannibal all disappear amid masses of tedious machinery. Without any invention or constructive power of his own, Silius copies with tasteless pedantry all the outworn traditions

of the heroic epic. What Homer or Virgil has done, he
must needs do too. The Romans are the Dardanians or
the Aeneadae : Juno interferes in Hannibal's favour, and
Venus, hidden in a cloud, watches the battle of the Trebia
from a hill. Hannibal is urged to war by a dream like that
of Agamemnon in the *Iliad;* he is equipped with a spear
" fatal to many thousands " of the enemy, and a shield, like
that of Aeneas, embossed with subjects from Carthaginian
history, and with the river Ebro flowing round the edge
as an ingenious variant of the Ocean-river on the shield
of Achilles. A Carthaginian fleet cruising off the coast of
Italy falls in with Proteus, who takes the opportunity of
prophesying the course of the war. Hannibal at Zama
pursues a phantom of Scipio, which flies before him and
disappears like that of Aeneas before Turnus. Such was
the degradation to which the noble epic machinery had
now sunk. Soon after the death of Silius the poem seems
to have fallen into merited oblivion ; there is a single
reference to it in a poet of the fifth century, and thereafter
it remained unknown or unheard of until a manuscript
discovered by Poggio Bracciolini brought it to light again
early in the fifteenth century.

The works of the other Flavian poets, Curiatius Maternus,
Saleius Bassus, Arruntius Stella, and the poetess Sulpicia,
are lost ; all else that survives of the verse of the period
is the work of a writer of a different order, but of considerable importance and value, the epigrammatist Martial. By
no means a poet of the first rank, hardly perhaps a poet
at all according to any strict definition, he has yet a genius
of his own which for many ages made him the chief and
almost the sole model for a particular kind of literature.

Marcus Valerius Martialis was born at Augusta Bilbilis
in Central Spain towards the end of the reign of Tiberius.
He came to Rome as a young man during the reign of
Nero, when his countrymen, Seneca and Lucan, were at
the height of their reputation.   Through their patronage

he obtained a footing, if not at court, yet among the wealthy amateurs who extended a less dangerous protection to men of letters. For some thirty-five years he led the life of a dependant; under Domitian his assiduous flattery gained for him the honorary tribunate which conferred equestrian rank, though not the rewards of hard cash which he would probably have appreciated more. The younger Pliny, who speaks of him with a slightly supercilious approval, repaid with a more substantial gratification a poem comparing him to Cicero. Martial's gift for occasional verse just enabled him to live up three pair of stairs in the city; in later years, when he had an income from booksellers as well as from private patrons, he could afford a tiny country house among the Sabine hills. Early in the reign of Domitian he began to publish regularly, bringing out a volume of epigrams every year. After the accession of Trajan he returned to his native town, from which, however, he continued to send fresh volumes of epigrams to his Roman publishers. There his talent for flattery at last bore substantial fruit; a rich lady of the neighbourhood presented him with a little estate, and though the longing for the country, which had grown on him in Rome, was soon replaced by a stronger feeling of regret for the excitement of the capital, he spent the remainder of his life in material comfort.

The collected works of Martial, as published after his death, which probably took place about the year 102, consist of twelve books of miscellaneous *Epigrams*, which are prefaced by a book of pieces called *Liber Spectaculorum*, upon the performances given by Titus and Domitian in the capital, especially in the vast amphitheatre erected by the former. At the end are added two books of *Xenia* and *Apophoreta*, distichs written to go with the Christmas presents of all sorts which were interchanged at the festival of the Saturnalia. These last are, of course, not "distinguished for a strong poetic feeling," any more than the cracker mottoes

of modern times. But the twelve books of *Epigrams*, while
they include work of all degrees of goodness and badness,
are invaluable from the vivid picture which they give of
actual daily life at Rome in the first century. Few writers
of equal ability show in their work such a total absence of
character, such indifference to all ideas or enthusiasms ;
yet this very quality makes the verse of Martial a more
perfect mirror of the external aspects of Roman life. A
certain intolerance of hypocrisy is the nearest approach
Martial ever makes to moral feeling. His perpetual flattery
of Domitian, though gross as a mountain — it generally takes
the form of comparing him with the Supreme Being, to the
disadvantage of the latter — has no more serious political
import than there is serious moral import in the almost
unexampled indecency of a large proportion of the epigrams.
The "candour" noted in him by Pliny is simply that of
a sheet of paper which is indifferent to what is written upon
it, fair or foul. He may claim the merit — nor is it an
inconsiderable one — of being totally free from pretence.
In one of the most graceful of his poems, he enumerates
to a friend the things which make up a happy life : " Be
yourself, and do not wish to be something else," is the line
which sums up his counsel. To his own work he extends
the same easy tolerance with which he views the follies and
vices of society. " A few good, some indifferent, the greater
number bad " — so he describes his epigrams ; what opening
is left after this for hostile criticism? If elsewhere he hints
that only indolence prevented him from producing more
important work, so harmless an affectation may be passed
over in a writer whose clearness of observation and mastery
of slight but lifelike portraiture are really of a high order.

By one of the curious accidents of literary history
Martial, as the only Latin epigrammatist who left a large
mass of work, gave a meaning to the word epigram from
which it is only now beginning to recover. The art,
practised with such infinite grace by Greek artists of almost

every age between Solon and Justinian, was just at this
period sunk to a low ebb.   The contemporary Greek
epigrammatists whose work is preserved in the Palatine
Anthology, from Nicarchus and Lucilius to Strato, all show
the same heaviness of handling and the same tiresome
insistence on making a point, which prevent Martial's
epigrams from being placed in the first rank.   But while in
any collection of Greek epigrammatic poetry these authors
naturally sink to their own place, Martial, as well by the
mere mass of his work — some twelve hundred pieces in all,
exclusive of the cracker mottoes — as by his animation and
pungent wit, set a narrow and rather disastrous type for
later literature.   He appealed strongly to all that was worst
in Roman taste — its heavy-handedness, its admiration of
verbal cleverness, its tendency towards brutality.   Half a
century later, Verus Caesar, that wretched creature whom
Hadrian had adopted as his successor, and whose fortunate
death left the Empire to the noble rule of Antoninus Pius,
called Martial " his Virgil : " the incident is highly significant
of the corruption of taste which in the course of the second
century concurred with other causes to bring Latin literature
to decay and almost to extinction.

Among the learned Romans of this age of great learning,
the elder Pliny, *aetatis suae doctissimus,* easily took the first
place.   Born in the middle of the reign of Tiberius, Gaius
Plinius Secundus of Comum passed his life in high public
employments, both military and civil, which took him
successively over nearly all the provinces of the Empire.
He served in Germany, in the Danubian provinces, in
Spain, in Gaul, in Africa, and probably also in Syria, on
the staff of Titus, during the Jewish war.   In August of
the year 79 he was in command of the fleet stationed at
Misenum when the memorable eruption of Vesuvius took
place.   In his zeal for scientific investigation he set sail for
the spot in a man-of-war, and, lingering too near the zone
of the eruption, was suffocated by the rain of hot ashes.

The account of his death, given by his nephew in a letter to the historian Tacitus, is one of the best known passages in the classics.

By amazing industry and a most rigid economy of time, Pliny combined with his continuous official duties an immense reading and a literary production of great scope and value. A hundred and sixty volumes of his extracts from writers of all kinds, written, we are told, on both sides of the paper in an extremely small hand, were bequeathed by him to his nephew. Besides works on grammar, rhetoric, military tactics, and other subjects, he wrote two important histories — one, in twenty books, on the wars on the German frontier, the other a general history of Rome in thirty-one books, from the accession of Nero to the joint triumph of Vespasian and Titus after the subjugation of the Jewish revolt. Both these valuable works are completely lost, nor is it possible to determine how far their substance reappears in Tacitus and Suetonius; the former, however, in both *Annals* and *Histories*, repeatedly cites him as an authority. But we fortunately possess the most important of his works, the thirty-seven books of his *Natural History*. This is not, indeed, a great work of literature, though its style, while sometimes heavy and sometimes mannered, is on the whole plain, straightforward, and unpretentious; but it is a priceless storehouse of information on every branch of natural science as known to the ancient world. It was published with a dedication to Titus two years before Pliny's death, but continued during the rest of his life to receive his additions and corrections. It was compiled from a vast reading. Nearly five hundred authors (about a hundred and fifty Roman, the rest foreign) are cited in his catalogue of authorities. The plan of this great encyclopedia was carefully thought out before its composition was begun. It opens with a general system of physiography, and then passes successively to geography, anthropology, human physiology, zoology and comparative physiology, botany, including agriculture and horticulture, medicine, mineralogy, and the fine arts.

After being long held as an almost infallible authority, Pliny, in more recent times, fell under the reproach of credulity and want of sufficient discrimination in the value of his sources. Further research has gone far to reinstate his reputation. Without having any profound original knowledge of the particular sciences, he had a naturally scientific mind. His tendency to give what is merely curious the same attention as what is essentially important, has incidentally preserved much valuable detail, especially as regards the arts; and modern research often tends to confirm the anecdotes which were once condemned as plainly erroneous and even absurd. Pliny has, further, the great advantage of being shut up in no philosophical system. His philosophy of life, and his religion so far as it appears, is that of his age, a moderate and rational Stoicism. Like his contemporaries, he complains of the modern falling away from nature and the decay of morals. But it is as the conscientious student and the candid observer that he habitually appears. In diligence, accuracy, and freedom from preconception or prejudice, he represents the highest level reached by ancient science after Aristotle and his immediate successors.

Of the more specialised scientific treatises belonging to this period, only two are extant, the three books on *Strategy* by Sextus Julius Frontinus, and a treatise by the same author on the public water-supply of Rome; both belong to strict science, rather than to literature. The schools of rhetoric and grammar continued to flourish : among many unimportant names that of Quintilian stands eminent, as not only a grammarian and rhetorician, but a fine critic and a writer of high substantive value.

Marcus Fabius Quintilianus of Calagurris, a small town on the Upper Ebro, is the last, and perhaps the most distinguished of that school of Spanish writers which bulks so largely in the history of the first century. He was educated at Rome, and afterwards returned to his native town as a teacher of rhetoric. There he made, or improved, the acquaintance of Servius Sulpicius Galba, proconsul of Tarraconensian Spain in the later years of Nero. When Galba was declared Emperor by the senate, he took Quintilian with him to Rome. There he was appointed a public teacher of rhetoric, with a salary from the privy purse. He retained his fame and his favour through the succeeding reigns. Domitian made him tutor to the two grand-nephews whom he destined for his own successors, and raised him to consular rank. For about twenty years he remained the most celebrated teacher in the capital, combining his professorship with a large amount of actual pleading in the law-courts. His published works belong to the later years of his life, when he had retired from the bar and from public teaching. His first important treatise, on the decay of oratory, *De Causis Corruptae Eloquentiae*, is not extant. It was followed, a few years later, in or about the year 93, by his great work, the *Institutio Oratoria*, which sums up the teaching and criticism of his life.

The contents of this work, which at once became the final and standard treatise on the theory and practice of Latin oratory, are very elaborate and complete. In the first book, Quintilian discusses the preliminary training required before the pupil is ready to enter on the study of his art, beginning with a sketch of the elementary education of the child from the time he leaves the nursery, which is even now of remarkable interest. The second book deals with the general principles and scope of the art of oratory, and continues the discussion of the aims and methods of education in its later stages. The five books from the third to the seventh are occupied with an exhaustive treatment of the matter of oratory, under the heads of what were known to the Roman schools by the names of *invention* and *disposition*. The greater part of these books is, of course, highly technical. The next four books, from the eighth to the eleventh, treat of the manner of oratory, or all that is included in the word *style* in its widest signification. It is in this part of the treatise that Quintilian, in relation to the course of general reading both in Greek and Latin that should be pursued by the young orator, gives the masterly sketch of Latin literature which is the most famous portion of the whole work. The twelfth book, which concludes the work, reverts to education in the highest and most extended sense, that of the moral qualifications of the great orator, and the exhaustive discipline of the whole nature throughout life which must be continued unfalteringly to the end.

Now that the formal study of rhetoric has ceased to be a part of the higher education, the more strictly technical parts of Quintilian's work, like those of the *Rhetoric* of Aristotle, have, in a great measure, lost their relevance to actual life, and with it their general interest to the world at large. Both the Greek and the Roman masterpiece are read now rather for their incidental observations upon human nature and the fundamental principles of art, than for instruction in a particular form of art which, in the course of time, has become obsolete. These observations, in Quintilian no less than in Aristotle, are often both luminous and profound. A collection of the memorable sentences of Quintilian, such as has been made by his modern editors, is full of sayings of deep wisdom and enduring value. *Nulla mansit ars qualis inventa est, nec intra initium stetit; Plerumque facilius est plus facere, quam idem; Nihil in studiis parvum est; Cito scribendo non fit ut bene scribatur, bene scribendo fit ut cito; Omnia nostra dum nascuntur placent, alioqui nec scriberentur;* — such sayings as these, expressed with admirable terseness and lucidity, are scattered all over the work, and have a value far beyond the limits of any single study. If they do not drop from Quintilian with the same curious negligence as they do from Aristotle (whose best things are nearly always said in a parenthesis), the advantage is not wholly with the Greek author; the more orderly and finished method of the Roman teacher marks a higher constructive literary power than that of Aristotle, whose singular genius made him indeed the prince of lecturers, but did not place him in the first rank of writers.

Beyond these incidental touches of wisdom and insight, which give an enduring value to the whole substance of the work, the chief interest for modern readers in the *Institutio Oratoria* lies in three portions which are, more or less, episodic to the strict purpose of the book, though they sum up the spirit in which it is written. These are the discussions on the education of children in the first, and on the larger education of mature life in the last book, and the critical sketch of ancient literature up to his own time, which occupies the first chapter of the tenth. Almost for the first time in history — for the ideal system of Plato, however brilliant and suggestive, stands on quite a different footing — the theory of education was, in this age, made a subject of profound thought and study. The precepts of Quintilian, if taken in detail, address themselves to the formation of a Roman of the Empire, and not a citizen of modern Europe. But their main spirit is independent of the accidents of any age or country. In the breadth of his ideas, and in the wisdom of much of his detailed advice, Quintilian takes a place in the foremost rank of educational writers. The dialogue on oratory written a few years earlier by Tacitus names, as the main cause of the decay of the liberal arts, not any lack of substantial encouragement, but the negligence of parents and the want of skill in teachers. To leave off vague and easy declamations against luxury and the decay of morals, and to fix on the great truth that bad education is responsible for bad life, was the first step towards a real reform. This Quintilian insists upon with admirable clearness. Nor has any

writer on education grasped more firmly or expressed more
lucidly the complementary truth that education, from the
cradle upwards, is something which acts on the whole
intellectual and moral nature, and whose object is the production of what the Romans called, in a simple form of
words which was full of meaning, "the good man." It
would pass beyond the province of literary criticism to
discuss the reasons why that reform never took place, or, if
it did, was confined to a circle too small to influence the
downward movement of the Empire at large. They belong
to a subject which is among the most interesting of all
studies, and which has hardly yet been studied with adequate fulness or insight, the social history of the Roman
world in the second century.

One necessary part of the education of the orator was
a course of wide and careful reading in the best literature ;
and it is in this special connection that Quintilian devotes
part of his elaborate discussion on style to a brief critical
summary of the literature of Greece and that of his own
country. The frequent citations which have already been
made from this part of the work may indicate the very
great ability with which it is executed. Though his special
purpose as a professor of rhetoric is always kept in view,
his criticism passes beyond this formal limit. He expresses,
no doubt, what was the general opinion of the educated
world of his own time ; but the form of his criticism is so
careful and so choice, that many of his brief phrases have
remained the final word on the authors, both in prose and
verse, whom he mentions in his rapid survey. His catalogue
is far from being, as it has been disparagingly called, a mere
"list of the best hundred books." It is the deliberate
judgment of the best Roman scholarship, in an age of wide
reading and great learning, upon the masterpieces of their
own literature. His own preference for certain periods and
certain manners is well marked. But he never forgets that
the object of criticism is to disengage excellences rather

than to censure faults : even his pronounced aversion from the style of Seneca and the authors of the Neronian age does not prevent him from seeing their merits, and giving these ungrudging praise.

It is, indeed, in Quintilian that the reaction from the early imperial manner comes to its climax. Statius had, to a certain degree, gone back to Virgil; Quintilian goes back to Cicero without hesitation or reserve. He is the first of the Ciceronians; Lactantius in the fourth century, John of Salisbury in the twelfth, Petrarch in the fourteenth, Erasmus in the sixteenth, all in a way continue the tradition which he founded; nor is it surprising that the discovery of a complete manuscript of the *Institutio Oratoria* early in the fifteenth century was hailed by scholars as one of the most important events of the Renaissance. He is not, however, a mere imitator of his master's style; indeed, his style is, in some features and for some purposes, a better one than his master's. It is as clear and fluent, and not so verbose. He cannot rise to the great heights of Cicero; but for ordinary use it would be difficult to name a manner that combines so well the Ciceronian dignity with the rich colour and high finish added to Latin prose by the writers of the earlier empire.

The body of criticism left by Quintilian in this remarkable chapter is the more valuable because it includes nearly all the great Latin writers. Classical literature, little as it may have seemed so at the time, was already nearing its end. With the generation which immediately followed, that of his younger contemporaries, the Silver Age closes, and a new age begins, which, though full of interest in many ways, is no longer classical. After Tacitus and the younger Pliny, the main stream dwindles and loses itself among quicksands. The writers who continue the pure classical tradition are few, and of inferior power; and the chief interest of Latin literature becomes turned in other directions, to the Christian writers on the one hand, and

on the other to those authors in whom we may trace the
beginning of new styles and methods, some of which bore
fruit at the time, while others remained undeveloped till
the later Middle Ages.   Why this final effort of purely
Roman culture, made in the Flavian era with such sustained
energy and ability, on the whole scarcely survived a single
generation, is a question to which no simple answer can be
given.   It brings us once more face to face with the other
question, which, indeed, haunts Latin literature from the
outset, whether the conquest and absorption of Greece by
Rome did not carry with it the seeds of a fatal weakness
in the victorious literature.   Up to the end of the Golden
Age fresh waves of Greek influence had again and again
given new vitality and enlarged power to the Latin language.
That influence had now exhausted itself; for the Latin
world Greece had no further message.   That Latin literature
began to decline so soon after the stimulating Greek influence ceased to operate, was partly due to external causes;
the empire began to fight for its existence before the end
of the second century, and never afterwards gained a pause
in the continuous drain of its vital force.   But there was
another reason more intimate and inherent; a literature
formed so completely on that of Greece paid the penalty
in a certain loss of independent vitality.   The gap between
the literary Latin and the actual speech of the mass of
Latin-speaking people became too great to bridge over.
Classical Latin poetry was, as we have seen, written
throughout in alien metres, to which indeed the language
was adapted with immense dexterity, but which still remained foreign to its natural structure.   To a certain degree
the same was even true of prose, at least of the more imaginative prose which was developed through a study of
the great Greek masters of history, oratory, and philosophy.
In the Silver Age Latin literature, feeling a great past behind
it, definitely tried to cut itself away from Greece and stand
on its own feet.   Quintilian's criticism implies throughout

that the two literatures were on a footing of substantial
equality; Cicero is sufficient for him, as Virgil is for Statius.
Even Martial, it has been noted, hardly ever alludes to
Greek authors, while he is full of references to those of his
own country. The eminent grammarians of the age,
Aemilius Asper, Marcus Valerius Probus, Quintus Asconius Pedianus, show the same tendency; their main work
was in commenting on the great Latin writers. The
elaborate editions of the Latin poets, from Lucretius to
Persius, produced by Probus, and the commentaries on
Terence, Cicero, Sallust, and Virgil by Asconius and
Asper, were the work of a generation to whom these
authors had become in effect the classics. But literature,
as the event proved not for the first or the last time, cannot
live long on the study of the classics alone.

III.

TACITUS.

THE end, however, was not yet; and in the generation which immediately followed, the single imposing figure of Cornelius Tacitus, the last of the great classical writers, adds a final and, as it were, a sunset splendour to the literature of Rome. The reigns of Nerva and Trajan, however much they were hailed as the beginning of a golden age, were really far less fertile in literary works than those of the Flavian Emperors; and the boasted restoration of freedom of speech was almost immediately followed by an all but complete silence of the Latin tongue. When to the name of Tacitus are added those of Juvenal and the younger Pliny, there is literally almost no other author — none certainly of the slightest literary importance — to be chronicled until the reign of Hadrian; and even then the principal authors are Greek, while mere compilers or grammarians like Gellius and Suetonius are all that Latin literature has to show. The beginnings of Christian literature in Minucius Felix, and of mediaeval literature in Apuleius and the author of the *Pervigilium Veneris*, rise in an age scanty in the amount and below mediocrity in the substance of its production.

Little is known of the birth and parentage of Tacitus beyond the mere fact that he was a Roman of good family. Tradition places his birth at Interamna early in the reign of Nero; he passed through the regular stages of an official career under the three Flavian Emperors. His marriage, towards the end of the reign of Vespasian, to the daughter and only surviving child of the eminent soldier and administrator, Gnaeus Julius Agricola, aided him in obtaining rapid promotion; he was praetor in the year in which Domitian celebrated the Secular Games, and rose to the dignity of the consulship during the brief reign of Nerva. He was then a little over forty. When still quite a young man he had written the dialogue on oratory, which is one of the most interesting of Latin works on literary criticism; but throughout the reign of Domitian his pen was wholly laid aside. The celebrated passage of the *Agricola* in which he accounts for this silence may or may not give an adequate account of the facts, but at all events gives the keynote of the whole of his subsequent work, and of that view of the imperial government of the first century which his genius has fixed ineradicably in the imagination of the world. Under Domitian a servile senate had ordered the works of the two most eminent martyrs of reactionary Stoicism, Arulenus Rusticus and Herennius Senecio, to be publicly burned in the forum; "thinking that in that fire they consumed the voice of the Roman people, their own freedom, and the conscience of mankind. Great indeed," he bitterly continues, "are the proofs we have given of what we can endure. The antique time saw to the utmost bounds of freedom, we of servitude; robbed by an inquisition of the common use of speech and hearing, we should have lost our very memory with our voice, were it as much in our power to forget as to be dumb. Now at last our breath has come back; yet in the nature of human frailty remedies are slower than their diseases, and genius and learning are more easily extinguished than recalled. Fifteen years have been taken out of our lives, while youth passed silently into age; and we are the wretched survivors, not only of those who have been taken away from us, but of ourselves." Even a colourless translation may give some

idea of the distilled bitterness of this tremendous indictment.   We must remember that they are the words of a
man in the prime of life and at the height of public distinction, under a prince of whose government he speaks in
terms of almost extravagant hope and praise, to realise the
spirit in which he addressed himself to paint, his lurid
portraits of Tiberius or Nero or Domitian.

The exquisitely beautiful memoir of his father-in-law, in
the introduction to which this passage occurs, was written
by Tacitus in the year which succeeded his own consulship,
and which saw the accession of Trajan.   He was then
already meditating a large historical work on the events of
his own lifetime, for which he had, by reading and reflection,
as well as by his own administrative experience, accumulated large materials.   The essay *De Origine Situ Moribus
ac Populis Germaniae* was published about the same time
or a little later, and no doubt represents part of the
material which he had collected for the chapters of his
history dealing with the German wars, and which, as much
of it fell outside the scope of a general history of Rome,
he found it worth his while to publish as a separate treatise.
The scheme of his work became larger in the course of its
progress.   As he originally planned it, it was to begin with
the accession of Galba, thus dealing with a period which
fell entirely within his own lifetime, and indeed within his
own recollection.   But after completing his account of the
six reigns from Galba to Domitian, he did not, as he had
at first proposed, go on to those of Nerva and Trajan, but
resumed his task at an earlier period, and composed an
equally elaborate history of the empire from the death of
Augustus down to the point where his earlier work began.
He still cherished the hope of resuming his history from
the accession of Nerva, but it is doubtful whether he lived
long enough to do so.   Allusions to the Eastern conquests
of Trajan in the *Annals* show that the work cannot have
been published till after the year 115, and it would seem —

though nothing is known as to the events or employments
of his later life — that he did not long survive that date.
But the thirty books of his *Annals* and *Histories*, themselves
splendid work for a lifetime, gave the continuous history
of the empire in the most crucial and on the whole the
most remarkable period of its existence, the eighty-two
years which succeeded the death of its founder.

As in so many other cases, this memorable work has
only escaped total loss by the slenderest of chances. As it
is, only about one-half of the whole work is extant, consisting of four large fragments. The first of these, which
begins at the beginning, breaks off abruptly in the fifteenth
year of the reign of Tiberius. A gap of two years follows,
and the second fragment carries on the history to Tiberius'
death. The story of the reign of Caligula is wholly lost;
the third fragment begins in the seventh year of Claudius,
and goes on as far as the thirteenth of Nero. The fourth,
consisting of the first four and part of the fifth book of
the earlier part of the work, contains the events of little
more than a year, but that the terrible "year of Emperors"
which followed the overthrow of Nero and shook the
Roman world to its foundations. A single manuscript has
preserved the last two of these four fragments; to the hand
of one nameless Italian monk of the eleventh century we
owe our knowledge of one of the greatest masterpieces of
the ancient world.

Not the least interesting point in the study of the writings
of Tacitus is the way in which we can see his unique style
gradually forming and changing from his earlier to his later
manner. The dialogue *De Oratoribus* is his earliest extant
work. Its scene is laid in or about the year 75. But
Tacitus was then little if at all over twenty, and it may have
been written some five or six years later. In this book the
influence of Quintilian and the Ciceronian school is strongly
marked; there is so much of Ciceronianism in the style
that many scholars have been inclined to assign it to some

other author, or have even identified it with the lost
treatise of Quintilian himself, on the *Causes of the Decay of
Eloquence.* But its style, while it bears the general colour
of the Silver Age, has also large traces of that compressed
and allusive manner which Tacitus later carried to such an
extreme degree of perfection. Full as it is of the *ardor
iuvenilis*, page after page recalling that Ciceronian manner
with which we are familiar in the *Brutus* or the *De Oratore*
by the balance of the periods, by the elaborate similes,
and by a certain fluid and florid evolution of what is
really commonplace thought, a touch here and there, like
contemnebat potius literas quam nesciebat, or *vitio malignitatis
humanae vetera semper in laude, praesentia in fastidio esse*,
or the criticism on the poetry of Caesar and Brutus, *non
melius quam Cicero, sed felicius, quia illos fecisse pauciores
sciunt*, anticipates the author of the *Annals*, with his mastery
of biting phrase and his unequalled power of innuendo. The
defence and attack of the older oratory are both dramatic,
and to a certain extent unreal; it is probable that the
dialogue does in fact represent the matter of actual discussions between the two principal interlocutors, celebrated
orators of the Flavian period, to which as a young student
Tacitus had himself listened. One phrase dropped by
Aper, the apologist of the modern school, is of special
interest as coming from the future historian; among the
faults of the Ciceronian oratory is mentioned a languor and
heaviness in narration — *tarda et iners structura in morem
annalium.* It is just this quality in historical composition
that Tacitus set himself sedulously to conquer. By every
artifice of style, by daring use of vivid words and elliptical
constructions, by studied avoidance of the old balance of
the sentence, he established a new historical manner which,
whatever may be its failings — and in the hands of any
writer of less genius they become at once obvious and
intolerable — never drops dead or says a thing in a certain
way because it is the way in which the ordinary rules of

style would prescribe that it should be said. A comparison has often been drawn between Tacitus and Carlyle in this matter. It may easily be pressed too far, as in some rather grotesque attempts made to translate portions of the Latin author into phrases chosen or copied from the modern; but there is enough likeness to give some colour even to these attempts. Both authors began by writing in the rather mechanical and commonplace style which was the current fashion during their youth; in both the evolution of the personal and inimitable manner from these earlier essays into the full perfection of the *Annals* and the *French Revolution* is a lesson in language of immense interest.

The fifteen silent years of Tacitus followed the publication of the dialogue on oratory. In the *Agricola* and *Germania* the distinctively Tacitean style is still immature, though it is well on the way towards maturity. The *Germania* is less read for its literary merit than as the principal extant account, and the only one which professes to cover the ground at all systematically, of Central Europe under the early Roman Empire. It does not appear whether, in the course of his official employments, Tacitus had ever been stationed on the frontier either of the Rhine or of the Danube. The treatise bears little or no traces of first-hand knowledge; nor does he mention his authorities, with the single exception of a reference to Caesar's *Gallic War*. We can hardly doubt that he made free use of the material amassed by Pliny in his *Bella Germaniae*, and it is quite possible that he really used few other sources. For the work, though full of information, is not critically written, and the historian constantly tends to pass into the moralist. The Ciceronian style has now completely worn away, but his manner is still as deeply rhetorical as ever. What he has in view throughout is to bring the vices of civilised luxury into stronger relief by a contrast with the idealised simplicity of the German tribes; and though his knowledge and his candour alike make him stop short of falsifying

facts, his selection and disposition of facts is guided less by
a historical than by an ethical purpose. His lucid and
accurate description of the amber of the Baltic seems merely
introduced to point a sarcastic reference to Roman luxury;
and the whole of the extremely valuable general account of
the social life of the Western German tribes is drawn in
implicit or expressed contrast to the elaborate social conventions of what he considers a corrupt and degenerate
civilisation. The exaggeration of the sentiment is more
marked than in any of his other writings; thus the fine
outburst, *Nemo illic vitia ridet, nec corrumpere et corrumpi
seculum vocatur,* concludes a passage in which he gravely
suggests that the invention of writing is fatal to moral
innocence; and though he is candid enough to note the
qualities of laziness and drunkenness which the Germans
shared with other half-barbarous races, he glosses over the
other quality common to savages, want of feeling, with the
sounding and grandiose commonplace, expressed in a
phrase of characteristic force and brevity, *feminis lugere
honestum est, viris meminisse.*

The *Agricola,* perhaps the most beautiful piece of
biography in ancient literature, stands on a much higher
level than the *Germania,* because here his heart was in the
work. The rhetorical bent is now fully under control,
while his mastery over "disposition" (to use the term of the
schools), or what one might call the architectural quality of
the book, could only have been gained by such large and
deep study of the art of rhetoric as is inculcated by Quintilian. The *Agricola* has the stateliness, the ordered
movement, of a funeral oration; the peroration, as it might
not unfairly be called, of the two concluding chapters,
reaches the highest level of the grave Roman eloquence,
and its language vibrates with a depth of feeling to which
Lucretius and Virgil alone in their greatest passages offer a
parallel in Latin. The sentence, with its subtle Virgilian
echoes, in which he laments his own and his wife's absence

from Agricola's death-bed — *omnia sine dubio, optime paren-
tum, adsidente amantissima uxore superfuere honori tuo ;
paucioribus tamen lacrimis comploratus es, et novissima in luce
desideraverunt aliquid oculi tui* — shows a new and strange
power in Latin. It is still the ancient language, but it
anticipates in its cadences the language of the Vulgate and
of the statelier mediaeval prose.

Together with this remarkable power over new prose
rhythms, Tacitus shows in the *Agricola* the complete mastery
of mordant and unforgettable phrase which makes his
mature writing so unique. Into three or four ordinary
words he can put more concentrated meaning than any
other author. The likeness and contrast between these
brief phrases of his and the "half-lines" of Virgil might
repay a long study. They are alike in their simple language,
which somehow or other is charged with the whole personality of the author ; but the personality itself is in the sharpest
antithesis. The Virgilian phrases, with their grave pity, are
steeped in a golden softness that is just touched with a
far-off trouble, a pathetic waver in the voice as if tears were
not far below it. Those of Tacitus are charged with
indignation instead of pity ; "like a jewel hung in ghastly
night," to use Shakespeare's memorable simile, or like the
red and angry autumnal star in the *Iliad*, they quiver and
burn. Phrases like the famous *ubi solitudinem faciunt pacem
appellant*, or the *felix opportunitate mortis*, are the concentrated utterance of a great but deeply embittered mind.

In this spirit Tacitus set himself to narrate the history of
the first century of the Empire. Under the settled equable
government of Trajan, the reigns of the Julio-Claudian house
rapidly became a legendary epoch, a region of prodigies
and nightmares and Titanic crimes. Even at the time
they happened many of the events of those years had thrown
the imagination of their spectators into a fever. The strong
taint of insanity in the Claudian blood seemed to have
communicated itself to the world ruled over by that extra-

ordinary series of men, about whom there was something
inhuman and supernatural. Most of them were publicly
deified before their death. The *Fortuna Urbis* took in them
successive and often monstrous incarnations. Augustus
himself was supposed to have the gift of divination; his
foreknowledge overleapt the extinction of his own house,
and foresaw, across a gap of fifty years, the brief reign of
Galba. Caligula threw an arch of prodigious span over the
Roman Forum, above the roofs of the basilica of Julius
Caesar, that from his house on the Palatine he might cross
more easily to sup with his brother, Jupiter Capitolinus.
Nero's death was for years regarded over half the Empire
as incredible; men waited in a frenzy of excited terror for
the reappearance of the vanished Antichrist. Even the
Flavian house was surrounded by much of the same supernatural atmosphere. The accession of Vespasian was
signalised by his performing public miracles in Egypt;
Domitian, when he directed that he should be formally
addressed as *Our Lord God* by all who approached him,
was merely settling rules for an established practise of court
etiquette. In this thunderous unnatural air legends of all
sorts sprung up right and left; foremost, and including
nearly all the rest, the legend of the Empire itself, which
(like that of the French Revolution) we are only now
beginning to unravel. The modern school of historians
find in authentic documents, written and unwritten, the
story of a continuous and able administration of the Empire
through all those years by the permanent officials, and
traces of a continuous personal policy of the Emperors
themselves sustaining that administration against the reactionary tendencies of the Senate. Even the massacres of
Nero and Domitian are held to have been probably dictated
by imperious public necessity. The confidential advisers
of the Emperors acted as a sort of Committee of Public
Safety, silent and active, while the credit or obloquy was
all heaped on a single person. It took three generations

to carry the imperial system finally out of danger; but when this end was at last attained, the era of the Good Emperors succeeded as a matter of course; much as in France, the success of the Revolution once fairly secured, the moderate government of the Directory and Consulate quietly succeeded to the Terror and the Revolutionary Tribunal.

Such is one view now taken of the early Roman Empire. Its weakness is that it explains too much. How or why, if the matter was really as simple as this, did the traditional legend of the Empire grow up and extinguish the real facts? Is it possible that the malignant genius of a single historian should outweigh, not only perishable facts, but the large body of imperialist literature which extends from the great Augustans down to Statius and Quintilian? Even if we set aside Juvenal and Suetonius as a rhetorician and a gossipmonger, that only makes the weight Tacitus has to sustain more overwhelming. It is hardly possible to overrate the effect of a single work of great genius; but the more we study works of great genius the more certain does it appear that they are all founded on real, though it may be transcendental, truth. Systems, like persons, are to be known by their fruits. The Empire produced, as the flower of its culture and in the inner circle of its hierarchy, the type of men of whom Tacitus is the most eminent example; and the indignant hatred it kindled in its children leaves it condemned before the judgment of history.

The surviving fragments of the *Annals* and *Histories* leave three great pictures impressed upon the reader's mind: the personality of Tiberius, the court of Nero, and the whole fabric and machinery of empire in the year of the four Emperors. The lost history of the reigns of Caligula and Domitian would no doubt have added two other pictures as memorable and as dramatic, but could hardly make any serious change in the main structure of

the imperial legend as it is successively presented in these
three imposing scenes.

The character and statesmanship of Tiberius is one of
the most vexed problems in Roman history; and it is
significant to observe how, in all the discussions about
it, the question perpetually reverts to another — the view
to be taken of the personality of the historian who wrote
nearly a century after Tiberius' accession, and was not
born till long after his death. In no part of his work
does Tacitus use his great weapon, insinuation of motive,
with such terrible effect. All the speeches or letters of
the Emperor quoted by him, almost all the actions he
records, are given with this malign sidelight upon them :
that, in spite of it, we lose our respect for neither Emperor
nor historian is strong evidence both of the genius of
the latter and the real greatness of the former. The case
of Germanicus Caesar is a cardinal instance. In the whole
account of the relations of Tiberius to his nephew there
is nothing in the mere facts as stated inconsistent with
confidence and even with cordiality. Tiberius pronounces
a long and stately eulogy on Germanicus in the senate
for his suppression of the revolt of the German legions.
He recalls him from the German frontier, where the
Roman supremacy was now thoroughly re-established, and
where the hot-headed young general was on the point
of entangling himself in fresh and dangerous conquests,
in order to place him in supreme command in the Eastern
provinces; but first he allows him the splendid pageant
of a Roman triumph, and gives an immense donative
to the population of the capital in his nephew's name.
Germanicus is sent to the East with *maius imperium* over
the whole of the transmarine provinces, a position more
splendid than any that Tiberius himself had held during
the lifetime of Augustus, and one that almost raised him to
the rank of a colleague in the Empire. Then Germanicus
embroils himself hopelessly with his principal subordinate,

the imperial legate of Syria, and his illness and death at Antioch put an end to a situation which is rapidly becoming impossible. His remains are solemnly brought back to Rome, and honoured with a splendid funeral; the proclamation of Tiberius fixing the termination of the public mourning is in its gravity and good sense one of the most striking documents in Roman history. But in Tacitus every word and action of Tiberius has its malignant interpretation or comment. He recalls Germanicus from the Rhine out of mingled jealousy and fear; he makes him viceroy of the East in order to carry out a diabolically elaborate scheme for bringing about his destruction. The vague rumours of poison or magic that ran during his last illness among the excitable and grossly superstitious populace of Antioch are gravely recorded as ground for the worst suspicions. That dreadful woman, the elder Agrippina, had, even in her husband's lifetime, made herself intolerable by her pride and jealousy; after her husband's death she seems to have become quite insane, and the recklessness of her tongue knew no bounds. To Tacitus all her ravings, collected from hearsay or preserved in the memoirs of her equally appalling daughter, the mother of Nero, represent serious historical documents; and the portrait of Tiberius is from first to last deeply influenced by, and indeed largely founded on, the testimony of a madwoman.

The three books and a half of the *Annals* which contain the principate of Nero are not occupied with the portraiture of a single great personality, nor are they full, like the earlier books, of scathing phrases and poisonous insinuations. The reign of Nero was, indeed, one which required little rhetorical artifice to present as something portentous. The external history of the Empire, till towards its close, was without remarkable incident. The wars on the Armenian frontier hardly affected the general quiet of the Empire; the revolt of Britain was an isolated

occurrence, and soon put down. The German tribes,
engaged in fierce internal conflicts, left the legions on
the Rhine almost undisturbed. The provinces, though
suffering under heavy taxation, were on the whole well
ruled. Public interest was concentrated on the capital;
and the startling events which took place there gave the
fullest scope to the dramatic genius of the historian. The
court of Nero lives before us in his masterly delineation.
Nero himself, Seneca and Tigellinus, the Empress-mother,
the conspirators of the year 65, form a portrait-gallery
of sombre magnificence, which surpasses in vivid power
the more elaborate and artificial picture of the reign of
Tiberius. With all his immense ability and his deep
psychological insight, Tacitus is not a profound political
thinker; as he approaches the times which fell within his
own personal knowledge he disentangles himself more and
more from the preconceptions of narrow theory, and gives
his dramatic gift fuller play. It is for this reason that
the *Histories*, dealing with a period which was wholly
within his own lifetime, and many of the main actors in
which he knew personally and intimately, are a greater
historical work than even the *Annals*. He moves with a
more certain step in an ampler field. The events of the
year 69, which occupy almost the whole of the extant
part of the *Histories*, offer the largest and most crowded
canvas ever presented to a Roman historian. And Tacitus
rises fully to the amplitude of his subject. It is in these
books that the material greatness of the Empire has found
its largest expression. In the *Annals* Rome is the core
of the world, and the provinces stretch dimly away from
it, shaken from time to time by wars or military revolts
that hardly touch the great central life of the capital.
Here, though the action opens indeed in the capital in that
wet stormy January, the main interest is soon transferred
to distant fields; the life of the Empire still converges on
Rome as a centre, but no longer issues from it as from

a common heart and brain. The provinces had been the
spoil of Rome; Rome herself is now becoming the spoil
of the provinces. The most splendid piece of narration
in the *Histories,* and one of the finest in the work of any
historian, is the story of the second battle of Bedriacum,
and the storm and sack of Cremona by the Moesian and
Pannonian legions. This is the central thought which
makes it so tragical. The little vivid touches in which
Tacitus excels are used towards this purpose with extraordinary effect; as in the incident of the third legion
saluting the rising sun — *ita in Suria mos est* — which brings
before our imagination the new and fatal character of
the great provincial armies, or the casual words of the
Flavian general, *The bath will soon be hot enough,* which
gave the signal for the burning of Cremona. In these
scenes the whole tragedy of the Empire rises before us.
The armies of the Danube and Rhine left the frontiers
defenceless while they met in the shock of battle on
Italian soil, still soaking with Roman blood and littered
with unburied Roman corpses; behind them the whole
armed strength of the Empire — *immensa belli moles* — was
gathering out of Gaul, Spain, Syria, and Hungary; and
before the year was out, the Roman Capitol itself, in a
trifling struggle between small bodies of the opposing
forces, went up in flame at the hands of the German troops
of Vitellius.

This great pageant of history is presented by Tacitus in
a style which, in its sombre yet gorgeous colouring, is
unique in literature. In mere grammatical mechanism it
bears close affinity to the other Latin writing of the period,
but in all its more intimate qualities it is peculiar to Tacitus
alone; he founded his own style, and did not transmit
it to any successor. The influence of Virgil over prose
reaches in him its most marked degree. Direct transfer-
ences of phrase are not infrequent; and throughout, as one
reads the *Histories,* one is reminded of the *Aeneid,* not only

by particular phrases, but by a more indefinable quality
permeating the style. The narrative of the siege and firing
of the Capitol, to take one striking instance, is plainly
from the hand of a writer saturated with the movement
and language of Virgil's *Sack of Troy*. A modern historian
might have quoted Virgil in a note; with Tacitus the
Virgilian reminiscences are interwoven with the whole
structure of his narrative. The whole of the three fine
chapters will repay minute comparison; but some of the
more striking resemblances are worth noting as a study
in language. *Erigunt aciem*, says the historian, *usque ad
primas Capitolinae arcis fores . . . in tectum egressi saxis
tegulisque Vitellianos obruebant . . . ni revolsas undique
statuas, decora maiorum, in ipso aditu obiecissent . . . vis
propior atque acrior ingruebat . . . quam non Porsena dedita
urbe neque Galli temerare potuissent . . . inrumpunt Vitelliani
et cuncta sanguine ferro flammisque miscent.* We seem to
be present once more at that terrible night in Troy —

Vestibulum ante ipsum primoque in limine Pyrrhus . . .
Evado ad summi fastigia culminis . . .
    . . . turres ac tecta domorum
Culmina convellunt . . .
    . . . veterum decora alta parentum
Devolvunt . . . nec saxa, nec ullum
Telorum interea cessat genus . . .
    . . . armorumque ingruit horror . . .
    . . . et iam per moenia clarior ignis
Auditur, propiusque aestus incendia volvunt . . .
Quos neque Tydides, nec Larissaeus Achilles,
Non anni domuere decem, non mille carinae . . .
Fit via vi; rumpunt aditus primosque trucidant
Inmissi Danai, et late loca milite complent.

These quotations indicate strikingly enough the way in
which Tacitus is steeped in the Virgilian manner and
diction. The whole passage must be read continuously to

realise the immense skill with which he uses it, and the tragic height it adds to the narrative.

Nor is the deep gloom of his history, though adorned with the utmost brilliance of rhetoric, lightened by any belief in Providence or any distinct hope for the future. The artificial optimism of the Stoics is alien from his whole temper; and his practical acquiescence in the existing system under the reign of Domitian only added bitterness to his inward revolt from it. The phrases of religion are merely used by him to darken the shades of his narrative; *Deum ira in rem Romanam,* one of the most striking of them, might almost be taken as a second title for his history. On the very last page of the *Annals* he concludes a brief notice of the ruin and exile of Cassius Asclepiodotus, whose crime was that he had not deserted an unfortunate friend, with the striking words, " Such is the even-handedness of Heaven towards good and evil conduct." Even his praises of the government of Trajan are half-hearted and incredulous; " the rare happiness of a time when men may think what they will, and say what they think," is to his mind a mere interlude, a brief lightening of the darkness before it once more descends on a world where the ambiguous power of fate or chance is the only permanent ruler, and where the gods intervene, not to protect, but only to avenge.

IV.

FROM the name of Tacitus that of Juvenal is inseparable.
The pictures drawn of the Empire by the historian and the
satirist are in such striking accordance that they create
a greater plausibility for the common view they hold than
could be given by any single representation; and while
Juvenal lends additional weight and colour to the Tacitean
presentment of the imperial legend, he acquires from it
in return an importance which could hardly otherwise have
been sustained by his exaggerated and glaring rhetoric.

As regards the life and personality of the last great
Roman satirist we are in all but total ignorance. Several
lives of him exist which are confused and contradictory in
detail. He was born at Aquinum, probably in the reign
of Nero; an inscription on a little temple of Ceres, dedicated by him there, indicates that he had served in the
army as commander of a Dalmatian cohort, and was super-
intendent (as one of the chief men of the town) of the
civic worship paid to Vespasian after his deification. The
circumstance of his banishment for offence given to an
actor who was high in favour with the Emperor is well
authenticated; but neither its place nor its time can be
fixed. It appears from the *Satires* themselves that they
were written late in life; we are informed that he reached
his eightieth year, and lived into the reign of Antoninus

Pius. Martial, by whom he is repeatedly mentioned, alludes to him only as a rhetorician, not as a satirist. The sixteen satires (of which the last is, perhaps, not genuine) were published at intervals under Trajan and Hadrian. They fall into two groups; the first nine, which are at once the most powerful and the least agreeable, being separated by a considerable interval of years from the others, in which a certain softening of tone and a tendency to dwell on the praise of virtue more than on the ignoble details of vice is united with a failing power that marks the approach of senility.

Juvenal is the most savage — one might almost say the most brutal — of all the Roman satirists. Lucilius, when he "scourged the town," did so in the high spirits and voluble diction of a comparatively simple age. Horace soon learned to drop the bitterness which appears in his earlier satires, and to make them the vehicle for his gentle wisdom and urbane humour. The writing of Persius was that of a student who gathered the types he satirised from books rather than from life. Juvenal brought to his task not only a wide knowledge of the world — or, at least, of the world of the capital — but a singular power of mordant phrase, and a mastery over crude and vivid effect that keeps the reader suspended between disgust and admiration. In the commonplaces of morality, though often elevated and occasionally noble, he does not show any exceptional power or insight; but his graphic realism, combined (as realism often is) with a total absence of all but the grimmest forms of humour, makes his verses cut like a knife. *Facit indignatio versum*, he truly says of his own work; with far less flexibility, he has all the remorselessness of Swift. That singular product of the last days of paganism, the epigrammatist Palladas of Alexandria, is the only ancient author who shows the same spirit. Of his earlier work the second and ninth satires, and a great part of the sixth, have a cold prurience and disgustingness of detail, that even Swift only approaches at his worst moments. Yet the sixth satire, at all events, is an undeniable masterpiece; however raw the colour, however exaggerated the drawing, his pictures of Roman life have a force that stamps them permanently on the imagination; his *Legend of Bad Women,* as this satire might be called, has gone far to make history.

It is in the third satire that his peculiar gift of vivid painting finds its best and easiest scope. In this elaborate indictment of the life of the capital, put into the mouth of a man who is leaving it for a little sleepy provincial town, he draws a picture of the Rome he knew, its social life and its physical features, its everyday sights and sounds, that brings it before us more clearly and sharply than even the Rome of Horace or Cicero. The drip of the water from the aqueduct that passed over the gate from which the dusty squalid Appian Way stretched through its long suburb; the garret under the tiles where, just as now, the pigeons sleeked themselves in the sun and the rain drummed on the roof; the narrow crowded streets, half choked with the builders' carts, ankle-deep in mud, and the pavement ringing under the heavy military boots of guardsmen; the tavern waiters trotting along with a pyramid of hot dishes on their head; the flowerpots falling from high window ledges; night, with the shuttered shops, the silence broken by some sudden street brawl, the darkness shaken by a flare of torches as some great man, wrapped in his scarlet cloak, passes along from a dinner-party with his long train of clients and slaves: these scenes live for us in Juvenal, and are perhaps the picture of ancient Rome that is most abidingly impressed on our memory. The substance of the satire is familiar to English readers from the fine copy of Johnson, whose *London* follows it closely, and is one of the ablest and most animated modern imitations of a classical original. The same author's noble poem on the *Vanity of Human Wishes* is a more free, but equally spirited rendering of the tenth satire, which stands at the head of the later portion of Juvenal's work. In this, and in those of the subsequent satires which do not show traces of declining power, notably the eleventh and thirteenth, the rhetoric is less gaudy and the thought rises to a nobler tone. The fine passage at the end of the tenth satire, where he points out what it is permitted mankind to pray for, and that in the thirteenth, where he paints the torments of conscience in the unpunished sinner, have something in them which combines the lofty ardour of Lucretius with the subtle psychological insight of Horace, and to readers in all ages have been, as they still remain, a powerful influence over conduct. Equally elevated in tone, and with a temperate gravity peculiar to itself, is the part of the fourteenth satire which deals with the education of the young. We seem to hear once more in it the enlightened eloquence of Quintilian ; in the famous *Maxima debetur puero reverentia* he sums up in a single memorable phrase the whole spirit of the instructor and the moralist. The allusions to childhood here and elsewhere show Juvenal on his most pleasing side ; his rhetorical vices had not infected the real simplicity of his nature, or his admiration for goodness and innocence. In his power over trenchant expression he rivals Tacitus himself. Some of his phrases, like the one just quoted, have obtained a world-wide currency, and even reached the crowning honour of habitual misquotation ; his *Hoc volo sic iubeo*, his *Mens sana in corpore sano*, his *Quis custodiet ipsos custodes ?* are more familiar than all but the best-known lines of Virgil and Horace. But perhaps his most characteristic lines are rather those where his moral indignation breaks forth in a sort of splendid violence quite peculiar to himself ; lines like —

> *Et propter vitam vivendi perdere causas,*

or —

> *Magnaque numinibus vota exaudita malignis,*

in which the haughty Roman language is still used with unimpaired weight and magnificence.

To pass from Juvenal to the other distinguished contemporary of Tacitus, the younger Pliny, is like exchanging the steaming atmosphere and gorgeous colours of a hothouse for the commonplace trimness of a suburban garden. The nephew and adopted son of his celebrated uncle, Pliny had received from his earliest years the most elaborate training which ever fell to the lot of mediocrity. His uncle's death left him at the age of seventeen already a finished pedant. The story which he tells, with obvious self-satisfaction, of how he spent the awful night of the eruption of Vesuvius in making extracts from Livy for his commonplace book, sets the whole man before us. He became a successful pleader in the courts, and passed through the usual public offices up to the consulate. At the age of fifty he was imperial legate of Bithynia : the extant official correspondence between him and the Emperor during this governorship shows him still unchanged ; upright and conscientious, but irresolute, pedantic, and totally unable to think and act for himself in any unusual circumstances. The contrast between Pliny's fidgety indecision and the quiet strength and inexhaustible patience of Trajan, though scarcely what Pliny meant to bring out, is the first and last impression conveyed to us by this curious correspondence. The nine books of his private letters, though prepared, and in many cases evidently written for publication, give a varied and interesting picture of the time. Here, too, the character of the writer in its virtues and its weakness is throughout unmistakeable. Pliny, the noble-minded citizen,—Pliny, the munificent patron,—Pliny, the eminent man of letters, — Pliny, the affectionate husband and humane master, — Pliny, the man of principle, is in his various phases the real subject of the whole collection. His opinions are always just and elegant ; few writers can express truisms with greater fervour. The letters to Tacitus with whom he was throughout life in close intimacy, are among the most interesting and the fullest of unintentional humour. Tacitus was the elder of the two; and Pliny, " when very young " — the words are his own, — had chosen him as his model and sought to follow his fame. " There were then many writers of brilliant genius; but you," he writes to Tacitus, " so strong was the affinity of our natures, seemed to me at once the easiest to imitate and the most worthy of imitation. Now we are named together; both of us have, I may say, some name in literature, for, as I include myself, I must be moderate in my praise of you." This to the author who had already published the *Histories!* Before so exquisite a self-revelation criticism itself is silenced.

The cult of Ciceronianism established by Quintilian is the real origin of the collection of Pliny's *Letters.* Cicero and Pliny had many weaknesses and some virtues in common, and the desire of emulating Cicero, which Pliny openly and repeatedly expresses, had a considerable effect in exaggerating his weaknesses. Cicero was vain, quick-tempered, excitable; his sensibilities were easily moved, and found natural and copious expression in the language of which he was a consummate master. Pliny, the most steady-going of mankind, sets himself to imitate this excitable temperament with the utmost seriousness; he cultivates sensibility, he even cultivates vanity. His elaborate and graceful descriptions of scenery — the fountain of Clitumnus or the villa overlooking the Tiber valley — are no more consciously insincere than his tears over the death of friends, or the urgency with which he begs his wife to write to him from the country twice a day. But these fine feelings are meant primarily to impress the public; and a public which could be impressed by the spectacle of a man giving a dinner-party, and actually letting his untitled guests drink the same wine that was being drunk at the head of the table, put little check upon lapses of taste.

Yet with all his affectations and fatuities, Pliny compels respect, and even a measure of admiration, by the real goodness of his character. Where a good life is lived, it hardly becomes us to be too critical of motives and springs of action ; and in Pliny's case the practice of domestic and civic virtue was accompanied by a considerable literary gift. Had we a picture drawn with equal copiousness and grace of the Rome of Marcus Aurelius half a century later, it would be a priceless addition to history. Pliny's world — partly because it is presented with such rich detail — reminds us, more than that of any other period of Roman history, of the society of our own day. To pass from Cicero's letters to his is curiously like passing from the eighteenth to the nineteenth century. In other respects, indeed, they have what might be called an eighteenth century flavour. Some of the more elaborate of them would fall quite naturally into place among the essays of the *Spectator* or the *Rambler;* in many others the combination of thin and lucid common-sense with a vein of calculated sensibility can hardly be paralleled till we reach the age of Rousseau.

Part of this real or assumed sensibility was the interest in scenery and the beauties of nature, which in Pliny, as in the eighteenth century authors, is cultivated for its own sake as an element in self-culture. In the words with which he winds up one of the most elaborate of his descriptive pieces, that on the lake of Vadimo in Tuscany — *Me nihil aeque ac naturae opera delectant* — there is an accent which hardly recurs till the age of the *Seasons* and of Gray's *Letters.* Like Gray, Pliny took a keen pleasure in exploring the more romantic districts of his country ; his description of the lake in the letter just mentioned is curiously like passages from the journal in which Gray records his discovery — for it was little less — of Thirlmere and Derwentwater. He views the Clitumnus with the eye of an accomplished landscape-gardener; he notes the cypresses on the hill, the ash and poplar groves by the water's edge ;

he counts the shining pebbles under the clear ice-cold water, and watches the green reflections of the overhanging trees; and finally, as Thomson or Cowper might have done, mentions the abundance of comfortable villas as the last charm of the landscape.

The munificent benefactions of Pliny to his native town of Comum, and his anxiety that, instead of sending its most promising boys to study at Milan — only thirty miles off — it should provide for them at home what would now be called a university education, are among the many indications which show us how Rome was diffusing itself over Italy, as Italy was over the Latin-speaking provinces. Under Hadrian and the Antonines this process went on with even growing force. Country life, or that mixture of town and country life afforded by the small provincial towns, came to be more and more of a fashion, and the depopulation of the capital had made insensible progress long before the period of renewed anarchy that followed the assassination of Commodus. Whether the rapid decay of Latin literature which took place after the death of Pliny and Tacitus was connected with this weakening of the central life of Rome, is a question to which we hardly can hazard a definite answer. Under the three reigns which succeeded that of Trajan, a period of sixty-four years of internal peace, of beneficent rule, of enlightened and humane legislation, the cultured society shown to us in Pliny's *Letters* as diffused all over Italy remained strangely silent. Of all the streams of tradition which descended on this age, the schools of law and grammar alone kept their course; the rest dwindle away and disappear. Sixty years pass without a single poet or historian, even of the second rate; one or two eminent jurists share the field with one or two inconsiderable extract-makers and epitomators, who barely rise out of the common herd of undistinguished grammarians. Among the obscure poets mentioned by Pliny, the name of Vergilius Romanus may excite a momentary curiosity; he

was the author of Terentian comedies, which probably did
not long survive the private recitations for which they
were composed. The epitome of the *History* of Pompeius
Trogus, made by the otherwise unknown Marcus Junianus
Justinus, has been already mentioned; like the brief and
poorly executed abridgment of Livy by Julius or Lucius
Annaeus Florus (one of the common text-books of the
Middle Ages), it is probably to be placed under Hadrian.
Javolenus Priscus, a copious and highly esteemed juridical
writer, and head of one of the two great schools of Roman
jurisprudence, is best remembered by the story of his witty
interruption at a public recitation, which Pliny (part of
whose character it was to joke with difficulty) tells with a
scandalised gravity even more amusing than the story itself.
His successor as head of the school, Salvius Julianus, was
of equal juristic distinction; his codification of praetorian
law received imperial sanction from Hadrian, and became
the authorised civil code. He was one of the instructors of
Marcus Aurelius. The wealth he acquired by his profession
was destined, in the strange revolutions of human affairs,
to be the purchase-money of the Empire for his great-
grandson, Didius Julianus, when it was set up at auction by
the praetorian guards. More eminent as a man of letters
than either of these is their contemporary Gaius, whose
Institutes of Civil Law, published at the beginning of the
reign of Marcus Aurelius, have ever since remained one of
the foremost manuals of Roman jurisprudence.

But the literary poverty of this age in Latin writing is
most strikingly indicated by merely naming its principal
author. At any previous period the name of Gaius Suetonius
Tranquillus would have been low down in the second rank:
here it rises to the first; nor is there any other name which
fairly equals his, either in importance or in interest. The
son of an officer of the thirteenth legion, Suetonius practised
in early life as an advocate, subsequently became one of
Hadrian's private secretaries, and devoted his later years to

literary research and compilation, somewhat in the mannei, though without the encyclopedic scope, of Varro. In his youth he had been an intimate friend of the younger Pliny, who speaks in high terms of his learning and integrity. The greater part of his voluminous writings are lost; they included many works on grammar, rhetoric, and archae- ology, and several on natural history and physical science. Fragments survive of his elaborate treatise *De Viris Illustribus,* an exhaustive history of Latin literature up to his own day: excerpts made from it by St. Jerome in his *Chronicle* are the source from which much of our informa- tion as to Latin authors is derived, and several complete lives have been prefixed to manuscripts of the works of the respective authors, and thus independently preserved. But his most interesting, and probably his most valuable work, the *Lives of the Twelve Caesars,* has made him one of the most widely known of the later classical writers. It was published under Hadrian in the year 120, and dedicated to his praetorian prefect, Septicius Clarus. Tacitus (perhaps because he was still alive) is never mentioned, and not certainly made use of. Both authors had access, in the main, to the same materials ; but the confidential position of Suetonius as Hadrian's secretary no doubt increased his natural tendency to collect stories and preserve all sorts of trivial or scandalous gossip, rather than make any attempt to write serious history. It is just this, however, which gives unique interest and value to the *Lives of the Caesars.* We can spare political insight or consecutive arrangement in an author who is so lavish in the personal detail that makes much of the life of history : who tells us the colour of Caesar's eyes, who quotes from a dozen private letters of Augustus, who shows us Caligula shouting to the moon from his palace roof, and Nero lecturing on the construction of the organ. There perhaps never was a series of biographies so crammed with anecdote. Nor is the style without a certain sort of merit, from its

entire and unaffected simplicity.   After all the fine writing
of the previous century it is, for a little while, almost a
relief to come on an author who is frankly without style,
and says what he has to say straightforwardly.   But it is
only the absorbing interest of the matter which makes this
kind of writing long endurable.   It is, in truth, the beginning
of barbarism ; and Suetonius measures more than half the
distance from the fine familiar prose of the Golden Age to
the base jargon of the authors of the *Augustan History* a
century and a half later, under Diocletian.

Amid the decay of imagination and of the higher qualities
of style, the tradition of industry and accuracy to some
degree survived.   The biographies of Suetonius show considerable research and absolute candour ; and the same
qualities, though united with a feebler judgment, appear in
the interesting miscellanies of his younger contemporary,
Aulus Gellius.   This work, published under the fanciful
title of *Noctes Atticae*, is valuable at once as a collection
of extracts from older writers and as a source of information
regarding the knowledge and studies of his own age.   Few
authors are more scrupulously accurate in quotation ; and
by this conscientiousness, as well as by his real admiration
for the great writers, he shows the pedantry of the time on
its most pleasing side.

The twenty books of the *Noctes Atticae* were the compilation of many years ; but the title was chosen from the fact
of the work having been begun during a winter spent by
the author at Athens, when about thirty years of age.   He
was only one among a number of his countrymen, old as
well as young, who found the atmosphere of that university
town more congenial to study than the noisy, unhealthy,
and crowded capital, or than the quiet, but ill-equipped,
provincial towns of Italy.   Athens once more became, for
a short time, the chief centre of European culture.   Herodes
Atticus, that remarkable figure who traced his descent to
the very beginnings of Athenian history and the semi-

mythical Aeacidae of Aegina, and who was consul of Rome
under Antoninus Pius, had taken up his permanent residence
in his native town, and devoted his vast wealth to the
architectural embellishment of Athens, and to a munificent
patronage of letters. Plutarch and Arrian, the two most
eminent authors of the age, both spent much of their time
there; and the Emperor Hadrian, by his repeated and
protracted visits — he once lived at Athens for three years
together — established the reputation of the city as a fashionable resort, and superintended the building of an entirely
new quarter to accommodate the great influx of permanent
residents. The accident of imperial patronage doubtless
added force to the other causes which made Greek take
fresh growth, and become for a time almost the dominant
language of the Empire. Though two centuries were still
to pass before the foundation of Constantinople, the centre
of gravity of the huge fabric of government was already
passing from Italy to the Balkan peninsula, and Italy
itself was becoming slowly but surely one of the Western
provinces. Nature herself seemed to have fixed the Eastern
limit of the Latin language at the Adriatic, and even in
Italy Greek was equally familiar with Latin to the educated
classes. Suetonius, Fronto, Hadrian himself, wrote in
Latin and Greek indifferently. Marcus Aurelius used Greek
by preference, even when writing of his predecessors and
the events of Roman history. From Plutarch to Lucian
the Greek authors completely predominate over the Latin.
In the sombre century which followed, both Greek and
Latin literature were all but extinguished; the partial
revival of the latter in the fourth century was artificial and
short-lived; and though the tradition of the classical manner
took long to die away, the classical writers themselves
completely cease with Suetonius. A new Latin, that of the
Middle Ages, was already rising to take the place of
the speech handed down by the Republic to the Empire.

V.

THE *ELOCUTIO NOVELLA.*

THOUGH the partial renascence in art and letters which took place in the long peaceful reign of Hadrian was on the whole a Greek, or, at all events, a Graeco-Roman movement, an attempt at least towards a corresponding movement in purely Latin literature, both in prose and verse, was made about the same time, and might have had important results had outward circumstances allowed it a reasonable chance of development. As it is, Apuleius and Fronto in prose, and the new school of poets, of whom the unknown author of the *Pervigilium Veneris* is the most striking and typical, represent not merely a fresh refinement in the artificial management of thought and language, but the appearance on the surface of certain native qualities in Latin, long suppressed by the decisive supremacy of the manner established as classical under the Republic, but throughout latent in the structure and temperament of the language. Just when Latin seemed to be giving way on all hands to Greek, the signs are first seen of a much more momentous change, the rise of a new Latin, which not only became a common speech for all Europe, but was the ground-work of the Romance languages and of half a dozen important national literatures. The decay of education, the growth of vulgarisms, and the degradation of the fine, but extremely artificial, literary language of the classical period, went hand in hand towards this changê with the extreme subtleties and refinements introduced by the ablest of the new writers, who were no longer content, like Quintilian and Pliny, to rest satisfied with the manner and diction of the Golden Age. The work of this school of authors is therefore of unusual interest; for they may not unreasonably be called a school, as working, though unconsciously, from different directions towards the same common end.

The theory of this new manner has had considerable light thrown upon it by the fragments of the works of Marcus Cornelius Fronto, recovered early in the present century by Angelo Mai from palimpsests in the Vatican and Ambrosian libraries at Rome and Milan. Fronto was the most celebrated rhetorician of his time, and exercised a commanding influence on literary criticism. The reign of the Spanish school was now over; Fronto was of African origin; and though it does not follow that he was not of pure Roman blood, the influence of a semi-tropical atmosphere and African surroundings altered the type, and produced a new strain, which we can trace later under different forms in the great African school of ecclesiastical writers headed by Tertullian and Cyprian, and even to a modified degree in Augustine himself. He was born in the Roman colony of Cirta, probably a few years after the death of Quintilian. He rose to a conspicuous position at Rome under Hadrian, and was highly esteemed by Marcus Antoninus, who not only elevated him to the consulship, but made him one of the principal tutors of the joint-heirs to the Empire, Marcus Aurelius and Lucius Verus. He died a few years before Marcus Aurelius. The recovered fragments of his writings, which are lamentably scanty and interrupted, are chiefly from his correspondence with his two imperial pupils. With both of them, and Marcus Aurelius especially, he continued in later years to be on the most intimate and affectionate relations. The elderly rhetorician, a martyr, as he keeps complaining, to gout, and the philosophic Emperor write to each other with the effusiveness of two school-girls. It is impossible to suspect Marcus Aurelius of insincerity, and it is easy to understand what a real fervour of admiration his saintly character might awaken in any one who had the privilege of watching and aiding its development; but the endearments exchanged in the letters that pass between " my dearest master " and " my life and lord " are such as modern taste finds it hard to sympathise with, or even to understand.

The single cause for complaint that Fronto had against his pupil was that, as he advanced in life, he gradually withdrew from the study of literature to that of philosophy. To Fronto, literature was the one really important thing in the world; and in his perpetual recurrence to this theme, he finds occasion to lay down in much detail his own literary theories and his canons of style. The *Elocutio Novella,* which he considered it his great work in life to expound and to practise, was partly a return upon the style of the older Latin authors, partly a new growth based, as theirs had been, on the actual language of common life. The prose of Cato and the Gracchi had been, in vocabulary and structure, the living spoken language of the streets and farms, wrought into shape in the hands of men of powerful genius. To give fresh vitality to Latin, Fronto saw, and saw rightly, that the same process of literary genius working on living material must once more take place. His mistake was in fancying it possible to go back again to the second century before Christ, and make a fresh start from that point as though nothing had happened in the meantime. In our own age we have seen a somewhat similar fallacy committed by writers who, in their admiration of the richness and flexibility of Elizabethan English, have tried to write with the same copiousness of vocabulary and the same freedom of structure as the Elizabethans. Between these and their object lies an insuperable barrier, the formed and finished prose of the eighteenth and nineteenth centuries; between Fronto and his lay the whole mass of what, in the sustained and secure judgment of mankind, is the classical prose of the Latin language, from Cicero to Tacitus. In the simplicity which he pursued there was something ineradicably artificial, and even unnatural, and the fresh resources from which he attempted to enrich the literary language and to form his new Latin resembled, to use his own striking simile, the exhausted and unwilling population from which the legions could only now be recruited by the most drastic conscription.

Yet if Fronto hardly succeeded in founding a new Latin, he was a powerful influence in the final collapse and disappearance of the old. His reversion to the style and language of pre-Ciceronian times was only a temporary fashion; but in the general decay of taste and learning it was sufficient to break the continuity of Latin literature. The bronze age of Ennius and Cato had been succeeded, in a broad and stately development, by the Golden and Silver periods. Under this fresh attack the Latin of the Silver Age breaks up and goes to pieces, and the failure of Fronto and his contemporaries to create a new language opens the age of the base metals. The collapse of the imperial system after the death of Marcus Aurelius is not more striking or more complete than the collapse of literature after that of his tutor.

Of the actual literary achievement of this remarkable critic, when he turned from criticism and took to construction, the surviving fragments give but an imperfect idea. Most of the fragments are from private letters; the rest are from rhetorical exercises, including those of the so-called *Principia Historiae*, a panegyric upon the campaigns and administration of Verus in the Asiatic provinces. But among the letters there are some of a more studied eloquence, which show pretty clearly the merits and defects of their author as a writer. In narrative he is below mediocrity:

his attempt to tell the story of the ring of Polycrates, after all allowance is made for its having been first told by Herodotus, is incredibly languid and tedious. Where his style reaches its highest level of force and refinement is in the more imaginative passages, and in the occasional general reflections where he makes the thought remarkable by a cadence of language that is at once unexpected and inevitable. *Novissimum homini sapientiam colenti amiculum est gloriae cupido : id novissimum exuitur* — the turn of phrase here is completely different from the way in which Cicero or Quintilian would have expressed the same idea. In the long letter urging the Emperor to take a brief rest from the wearing cares of government during a few days that he was spending at a little seaside town in Etruria, there occurs what is, perhaps, the most characteristic single passage that could be quoted, the allegory of the Creation of Sleep. " Now," he writes, " if you would like to hear a little fable, listen." The fable which he proceeds to relate, in its delicacy of phrasing and its curiously romantic flavour, has received an admirable and sympathetic rendering from the late Mr. Pater.* Part of his version — the passage is too long to quote in full — will show more clearly than abstract criticism the distinctively romantic or mediaeval note which, except in so far as it had been anticipated by the genius of Plato and Virgil, appears now in literature almost for the first time.

" They say that our father Jupiter, when he ordered the world at the beginning, divided time into two parts exactly equal ; the one part he clothed with light, the other with darkness ; he called them Day and Night ; and he assigned rest to the night and to the day the work of life. At that time Sleep was not yet born, and men passed the whole of their lives awake : only, the quiet of the night was ordained for them, instead of sleep. But it came to pass, little by little, being that the minds of men are restless, that they

* *Marius the Epicurean*, chap. xiii.

carried on their business alike by night as by day, and gave
no part at all to repose. . . . Then it was that Jupiter formed
the design of creating Sleep; and he added him to the
number of the gods, and gave him the charge over night and
rest, putting into his hands the keys of human eyes.   With
his own hands he mingled the juices wherewith Sleep should
soothe the hearts of mortals — herb of Enjoyment and herb
of Safety, gathered from a grove in Heaven ; and, from the
meadows of Acheron, the herb of Death ; expressing from
it one single drop only, no bigger than a tear that one
might hide.   'With this juice,' he said, ' pour slumber upon
the eyelids of mortals.   So soon as it hath touched them
they will lay themselves down motionless, under thy power.
But be not afraid : they will revive, and in a while stand
up again upon their feet.'   After that, Jupiter gave wings to
Sleep, attached, not to his heels like Mercury's, but to his
shoulders like the wings of Love.   For he said, ' It becomes
thee not to approach men's eyes as with the noise of a
chariot and the rushing of a swift courser, but with placid
and merciful flight, as upon the wings of a swallow — nay !
not so much as with the fluttering of a dove.' "

Alike in the naïve and almost childlike simplicity of its
general structure, and in its minute and intricate ornament,
like that of a diapered wall or a figured tapestry, where
hardly an inch of space is ever left blank — this new style is
much more akin to the manner of the thirteenth or fourteenth century than to the classical.   A similar quality is
shown, not more strikingly, but on a larger scale and with a
more certain touch, in the celebrated prose romance of
Fronto's contemporary, Lucius Apuleius.

Like Fronto, Apuleius was of African origin.   He was
born at the Roman colony of Madaura in Numidia, and
educated at Carthage, from which he proceeded afterwards
to the university of Athens.   The epithets of *semi-Numida*
and *semi-Gaetulus*, which he applies to himself, indicate
that he fully felt himself to belong to a civilisation which

was not purely European.   Together with the Graeco-Syrian
Lucian, this Romano-African represents the last extension
which ancient culture took before finally fading away or
becoming absorbed in new forms.   Both were by profession
travelling lecturers ; they were the nearest approach which
the ancient world made to what we should now call the
higher class of journalist.   Lucian, in his later life — like a
journalist nowadays who should enter Parliament — combined his profession with high public employment ; but
Apuleius, so far as is known, spent all his life in writing and
lecturing.   Though he was not strictly either an orator or a
philosopher, his works include both speeches and philosophical treatises ; but his chief distinction and his permanent
interest are as a novelist both in the literal and in the
accepted sense of the word — a writer of prose romances in
which he carried the *novella elocutio* to the highest point it
reached.   He was born about the year 125 ; the *Meta-*
morphoses, his most famous and his only extant romance,
was written at Rome before he was thirty, soon after he
had completed his course of study at Athens.   The philosophical or mystical treatises of his later life, *On the*
Universe, On the God of Socrates, On Plato and his Doctrine,
do not rise above the ordinary level of the Neo-Platonist
school, Platonism half understood, mixed with fanciful
Orientalism, and enveloped in a maze of verbiage.   That
known as the *Apologia*, an elaborate literary amplification
of the defence which he had to make before the proconsul
of Africa against an accusation of dealing in magic, is the
only one which survives of his oratorical works ; and his
miscellaneous writings on many branches of science and
natural history, which are conjectured to have formed a sort
of encyclopedia like those of Celsus and Pliny, are all but
completely lost : but the *Florida*, a collection, probably
made by himself, of twenty-four selected passages from the
public lectures which he delivered at Carthage, give an idea
of his style as a lecturer, and of the scope and variety of

his talent. The Ciceronian manner of Q intilian and his school has now completely disappeared. The new style may remind one here and there of Seneca, but the resemblance does not go far. Fronto, who speaks of Cicero with grudging and lukewarm praise, regards Seneca as on the whole the most corrupt among Roman writers, and Apuleius probably held the same view. He produces his rhetorical effects, not by daring tropes or accumulations of sonorous phrases, but by a perpetual refinement of diction which keeps curiously weighing and rejecting words, and giving every other word an altered value or an unaccustomed setting. The effect is like that of strange and rather barbarous jewellery. A remarkable passage, on the power of sight possessed by the eagle, may be cited as a characteristic specimen of his more elaborate manner. *Quum se nubium tenus altissime sublimavit,* he writes, *evecta alis totum istud spatium, qua pluitur et ningitur, ultra quod cacumen nec fulmini nec fulguri locus est, in ipso, ut ita dixerim, solo aetheris et fastigio hiemis . . . nutu clementi laevorsum vel dextrorsum tota mole corporis labitur . . . inde cuncta despiciens, ibidem pinnarum eminus indefesso remigio, ac paulisper cunctabundo volatu paene eodem loco pendula circumtuetur et quaerit quorsus potissimum in praedam superne se proruat fulminis vice, de caelo improvisa simul campis pecua, simul montibus feras, simul urbibus homines, uno obtutu sub eodem impetu cernens.* The first thing that strikes a reader accustomed to classical Latin in a passage like this is the short broken rhythms, the simple organism of archaic prose being artificially imitated by carefully and deliberately breaking up all the structure which the language had been wrought into through the handling of centuries. The next thing is that half the phrases are, in the ordinary sense of the word, barely Latin. Apuleius has all the daring, though not the genius, of Virgil himself in inventing new Latin or using old Latin in new senses. But Virgil is old Latin to him no less than Ennius or Pacuvius; in this very passage, with its elaborate archaisms, there are three phrases taken directly from the first book of the *Aeneid*.

In the *Metamorphoses* the elaboration of the new style culminates. In its main substance this curious and fantastic romance is a translation from a Greek original. Its precise relation to the version of the same story, extant in Greek under the name of Lucian, has given rise to much argument, and the question cannot be held to be conclusively settled; but the theory which seems to have most in its favour is that both are versions of a lost Greek original. Lucian applied his limpid style and his uncommon power of narration to rewrite what was no doubt a ruder and more confused story. Apuleius evidently took the story as a mere groundwork which he might overlay with his own fantastic embroidery. He was probably attracted to it by the supernatural element, which would appeal strongly to him, not merely as a professed mystic and a dabbler in magic, but as a *décadent* whose art sought out strange experiences and romantic passions no less than novel rhythms and exotic diction. Under the light touch of Lucian the supernaturalism of the story is merely that of a fairy-tale, not believed in or meant to be believed; in the *Metamorphoses* a brooding sense of magic is over the whole narrative. In this spirit he entirely remodels the conclusion of the story. The whole of the eleventh book, from the vision of the goddess, with which it opens, to the reception of the hero at the conclusion into the fellowship of her holy servants, is conceived at the utmost tension of mystical feeling. " With stars and sea-winds in her raiment," flower-crowned, shod with victorious palm, clad, under the dark splendours of her heavy pall, in shimmering white silk shot with saffron and rose like flame, an awful figure rises out of the moonlit sea: *En adsum,* comes her voice, *rerum natura parens, elementorum omnium domina, seculorum progenies initialis, summa numinum, regina manium, prima caelitum, deorum dearumque facies uniformis, quae caeli*

*luminosa culmina, maris salubria flamina, inferorum de-
plorata silentia nutibus meis dispenso.* It was in virtue of
such passages as that from which these words are quoted
that Apuleius came to be regarded soon after his death as
an incarnation of Antichrist, sent to perplex the worshippers
of the true God. Already to Lactantius he is not a curious
artist in language, but a magician inspired by diabolical
agency; St. Augustine tells us that, like Apollonius of
Tyana, he was set up by religious paganism as a rival to
Jesus Christ.

Of the new elements interwoven by Apuleius in the story
of the transformations and adventures of Lucius of Patrae
(Lucius of Madaura, he calls him, thus hinting, to the
mingled awe and confusion of his readers, that the events
had happened to himself), the fervid religion of the conclusion is no doubt historically the most important; but
that which made it universal and immortal is the famous
story of *Cupid and Psyche*, which fills nearly two books of
the *Metamorphoses*. With the strangeness characteristic
of the whole work, this wonderful and exquisitely told story
is put in the mouth of a half crazy and drunken old woman,
in the robbers' cave where part of the action passes. But
her first half-dozen words, the *errant in quadam civitate rex
et regina*, lift it in a moment into the golden world of pure
romance. The story itself is in its constituent elements a
well-known specimen of the *märchen*, or popular tale, which
is not only current throughout the Aryan peoples, but may
be traced in the popular mythology of all primitive races.
It is beyond doubt in its essential features of immemorial
antiquity; but what is unique about it is its sudden appearance in literature in the full flower of its most elaborate
perfection. Before Apuleius there is no trace of the story
in Greek or Roman writing; he tells it with a daintiness
of touch and a wealth of fanciful ornament that have left
later story-tellers little or nothing to add. The version by
which it is best known to modern readers, that in the

Earthly Paradise, while, after the modern poet's manner, expanding the descriptions for their own sake, follows Apuleius otherwise with exact fidelity.

In the more highly wrought episodes, like the *Cupid and Psyche*, the new Latin of Apuleius often approximates nearly to assonant or rhymed verse. Both rhyme and assonance were to be found in the early Latin which he had studied deeply, and may be judged from incidental fragments of the popular language never to have wholly disappeared from common use during the classical period. Virgil, in his latest work, as has been noticed, shows a tendency to experiment in combining their use with that of the Graeco-Latin rhythms. The combination, in the writing of the new school, of a sort of inchoate verse with an elaborate and even pedantic prose was too artificial to be permanent; but about the same time attempts were made at a corresponding new style in regular poetry. Rhymed verse as such does not appear till later; the work of the *novelli poetae*, as they were called by the grammarians, partly took the form of reversion to the trochaic metres which were the natural cadence of the Latin language, partly of fresh experiments in hitherto untried metres, in both cases with a large employment of assonance, and the beginnings of an accentual as opposed to a quantitative treatment. Of these experiments few have survived; the most interesting is a poem of remarkable beauty preserved in the Latin Anthology under the name of the *Pervigilium Veneris*. Its author is unknown, nor can its date be determined with certainty. The worship of Venus Genetrix, for whose spring festival the poem is written, had been revived on a magnificent scale by Hadrian; and this fact, together with the internal evidence of the language, make-it assignable with high probability to the age of the Antonines. The use of the preposition *de*, almost as in the Romance languages, where case-inflexions would be employed in classical Latin, has been held to argue an African origin;

while its remarkable mediaevalisms have led some critics,
against all the other indications, to place its date as low as
the fourth or even the fifth century.

The *Pervigilium Veneris* is written in the trochaic septe-
narian verse which had been freely used by the earliest
Roman poets, but had since almost dropped out of literary
use. With the revival of the trochaic movement the long
divorce between metrical stress and spoken accent begins
to break down. The metre is indeed accurate, and even
rigorous, in its quantitative structure; but instead of the
prose and verse stresses regularly clashing as they do in
the hexameter or elegiac, they tend broadly towards coin-
ciding, and do entirely coincide in one-third of the lines of
the poem. We are on the very verge of the accentual
Latin poetry of the Middle Ages, and the affinity is made
closer by the free use of initial and terminal assonances,
and even of occasional rhyme. The use of stanzas with
a recurring refrain was not unexampled; Virgil, following
Theocritus and Catullus, had employed the device with
singular beauty in the eighth *Eclogue;* but this is the first
known instance of the refrain being added to a poem in
stanzas of a fixed and equal length; * it is more than halfway towards the structure of an eleventh-century Provençal
alba. The keen additional pleasure given by rhyme was
easily felt in a language where accidental rhymes come so
often as they do in Latin, but the rhyme here, so far as
there is any, is rather incidental to the way in which the
language is used, with its silvery chimes and recurrences,
than sought out for its own sake; there is more of actual
rhyming in some of the prose of Apuleius. The refrain
itself —

Cras amet qui nunquam amavit, quique amavit cras amet —

---

* In the poem as it has come down to us the refrain comes in at
irregular intervals; but the most plausible reconstitution of a somewhat corrupt and disordered text makes it recur after every fourth line,
thus making up the twenty-two stanzas mentioned in the title.

has its internal recurrence, the folding back of the musical
phrase upon itself; and as it comes over and over again
it seems to set the whole poem swaying to its own music.
In one of the most remarkable of his lyrics (like this poem,
a song of spring), Tennyson has come very near, as near
perhaps as it is possible to do in words, towards explaining
the actual process through which poetry comes into existence : *The fairy fancies range, and lightly stirr'd, Ring little
bells of change from word to word.* In the *Pervigilium
Veneris* with its elaborate simplicity — partly a conscious
literary artifice, partly a real reversion to the childhood of
poetical form — this process is, as it were, laid bare before
our eyes ; the ringing phrases turn and return, and expand
and interlace and fold in, as though set in motion by a
strain of music.

Cras amet qui nunquam amavit, quique amavit cras amet;
Ver novum, ver iam canorum, ver renatus orbis est;
Vere concordant amores, vere nubunt alites
Et nemus comam resolvit de maritis imbribus :

> *Cras amet qui nunquam amavit, quique amavit cras*
> *amet —*

in these lines of clear melody the poem opens, and the
rest is all a series of graceful and florid variations or em-
broideries upon them ; the first line perpetually repeating
itself through the poem like a thread of gold in the pattern
or a phrase in the music. In the soft April night the
tapering flame-shaped rosebud, soaked in warm dew, swells
out and breaks into a fire of crimson at dawn.

> *Facta Cypridis de cruore deque Amoris osculo*
> *Deque gemmis deque flammis deque solis purpuris*
> *Cras ruborem qui latebat veste tectus ignea*
> *Unico marita nodo non pudebit solvere.*

Flower-garlanded and myrtle-shrouded, the Spring worshippers go dancing through the fields that break before

them into a sheet of flowers ; among them the boy Love goes, without his torch and his arrows ; amid gold-flowered broom, under trees unloosening their tresses, in myrtle-thicket and poplar shade, the whole land sings with the voices of innumerable birds.   Then with a sudden sob the pageant ceases : —

> *Illa cantat, nos tacemus : quando ver venit meum ?*
> *Quando fiam uti chelidon ut tacere desinam ?*

A second spring, in effect, was not to come for poetry till a thousand years later ; once more then we hear the music of this strange poem, not now in the clear bronze utterance of a mature and magnificent language, but faintly and haltingly, in immature forms that yet have notes of new and piercing sweetness.

> *Bels dous amicx, fassam un joc novel*
> *Ins el jardi on chanton li auzel—*

so it rings out in Southern France, "in an orchard under the whitethorn leaf ; " and in England, later, but yet a century before Chaucer, the same clear note is echoed, *bytuene Mershe ant Averil, whan spray bigineth to spring.*

But in the Roman Empire under the Antonines the soil, the race, the language, were alike exhausted.   The anarchy of the third century brought with it the wreck of the whole fabric of civilisation ; and the new religion, already widely diffused and powerful, was beginning to absorb into itself on all sides the elements of thought and emotion which ended towards a new joy and a living art.

VI.

EARLY LATIN CHRISTIANITY: MINUCIUS FELIX, TERTULLIAN, LACTANTIUS.

THE new religion was long in adapting itself to literary form; and if, between the era of the Antonines and that of Diocletian, a century passes in which all the important literature is Christian, this is rather due to the general decay of art and letters, than to any high literary quality in the earlier patristic writing. Christianity began among the lower classes, and in the Greek-speaking provinces of the Empire; after it reached Rome, and was diffused through the Western provinces, it remained for a long time a somewhat obscure sect, confined, in the first instance, to the small Jewish or Graeco-Asiatic colonies which were to be found in all centres of commerce, and spreading from them among the uneducated urban populations. The persecution of Nero was directed against obscure people, vaguely known as a sort of Jews, and the martyrdom of the two great apostles was an incident that passed without remark and almost without notice. Tacitus dismisses the Christians in a few careless words, and evidently classes the new religion with other base Oriental superstitions as hardly worth serious mention. The well-known correspondence between Pliny and Trajan, on the subject of the repressive measures to be taken against the Christians of Bithynia, indicates that Christianity had, by the beginning of the second century, taken a large and firm footing in the Eastern

248 Latin Literature. [III.

provinces ; but it is not till a good many years later that we
have any certain indication of its obtaining a hold on the
educated classes. The legend of the conversion of Statius
seems to be of purely mediaeval origin. Flavius Clemens, the
cousin of the Emperor Domitian, executed on the ground
of "atheism" during the year of his consulship, is claimed,
though without certainty, as the earliest Christian martyr of
high rank. Even in the middle of the second century, the
Church of Rome mainly consisted of people who could
barely speak or write Latin. The Muratorian fragment,
the earliest Latin Christian document, which general
opinion dates within a few years of the death of Marcus
Aurelius, and which is part of an extremely important
official list of canonical writings issued by the authority of
the Roman Church, is barbarous in construction and diction.
It is in the reign of Commodus, amid the wreck of all other
literature, that we come on the first Christian authors.
Victor, Bishop of Rome from the year 186, is mentioned by
Jerome as the first author of theological treatises in Latin ;
taken together with his attempt to excommunicate the
Asiatic Churches on the question, already a burning one,
of the proper date of keeping Easter, this shows that the
Latin Church was now gaining independent force and
vitality.

Two main streams may be traced in the Christian literature which begins with the reign of Commodus. On the
one hand, there is what may be called the African school,
writing in the new Latin ; on the other, the Italian school,
which attempted to mould classical Latin to Christian use.
The former bears a close affinity in style to Apuleius, or,
rather, to the movement of which Apuleius was the most
remarkable product ; the latter succeeds to Quintilian and
his contemporaries as the second impulse of Ciceronianism.
The two opposing methods appear at their sharpest contrast
in the earliest authors of each, Tertullian and Minucius
Felix. The vast preponderance of the former, alike in volume

of production and fire of eloquence, offers a suggestive
parallel to the comparative importance of the two schools
in the history of ecclesiastical Latin. Throughout the
third and fourth centuries the African school continues to
predominate, but it takes upon itself more of the classical
finish, and tames the first ferocity of its early manner.
Cyprian inclines more to the style of Tertullian ; Lactantius,
" the Christian Cicero," reverts strongly towards the classical
forms : and finally, towards the end of the fourth century,
the two languages are combined by Augustine, in proportions which, throughout the Middle Ages, form the accepted
type of the language of Latin Christianity.

In a fine passage at the opening of the fifth book of his
Institutes of Divinity, Lactantius regrets the imperfect
literary support given to Christianity by his two eminent
predecessors. The obscurity and harshness of Tertullian,
he says (and to this may be added his Montanism, which
fluctuated on the edge of heresy), prevent him from being
read or esteemed as widely as his great literary power
deserves ; while Minucius, in his single treatise, the *Octavius*,
gave a brilliant specimen of his grace and power as a
Christian apologist, but did not carry out the task to its full
scope. This last treatise is, indeed, of unique interest, not
only as a fine, if partial, vindication of the new religion,
but as the single writing of the age, Christian or pagan,
which in style and diction follows the classical tradition,
and almost reaches the classical standard. As to the life
of its author, nothing is known beyond the scanty indications given in the treatise itself. Even his date is not
wholly certain, and, while the reign of Commodus is his
most probable period, Jerome appears to allude to him as
later than Tertullian, and some modern critics incline to
place the work in the reign of Alexander Severus.

The *Octavius* is a dialogue in the Ciceronian manner,
showing especially a close study of the *De Natura
Deorum*. A brief and graceful introduction gives an

account of the scene of the dialogue. The narrator, with his two friends, Octavius and Caecilius, the former a Christian, the latter a somewhat wavering adherent of the old faith, are taking a walk on the beach near Ostia on a beautiful autumn morning, watching the little waves lapping on the sand, and boys playing duck-and-drake with pieces of tile, when Caecilius kisses his hand, in the ordinary pagan usage, to an image of Serapis which they pass. The incident draws them on to a theological discussion. Caecilius sets forth the argument against Christianity in detail, and Octavius replies to him point by point; at the end, Caecilius professes himself overcome, and declares his adhesion to the faith of his friend. Both in the attack and in the defence it is only the rational side of the new doctrine which is at issue. The unity of God, the resurrection of the body, and retribution in a future state, make up the sum of Christianity as it is presented. The name of Christ is not once mentioned, nor is his divinity directly asserted. There is no allusion to the sacraments, or to the doctrine of the Redemption; and Octavius neither quotes from nor refers to the writings of either Old or New Testament. Among early Christian writings, this method of treatment is unexampled elsewhere. The work is an attempt to present the new religion to educated opinion as a reasonable philosophic system; as we read it, we might be in the middle of the eighteenth century. With this temperate rationalism is combined a clearness and purity of diction, founded on the Ciceronian style, but without Cicero's sumptuousness of structure, that recalls the best prose of the Silver Age.

The author of the *Octavius* was a lawyer, who practised in the Roman courts. The literary influence of Quintilian no doubt lasted longer among the legal profession, for whose guidance he primarily wrote, than among the grammarians and journalists, who represent in this age the general tendency of the world of letters. But even in the legal profession the new Latin had established itself, and, except in the capital, seems to have almost driven out the classical manner. Its most remarkable exponent among Christian writers was, up to the time of his conversion, a pleader in the Carthaginian law-courts.

Quintus Septimius Florens Tertullianus was born at Carthage towards the end of the reign of Antoninus Pius. When he was a young man, the fame of Apuleius as a writer and lecturer was at its height; and though Tertullian himself never mentions him (as Apuleius, on his side, never refers in specific terms to the Christian religion), they must have been well known to each other, and their antagonism is of the kind which grows out of strong similarities of nature. Apuleius passed for a magician: Tertullian was a firm believer in magic, and his conversion to Christianity was, he himself tells us, very largely due to confessions of its truth extorted from demons, at the strange spiritualistic *séances* which were a feature of the time among all classes. His conversion took place in the last year of Commodus. The tension between the two religions — for in Africa, at all events, the old and the new were followed with equally fiery enthusiasm — had already reached breaking point. A heathen mob, headed by the priestesses of the *Mater et Virgo Caelestis*, the object of the ecstatic worship afterwards transferred to the mother of Christ, had two or three years before besieged the proconsul of Africa in his own house because he refused to order a general massacre of the Christians. In the anarchy after the assassination of Commodus, the persecution broke out, and continued to rage throughout the reign of Septimius Severus. It was in these years that Tertullian poured forth the series of apologetic and controversial writings whose fierce enthusiasm and impetuous eloquence open the history of Latin Christianity. The *Apologeticum*, the greatest of his earlier works, and, upon the whole, his masterpiece, was composed towards the beginning of this persecution, in the last years of the second century. The terms in which its purport is stated, *Quod religio Christiana damnanda non sit, nisi qualis sit prius intelligatur,* might lead one to expect a grave and reasoned defence of the new doctrine, like that of the *Octavius*. But Tertullian's strength is in attack, not in defence ; and his apology passes almost at once into a fierce indictment of paganism, painted in all the gaudiest colours of African rhetoric. Towards the end, he turns violently upon those who say that Christianity is merely a system of philosophy : and writers like Minucius are included with the eclectic pagan schoolmen in his condemnation. Here, for the first time, the position is definitely taken which has since then had so vast and varied an influence, that the Holy Scriptures are the source of all wisdom, and that the poetry and philosophy of the Graeco-Roman world were alike derived or perverted from the inspired writings of the Old Testament. Moses was five hundred years before Homer ; and therefore, runs his grandiose and sweeping fallacy, Homer is derived from the books of Moses. The argument, strange to say, has lived almost into our own day.

In thus breaking with heathen philosophy and poetry, Tertullian necessarily broke with the literary traditions of Europe for a thousand years. The Holy Scriptures, as a canon of revealed truth, became incidentally but inevitably a canon of literary style likewise. Writings soaked in quotations from the Hebrew poets and prophets could not but be affected by their style through and through. A current Latin translation of the Old and New Testament — the so-called *Itala*, which itself only survives as the ground-work of later versions — had already been made, and was in wide use. Its rude literal fidelity imported into Christian Latin an enormous mass of Grecisms and Hebraisms — the latter derived from the original writings, the former from the Septuagint version of the Old Testament — which combined with its free use of popular language and its relaxed grammar to force the new Latin further and further away from the classical tradition. The new religion, though it met its educated opponents in argument and outshone them in rhetorical embellishment, still professed, after the example of its first founders, to appeal mainly to the simple and the poor. "Stand forth, O soul!" cries Tertullian in another treatise of the same period; "I appeal to thee, not as wise with a wisdom formed in the schools, trained in libraries, or nourished in Attic academy or portico, but as simple and rude, without polish or culture; such as thou art to those who have thee only, such as thou art in the cross-road, the highway, the dockyard."

In the ardour of its attacks upon the heathen civilisation, the rising Puritanism of the Church bore hard upon the whole of culture. As against the theatre and the gladiatorial games, indeed, it occupied an unassailable position. There is a grim and characteristic humour in Tertullian's story of the Christian woman who went to the theatre and came back from it possessed with a devil, and the devil's crushing reply, *In meo eam inveni,* to the expostulation of the exorcist; a nobler passion rings in his pleading against the butcheries of the amphitheatre, "Do you wish to see blood? Behold Christ's!" His declamations against worldly luxury and ornament in the sumptuous pages of the *De Cultu Feminarum* are not more sweeping or less sincere than those of Horace or Juvenal; but the violent attack made on education and on literature itself in the *De Idololatria* shows the growth of that persecuting spirit which, as it gathered material force, destroyed ancient art and literature wherever it found them, and which led Pope Gregory, four hundred years later, to burn the magnificent library founded by Augustus. *Nos sumus in quos decucurrerunt fines seculorum,* "upon us the ends of the world are come," is the burden of Tertullian's impassioned argument. What were art and letters to those who waited, from moment to moment, for the glory of the Second

Coming? Yet for ten years or more he continued to pour forth his own brilliant essays; and while the substance of his teaching becomes more and more harsh and vindictive, the force of his rhetoric, his command over irony and invective, the gorgeous richness of his vocabulary, remain as striking as ever. In the strange and often romantic psychology of the *De Anima,* and in the singular clothes-philosophy of the *De Pallio,* he appears as the precursor of Swedenborg and Teufelsdröckh. A remarkable passage in the former treatise, in which he speaks of the growing pressure of over-population in the Empire, against which wars, famines, and pestilences had become necessary if unwelcome remedies, may lead us to reconsider the theory, now largely accepted, that the Roman Empire decayed and perished for want of men. With the advance of years his growing antagonism to the Catholic Church is accompanied by a further hardening of his style. The savage Puritanism of the *De Monogamia* and *De Ieiunio* is couched in a scholastic diction where the tradition of culture is disappearing; and in the gloomy ferocity of the *De Pudicitia,* probably the latest of his extant works, he comes to a final rupture alike with Catholicism and with humane letters.

The African school of patristic writers, of which Tertullian is at once the earliest and the most imposing figure, and of which he was indeed to a large degree the direct founder, continued for a century after his death to include the main literary production of Latin Christianity. Thascius Caecilius Cyprianus, Bishop of Carthage from the year 248, though a pupil and an admirer of Tertullian, reverts in his own writings at once to orthodoxy and to an easy and copious diction. In earlier youth he had been a professor of rhetoric; after his conversion in mature life, he gave up all his wealth to the poor, and devoted his great literary gifts to apologetic and hortatory writings. He escaped the Decian persecution by retiring from Carthage; but a few years later he was executed in the renewed outbreak of judicial

massacres which sullied the short and disastrous reign of
Valerian.   Forty years after Cyprian's death the rhetorician
Arnobius of Sicca in Numidia renewed the attack on paganism, rather than the defence or exposition of Christianity,
in the seven books *Adversus Nationes,* which he is said to
have written as a proof of the sincerity of his conversion.
"Uneven and ill-proportioned," in the phrase of Jerome,
this work follows neither the elaborate rhetoric of the early
African school, nor the chaster and more polished style of
Cyprian, but rather renews the inferior and slovenly manner
of the earlier antiquarians and encyclopedists.   A free use
of the rhetorical figures goes side by side with a general
want of finish and occasional lapses into solecism.   His
literary gift is so small, and his knowledge of the religion
he professes to defend so slight and so excessively inaccurate,
that theologians and men of letters for once agree that his
main value consists in the fragments of antiquarian information which he preserves.   But he has a further claim to
notice as the master of a celebrated pupil.

Lucius Caecilius Firmianus Lactantius, a name eminent
among patristic authors, and not inconsiderable in humane
letters, had, like Cyprian, been a professor of rhetoric, and
embraced Christianity in mature life.   That he was a pupil
of Arnobius is established by the testimony of Jerome ; his
African birth is only a doubtful inference from this fact.
Towards the end of the third century he established a
school at Nicomedia, which had practically become the
seat of empire under the rule of Diocletian ; and from
there he was summoned to the court of Gaul to superintend
the education of Crispus, the ill-fated son of Constantine.
The new religion had passed through its last and sharpest
persecution under Diocletian ; now, of the two joint-
emperors Constantine openly favoured the Christians, and
Licinius had been forced to relax the hostility towards
them which he had at first shown.   As it permeated the
court and saw the reins of government almost within its

grasp the Church naturally dropped some of the anathema-
tising spirit in which it had regarded art and literature in
the days of its earlier struggles. Lactantius brought to its
service a taste trained in the best literary tradition; and
while some doubt was cast on his dogmatic orthodoxy as
regards the precise definition of the Persons of the Trinity,
his pure and elegant diction was accepted as a model for
later writers. His greatest work, the seven books of the
Institutes of Divinity, was published a few years before
the victory of Constantine over Maxentius outside the
walls of Rome, which was the turning-point in the contest
between the two religions. It is an able exposition of
Christian doctrine in a style which, for eloquence, copiousness, and refinement, is in the most striking contrast
to the wretched prose produced by contemporary pagan
writers. The influence of Cicero is obvious and avowed
throughout; but the references in the work show the
author to have been familiar with the whole range of the
Latin classics, poets as well as prose writers. Ennius,
the comedians and satirists, Virgil and Horace, are cited by
him freely; he even dares to praise Ovid. In his treatise
On God's Workmanship — De Opificio Dei — the arguments
are often borrowed with the language from Cicero, but
Lucretius is also quoted and combated. The more
fanatical side of the new religion appears in the curious
work, *De Mortibus Persecutorum*, written after Constantine
had definitely thrown in his lot with Christianity. It is
famous as containing the earliest record of the vision of
Constantine before the battle of the Mulvian Bridge; and
its highly coloured account of the tragical fates of the
persecuting Emperors, from Nero to Diocletian, had a large
effect in fixing the tradition of the later Empire as viewed
throughout the Middle Ages. The long passionate pro-
test of the Church against heathen tyranny breaks out
here into equally passionate exultation; the Roman Empire
is already seen, as it was later by St. Augustine, fading and

crumbling away with the growth of the new and imperial
City of God.

Besides the large and continuous volume of its prose
production, the Latin Church of the third century also
made its first essays in poetry. They are both rude and
scanty; it was not till late in the fourth century that
Christian poetry reached its full development in the hymns
of Ambrose and Prudentius, and the hexameter poems of
Paulinus of Nola. The province of Africa, fertile as it was
in prose writers, never produced a poet of any eminence.
The pieces in verse — they can hardly be called poems —
ascribed to Tertullian and Cyprian are forgeries of a late
period.   But contemporary with them is an African verse
writer of curious linguistic interest, Commodianus. A
bishop of Marseilles, who wrote, late in the fifth century,
a continuation of St. Jerome's catalogue of ecclesiastical
writers, mentions his work in a very singular phrase:
"After his conversion," he says, "Commodianus wrote
a treatise against the pagans in an intermediate language
approximating to verse," *mediocri sermone quasi versu.* This
treatise, the *Carmen Apologeticum adversus Iudaeos et Gentes*,
is extant, together with other pieces by the same author.
It is a poem of over a thousand lines, which the allusions
to the Gothic war and the Decian persecution fix as
having been written in or very near the year 250. It is
written in hexameters, composed on a system which wavers
between the quantitative and accentual treatment. These
are almost evenly balanced. The poem is thus a document
of great importance in the history of the development of
mediaeval out of classical poetry. Though not, of course,
without his barbarisms, Commodianus was obviously neither
ignorant nor careless of the rules of classical versification,
some of which — for instance, the strong caesura in the
middle of the third foot — he retains with great strictness.
His peculiar prosody is plainly deliberate. Only a very
few lines are wholly quantitative, and none are wholly

accentual, except where accent and quantity happen to
coincide.   Much of the pronunciation of modern Italian
may be traced in his remarkable accentuation of some
words ; like Italian, he both throws back the accent off a
long syllable and slides it forward upon a short one.
Assonance is used freely, but there is not more rhyming
than is usual in the poetry of the late empire.   Not only in
pronunciation, but in grammatical inflexion, the beginnings
of Italian here and there appear.   The case-forms of the
different declensions are beginning to run into one another :
the plural, for example, of *insignis* is no longer *insignes*, but,
as in Italian, *insigni ;* and the case-inflexions themselves
are dwindling away before the free use of prepositions,
which was already beginning to show itself in the *Pervigilium
Veneris.*

Popular poetry was now definitely asserting itself alongside of book-poetry formed on the classical model.   But
authors who kept up a high literary standard in prose
continued to do so in verse also.   The elegiac piece
De Ave Phoenice, found in early mediaeval collections under
the name of Lactantius, and accepted as his by recent
critics, is written in accurate and graceful elegiac couplets,
which are quite in accordance with the admiration Lactantius, in his work *On the Wrath of God,* expresses for
Ovid.   It is perhaps the earliest instance outside the field
of prose of the truce or coalition which was slowly forming itself between the new religion and the old culture.
Beyond a certain faint and almost impalpable mysticism,
which hints at the legend of the Phoenix as symbolical
of the doctrine of the Resurrection, there is nothing in the
poem which is distinctively Christian.   Phoebus and the
lyre of Cyllene are invoked, as they might be by a pagan
poet.   But the language is from beginning to end full of
Christian or, at least, scriptural reminiscences, which could
only be possible to a writer familiar with the Psalter.
The description with which the poems opens of the Earthly

Paradise, a " land east of the sun," where the bird has its home, has mingled touches of the Elysium of Homer and Virgil, and the New Jerusalem of the Revelation; as in the Psalms, the sun is a bridegroom coming out of his chamber, and night and day are full of a language that is not speech.

In the literary revival of the latter half of the fourth century these tendencies have developed themselves, and taken a more mature but a less interesting form. After Christianity had become formally and irrevocably the State religion, it took over what was left of Latin culture as part of the chaotic inheritance which it had to accept as the price for civil establishment. A heavy price was paid on both sides when Constantine, in Dante's luminous phrase, " turned the eagles." The Empire definitively parted with the splendid administrative and political tradition founded on the classical training and the Stoic philosophy; though shattered as it had been in the anarchy of the third century, that was perhaps in any case irrecoverable. The Church, on its side, drew away in the persons of its leaders from its earlier tradition, with all that it involved in the growth of a wholly new thought and art, and armed or hampered itself with that classicalism from which it never again got quite free. It is in the century before Constantine, therefore, when old and new were in the sharpest antagonism, and yet were both full of a strange ferment — the ferment of dissolution in the one case, in the other that of quickening — that the end of the ancient world, and with it the end of Latin literature as such, might reasonably be placed. But the first result of the alliance between the Empire and the Church was to give added dignity to the latter and renewed energy to the former. The partial revival of letters in the fourth century may induce us to extend the period of the ancient Latin literature so far as to include Ausonius and Claudian as legitimate, though remote, successors of the Augustan poets.

VII.

For a full century after the death of Marcus Aurelius, Latin literature was, apart from the Christian writers, practically extinct. The authors of the least importance, or whose names even are known to any but professional scholars, may be counted on the fingers of one hand. The stream of Roman law, the one guiding thread down those dark ages, continued on its steady course. Papinian and Ulpian, the two foremost jurists of the reigns of Septimius and Alexander Severus, bear a reputation as high as that of any of their illustrious predecessors. Both rose to what was in this century the highest administrative position in the Empire, the prefecture of the praetorian guards. Papinian, a native it seems of the Syrian town of Emesa, and a kinsman of the Syrian wife of Septimius Severus, was the author of numerous legal works, both in Greek and Latin. Under Severus he was not only commander of the household troops, but discharged what we should now call the duties of Home Secretary. His genius for law was united with an independence of judgment and a sense of equity which rose beyond the limits of formal jurisprudence, and made him one of the great humanising influences of his profession. He was murdered, with circumstances of great brutality, by the infamous Caracalla, almost immediately after his accession to sole power. Domitius Ulpianus, Papinian's successor as the head of Latin jurists, was also a Syrian by birth.   Already an assessor to Papinian, and a member of the imperial privy council, he was raised to the praetorian prefecture and afterwards removed from it by his countryman, the Emperor Heliogabalus, but reinstated by Alexander Severus, under whom he was second ruler of the Empire till killed in a revolt of the praetorian guards in the year 228.   He was succeeded in the prefecture by Julius Paulus, a jurist of almost equal eminence, though inferior to Ulpian in style and literary grace.   Roman law practically remained at the point where these three eminent men left it, or only followed in their footsteps, until its final systematisation under Justinian.

Beyond the field of law, such prose as was written in this century was mainly Greek.   The historical works of Herodian and Dio Cassius, poor in quality as they are, seem to have excelled anything written at the same time in Latin.   Their contemporary, Marius Maximus, continued the series of biographies of the Emperors begun by Suetonius, carrying it down from Nerva to Heliogabalus ; but the work, such as it was, is lost, and is only known as the main source used by the earlier compilers of the *Augustan History*. Verse-making had fallen into the hands of inferior gram- marians.   Of their numerous productions enough survives to indicate that a certain technical skill was not wholly lost. The metrical treatises of Terentianus Maurus, a scholar of the later years of the second century, show that the science of metre was studied with great care, not only in its common forms, but in the less familiar lyric measures.   The didactic poem on the art of medicine by Quintus Sammonicus Serenus, the son of an eminent bibliophile, and the friend of the Emperor Alexander Severus, though of little poetical merit, is written in graceful and fluent verse.   If of little merit as poetry, it is of even less as science.   Medicine had sunk lower towards barbarism than versification, when a sovereign remedy against fevers was described in these polished lines :—

Inscribis chartae quod dicitur Abracadabra,
Saepius et subter repetis, sed detrahe summam
Et magis atque magis desint elementa figuris,
Singula quae semper rapies et cetera figes
Donec in angustum redigatur litera conum:
His lino nexis collum redimire memento.

Nor is his alternative remedy of a piece of coral hung round the patient's neck much more rational.   The drop from the science of Celsus is much more striking here than the drop from the art of Celsus' contemporary Manilius.   An intermittent imperial patronage of letters lingered on.   The elder and younger Gordian (the latter a pupil of Sammonicus' father, who bequeathed his immense library to him) had some reputation as writers.   Clodius Albinus, the governor of Britain who disputed the empire with Septimius Severus, was a devoted admirer of Apuleius, and wrote romances in a similar manner, which, according to his biographer, had no inconsiderable circulation.

Under Diocletian and his successors there was a slight and partial revival of letters, which chiefly showed itself on the side of verse.   The *Cynegetica*, a didactic poem on hunting, by the Carthaginian poet Marcus Aurelius Olympius Nemesianus, is, together with four bucolic pieces by the same author, the chief surviving fragment of the main line of Virgilian tradition.   The *Cynegetica*, in spite of its good taste and its excellent versification, is on the whole a dull performance; but in the other pieces, the pastoral form gives the author now and then an opportunity of introducing a little touch of the romantic tone which is partly imitated from Virgil, but partly natural to the new Latin.

Perdit spina rosas nec semper lilia candent
Nec longum tenet uva comas nec populus umbras;
Donum forma breve est, nec se quod commodet annis: —

in these graceful lines the copied Virgilian cadence is

united with the directness and the real or assumed simplicity
which belongs to the second childhood of Latin literature,
and which is so remarkable in the authors who founded the
new style.   The new style itself was also largely practised,
but only a few scattered remnants survive.   Tiberianus,
Count of Africa, Vicar of Spain, and praetorian prefect of
Gaul (the whole nomenclature of the Empire is now passing
from the Roman to the mediaeval type) under Constantine
the Great, is usually identified with the author of some of
the most strikingly beautiful of these fragmentary pieces.
A descriptive passage, consisting of twenty lines of finely
written trochaics, reminds one of the *Pervigilium Veneris* in
the richness of its language and the delicate simplicity of
its style.   The last lines may be quoted for their singular
likeness to one of the most elaborately beautiful stanzas
of the *Faerie Queene*, that which describes the sounds
"consorted in one harmony" which Guyon hears in the
gardens of Acrasia : —

> *Has per umbras omnis ales plus canora quam putes*
> *Cantibus vernis strepebat et susurris dulcibus :*
> *Hic loquentis murmur amnis concinebat frondibus*
> *Quas melos vocalis aurae, musa Zephyri, moverat :*
> *Sic euntem per virecta pulcra odora et musica*
> *Ales amnis aura lucus flos et umbra iuverat.*

The principal prose work, however, which has come down
from this age, shows a continued and even increased degradation of style.   The so-called *Historia Augusta*, a series
of memoirs, in continuation of Suetonius' *Lives of the Twelve
Caesars*, of the Roman Emperors from Hadrian to Numerian
(A.D. 117–284), was begun under Diocletian and finished
under Constantine by six writers — Aelius Spartianus, Julius
Capitolinus, Vulcacius Gallicanus, Trebellius Pollio, Aelius
Lampridius, and Flavius Vopiscus.   Most of them, if not
all, were officials of the imperial court, and had free access
to the registers of the senate as well as to more private

sources of information. The extreme feebleness of the contents of this curious work is only exceeded by the poverty and childishness of the writing. History had sunk into a collection of trivial gossip and details of court life, couched in a language worthy of a second-rate chronicler of the Dark Ages. The mere outward circumstances of the men whose lives they narrated — the *purpurati Augusti*, as one of the authors calls them in a romantically sonorous phrase — were indeed of world-wide importance, and among the masses of rubbish of which the memoirs chiefly consist there is included much curious information and striking incident. But their main interest is in the light they throw on the gradual sinking of the splendid administrative organisation of the second century towards the sterile Chinese hierarchy of the Byzantine Empire, and the concurrent degradation of paganism, both as a political and a religious system.

Vopiscus, the last of the six authors, apologises, in drawing the work to a close, for his slender literary power, and expresses the hope that his material at least may be found useful to some "eloquent man who may wish to unlock the actions of princes." What he had in his mind was probably not so much regular history as the panegyrical oratory which about this same time became a prominent feature of the imperial courts, and gave their name to a whole school of writers known as the Panegyrici. Gaul, for a long time the rival of Africa as the nurse of judicial oratory, was the part of the Empire where this new form of literature was most assiduously cultivated. Up to the age of Constantine, it had enjoyed practical immunity from barbarian invasion, and had only had a moderate share of the civil wars which throughout the third century desolated all parts of the Empire. In wealth and civilisation, and in the arts of peace, it probably held the foremost place among the provinces. Marseilles, Narbonne, Toulouse, Bordeaux, Autun, Rheims, and Trèves all possessed famous and flourishing schools of oratory. The last-named town was

after the supreme power had been divided among two or
more Augusti, a frequent seat of the imperial government
of the Western provinces, and, like Milan, became a more
important centre of public life than Rome.   Of the extant
collection of panegyrics, two were delivered there before
Diocletian's colleague, the Emperor Maximianus.   A florid
Ciceronianism was the style most in vogue, and the phrase-
ology, at least, of the old State religion was, until the
formal adoption of Christianity by the government, not
only retained, but put prominently forward.   Eumenius of
Autun, the author of five or more pieces in the collection,
delivered at dates between the years 297 and 311, is the
most distinguished figure of the group.   His fluent and
ornate Latin may be read with some pleasure, though the
purpose of the orations leaves them little value as a record
of facts or a candid expression of opinions.   Under the
influence of these nurseries of rhetoric a new Gallic school
of Christian writers rose and flourished during the fourth
century.   Hilarius of Poitiers, the most eminent of the
Gallic bishops of this period, wrote controversial and
expository works in the florid involved style of the neo-
Ciceronian orators, which had in their day a high reputation.
As the first known author of Latin hymns, he is the precursor of Ambrose and Prudentius.   Ambrose himself,
though as Bishop of Milan he belongs properly to the
Italian school of theological writers, was born and probably
educated at Trèves.   But the literature of the province
reached its highest point somewhat later, in one of the most
important authors of the century, Decimus Magnus Ausonius
of Bordeaux.

Ausonius was of Gallic blood by both parents ; he was
educated in grammar and rhetoric at the university of
Bordeaux, and was afterwards for many years professor of
both subjects at that of Trèves.   As tutor to Gratian, son
and successor of the Emperor Valentinian, he established
himself ir court favour, and fulfilled many high State offices

After Gratian was succeeded by Theodosius he retired to a lettered ease near his native town, where he lived till nearly the end of the century. His numerous poetical works are of the most miscellaneous kind, ranging from Christian hymns and elegies on deceased relations to translations from the Greek Anthology and centos from Virgil. Among them the volume of *Idyllia* constitutes his chief claim to eminence, and gives him a high rank among the later Latin poets. The gem of this collection is the famous *Mosella*, written at Trèves about the year 370. The most beautiful of purely descriptive Latin poems, it is unique in the felicity with which it unites Virgilian rhythm and diction with the new romantic sense of the beauties of nature. The feeling for the charm of landscape which we had occasion to note in the letters of the younger Pliny is here fully developed, with a keener eye and an enlarged power of expression. Pliny's description of the Clitumnus may be interestingly compared with the passage of this poem in which Ausonius recounts, with fine and observant touches, the beauties of his northern river — the liquid lapse of waters, the green wavering reflections, the belt of crisp sand by the water's edge and the long weeds swaying with the stream, the gleaming gravel-beds under the water with their patches of moss and the quick fishes darting hither and thither over them; or the oftener-quoted and not less beautiful lines where he breaks into rapture over the sunset colouring of stream and bank, and the glassy water where, at evening, all the hills waver and the vine-tendril shakes and the grape-bunches swell in the crystal mirror. In virtue of this poem Ausonius ranks not merely as the last, or all but the last, of Latin, but as the first of French poets. His feeling for the country of his birth has all the romantic patriotism which we are accustomed to associate with a much earlier or a much later age. The language of Du Bellay in the sixteenth century —

Plus que le marbre dur me plaist l'ardoise fine,
   Plus mon Loire Gaulois que le Tybre Latin —

is anticipated here.   The softer northern loveliness, *la douceur Angevine*, appeals to Ausonius more than all the traditional beauties of Arcadia or Sicily.   It is with the Gallic rivers that he compares his loved Moselle : *Non tibi se Liger anteferet, non Axona praeceps . . . te sparsis incerta Druentia ripis.*

   O lordly flow the Loire and Seine
      And loud the dark Durance ! —

we seem to hear the very words of the modern ballad : and at the end of the poem his imagination returns, with the fondness of a lover, to the green lakes and sounding streams of Aquitaine, and the broad sea-like reaches of his native Garonne.

   In this poem, alike by the classic beauty of his language and the modernism of his feeling, Ausonius marks one of the great divisions in the history of poetry.   He is the last of the poets of the Empire which was still nominally co-extensive with the world, which held in itself East and West, the old and the new.   The final division of the Roman world, which took place in the year 395 between the two sons of Theodosius, synchronises with a division as definite and as final between classical and mediaeval poetry ; and in the last years of the fourth century the parting of the two streams, the separation of the dying from the dawning light, is placed in sharp relief by the works of two con-temporary poets, Claudian and Prudentius.   The singular and isolated figure of Claudian, the posthumous child of the classical world, stands alongside of that of the first great Christian poet like the figures which were fabled to stand, regarding the rising and setting sun, by the Atlantic gates where the Mediterranean opened into the unknown Western seas.

   Claudius Claudianus was of Asiatic origin, and lived at

Alexandria until, in the year of the death of Theodosius, he passed into Italy and became the laureate of the court of Milan. Till then he had, according to his own statement, written in Greek, his life having been passed wholly in the Greek-speaking provinces. But immediately on his arrival at the seat of the Western or Latin Empire he showed himself a master of the language and forms of Latin poetry such as had not been known since the end of the first century. His poems, so far as they can be dated, belong entirely to the next ten years. He is conjectured not to have long survived the downfall of his patron Stilicho, the great Vandal general who, as guardian of the young Emperor Honorius, was practically ruler of the Western Empire. He was the last eminent man of letters who was a professed pagan.

The historical epics which Claudian produced in rapid succession during the last five years of the fourth and the first five of the fifth century are now little read, except by historians who refer to them for details of the wars or court intrigues of the period. A hundred years ago, when Statius and Silius Italicus formed part of the regular course of classical study, he naturally and properly stood alongside of them. His Latin is as pure as that of the best poets of the Silver Age ; in wealth of language and in fertility of imagination he is excelled, if at all, by Statius alone. Alone in his age he inherits the scholarly tradition which still lingered among the libraries of Alexandria. Nonnus, the last and not one of the least learned and graceful of the later Greek epicists, who probably lived not long after Claudian, was also of Egyptian birth and training, and he and Claudian are really the last representatives of that Alexandrian school which had from the first had so large and deep an influence over the literature of Rome. The immense range of time covered by Greek literature is brought more vividly to our imagination when we consider that this single Alexandrian school, which began late in

the history of Greek writing and came to an end centuries
before its extinction, thus completely overlaps at both ends
the whole life of the literature of Rome, reaching as it
does from before Ennius till after Claudian.

These historical epics of Claudian's — *On the Consulate of
Stilicho, On the Gildonic War, On the Pollentine War, On
the Third, Fourth, and Sixth Consulates of Honorius* — are
accompanied by other pieces, written in the same stately
and harmonious hexameter, of a more personal interest :
invectives against Rufinus and Eutropius, the rivals of his
patron ; a panegyric on Stilicho's wife, Serena, the niece
of Theodosius ; a fine epithalamium on the marriage of
Honorius with Maria, the daughter of Stilicho and Serena ;
and also by a number of poems in elegiac metre, in which
he wrote with equal grace and skill, though not with so
singular a mastery. Among the shorter elegiac pieces,
which are collected under the title of *Epigrams*, one, a poem
on an old man of Verona who had never travelled beyond
his own little suburban property, is among the jewels of
Latin poetry. The lines in which he describes this quiet
garden life —

> *Frugibus alternis, non consule computat annum ;*
> *Auctumnum pomis, ver sibi flore notat ;*
> *Idem condit ager soles idemque reducit,*
> *Metiturque suo rusticus orbe diem,*
> *Ingentem meminit parvo qui germine quercum*
> *Aequaevumque videt consenuisse nemus —*

are in grace and feeling like the very finest work of
Tibullus ; and the concluding couplet —

> *Erret, et extremos alter scrutetur Hiberos,*
> *Plus habet hic vitae, plus habet ille viae —*

though, in its dependence on a verbal point, it may not
satisfy the purest taste, is not without a dignity and pathos
that are worthy of the large manner of the classical period.

Claudian used the heroic hexameter for mythological as well as historical epics. Of his *Gigantomachia* we possess only an inconsiderable fragment; but the three books of the unfinished *Rape of Proserpine* are among the finest examples of the purely literary epic. The description of the flowery spring meadows where Proserpine and her companions gather blossoms for garlands is a passage perpetually quoted. It is interesting to note how the rising tide of romanticism has here, as elsewhere, left Claudian wholly untouched. The passage, though elaborately ornate, is executed in the clear hard manner of the Alexandrian school; it has not a trace of that sensitiveness to nature which vibrates in the *Pervigilium Veneris.* We have gone back for a moment to that poetical style which perpetually reminds us of the sculptured friezes of Greek art, severe in outline, immensely adroit and learned in execution, but a little chilly and colourless except in the hands of its greatest masters. After paying to the full the tribute of admiration which is due to Claudian's refined and dignified workmanship, we are still left with the feeling that this kind of poetry was already obsolete. It is not only that, as has been remarked with truth of his historical epics, the elaboration of the treatment is disproportionate to the importance or interest of the subject. *Materiam superabat opus* might be said with equal truth of much of the work of his predecessors. But a new spirit had by this time penetrated literature, and any poetry wholly divorced from it must be not only artificial — for that alone would prove nothing against it — but unnatural. Claudian is a precursor of the Renaissance in its narrower aspect; the last of the classics, he is at the same time the earliest, and one of the most distinguished, of the classicists. It might seem a mere chance whether his poetry belonged to the fourth or to the sixteenth century.

In Claudian's distinguished contemporary, the Spanish poet Aurelius Prudentius Clemens, Christian Latin poetry

reached complete maturity. His collected poems were
published at Rome in 404, the year celebrated by Claudian
as that of the sixth consulship of Honorius. Before Prudentius, Christian poetry had been slight in amount and
rude or tentative in manner. We have already had occasion to notice its earliest efforts in the rude verses of
Commodianus. The revival of letters in the fourth century,
so far as it went, affected Christian as well as secular
poetry. Under Constantine, a Spanish deacon, one Gaius
Vettius Aquilinus Juvencus, put the Gospel narrative into
respectable hexameters, which are still extant. The poems
and hymns which have come down under the name of
Bishop Hilary of Poitiers are probably spurious, and a
similar doubt attaches to those ascribed to the eminent
grammarian and rhetorician, Gaius Marius Victorinus, after
his conversion. Before Prudentius published his collection,
the hymns of St. Ambrose had been written, and were
in use among the Western Churches. But these, though
they formed the type for all later hymn-writers, were few
in number. Out of the so-called Ambrosian hymns a
rigorous criticism only allows five or six as authentic.
These, however, include two world-famed pieces, still in
daily use by the Church, the *Aeterne rerum Conditor* and
the *Deus Creator omnium*, and the equally famous *Veni
Redemptor.*

To the form thus established by St. Ambrose, Prudentius,
in his two books of lyrical poems, gave a larger volume
and a more sustained literary power. The *Cathemerina*,
a series of poems on the Christian life, and the *Periste-
phanon*, a book of the praise of Christian martyrs — St.
Lawrence, St. Vincent, St. Agnes, among other less celebrated names — at once represent the most substantial
addition made to Latin lyrical poetry since Horace, and
the complete triumph of the new religion. They are not,
like the Ambrosian hymns, brief pieces meant for actual
singing in churches. Out of the twenty-six poems only

three are under one hundred lines in length, and that on
the martyrdom of St. Romanus of Antioch runs to no less
than eleven hundred and forty, almost the proportions of
a small epic. But in the brilliance and vigour of their
language, their picturesque style, and the new joy that,
in spite of their asceticism, burns throughout them, they
gave an impulse of immense force towards the development
of Christian literature. In merely technical quality they
are superior to any poetry of the time, Claudian alone
excepted ; in their fulness of life, in the exultant tone which
kindles and sustains them, they make Claudian grow pale
like a candle-flame at dawn.

With Prudentius, however, as with Claudian, we have
almost passed beyond the strict limit of a history of ancient
Latin literature : and any fuller discussion, either of these
remarkable lyrical pieces, or of his more voluminous expository or controversial treatises in hexameter, properly
belongs to a history of the Christian Church. The two
most eminent and copious prose writers of the later fourth
century, Jerome and Augustine, occupy the same ambiguous position. Apart from them, and from the less
celebrated Christian writers who were their predecessors or
contemporaries, the prose of the fourth century is both
small in amount and insignificant in quality. The revival
in verse composition which followed the settlement of the
Empire under Constantine scarcely spread to the less
imitable art of prose. The school of eminent Roman
grammarians who flourished about the middle of the
century, and among whom Servius and Donatus are the
leading names, while they commented on ancient masterpieces with inexhaustible industry, and often with really
sound judgment, wrote themselves in a base and formless
style. A few authors of technical manuals and epitomes
of history rise a little above the common level, or have
a casual importance from the contents of their works. The
treatises on husbandry by Palladius, and on the art of war

by Flavius Vegetius Renatus, became, to a certain degree,
standard works; the little handbooks of Roman history
written in the reigns of Constantius and Valens by Aurelius
Victor and Eutropius are simple and unpretentious, but
have little positive merit. The age produced but one
Latin historian, Ammianus Marcellinus. Like Claudian,
he was of Asiatic origin, and Greek-speaking by birth, but,
in the course of his service on the staff of the captain-
general of the imperial cavalry, had spent much of his life
in the Latin provinces of Gaul and Italy; and his history
was written at Rome, where he lived after retiring from
active service. The task he set himself, a history of the
Empire, in continuation of that of Tacitus, from the accession of Nerva to the death of Valens, was one of great
scope and unusual complexity. He brought to it some
at least of the gifts of the historian : intelligence, honesty,
tolerance, a large amount of good sense. But his Latin,
which he never came to write with the 'ease of a native,
is difficult and confused; and to this, probably, should be
ascribed the early disappearance of the greater part of his
history. The last eighteen books, containing the history
of only five and twenty years, have survived. The greater
part of the period which they cover is one of decay and
wretchedness; but the account they give of the reign of
Julian (whom Ammianus had himself accompanied in his
Persian campaign) is of great interest, and his portrait of
the feeble incapable rule of Julian's successors, distracted
between barbarian inroads and theological disputes, is
drawn with a firm and almost a masterly hand.

The Emperor Valens fell, together with nearly the whole
of a great Roman army, in the disastrous battle of Adria-
nople. A Visigothic horde, to the number of two hundred
thousand fighting men, had crossed the Danube; and the
Huns and Alans, names even more terrible, joined the standards of Fritigern with a countless host of Mongolian cavalry.
The heart of the Empire lay helpless; Constantinople itself

was besieged by the conquerors. The elevation of Theodosius to the purple bore back for a time the tide of
disaster; once more the civilised world staggered to its
feet, but with strength and courage fatally broken. At
this dramatic moment in the downfall of the Roman Empire
the last of the Latin historians closes his narrative.

VIII.

THE BEGINNINGS OF THE MIDDLE AGES.

In August 410, while the Emperor Honorius fed his poultry among the impenetrable marshes of Ravenna, Rome was sacked by a mixed army of Goths and Huns under the command of Alaric. Eight hundred years had elapsed since the imperial city had been in foreign possession; and, though it had ceased to be the actual seat of government, the shock spread by its capture through the entire Roman world was of unparalleled magnitude. Six years later, a wealthy and distinguished resident, one Claudius Rutilius Namatianus, was obliged to take a journey to look after the condition of his estates in the south of France, which had been devastated by a band of wandering Visigoths. A large portion is extant of the poem in which he described this journey, one of the most charming among poems of travel, and one of the most interesting of the fragments of early mediaeval literature. Nowhere else can we see portrayed so strongly the fascination which Rome then still possessed for the whole of Western Europe, and the adoration with which she was still regarded as mother and light of the world. The magical statue had been cast away, with other heathen idols, from the imperial bedchamber; but the *Fortuna Urbis* itself, the mystical divinity which the statue represented, still exercised an overwhelming influence over men's imagination. After all the praises lavished on her for centuries by so many of her illustrious

children, it was left for this foreigner, in the age of her
decay, to pay her the most complete and most splendid
eulogy : —

> *Quod regnas minus est quam quod regnare mereris;*
> *Excedis factis grandia fata tuis :*
> *Nam solis radiis aequalia munera tendis,*
> *Qua circumfusus fluctuat oceanus.*
> *Fecisti patriam diversis gentibus unam :*
> *Profuit invitis te dominante capi;*
> *Dumque offers victis proprii consortia iuris,*
> *Urbem fecisti quod prius orbis erat.*

In this noble apostrophe Rutilius addressed the fading
mistress of the world as he passed lingeringly through the
Ostian gate. Far away in Northern Africa, the most
profound thinker and most brilliant writer of the age, as
deeply but very differently moved by the ancestral splendours of the city and the tragedy of her fall, was then
composing, with all the resources of his vast learning and
consummate dialectical skill, the epitaph of the ancient
civilisation. It was the capture of Rome by Alaric which
induced St. Augustine to undertake his work on the *City
of God.* "In this middle age," he says, — *in hoc interim
seculo* — the two cities with their two citizenships, the
earthly and the heavenly, are inextricably enwound and
intermingled with each other. Not until the Last Judgment will they be wholly separated; but the philosophy of
history is to trace the steps by which the one is slowly
replaced by, or transformed into, the other. The earthly
Empire, all the splendid achievement in thought and arts
and deeds of the Roman civilisation, already fades away
before that City of God on which his eyes are fixed —
*gloriosissimam Civitatem Dei, sive in hoc temporum cursu
cum inter impios peregrinatur ex fide vivens, sive in illa
stabilitate sedis aeternae, quam nunc exspectat per patientiam,
quoadusque iustitia convertatur in iudicium.*

The evolution of this change was, even to the impassioned faith of Augustine, slow, intermittent, and fluctuating : nor, among many landmarks and turning-points, is it easy to fix any single one as definitely concluding the life of the ancient world, and marking the beginning of what St. Augustine for the first time called by the name, which has ever since adhered to it, of the Middle Age. The old world slid into the new through insensible gradations. In nearly all Latin literature after Virgil we may find traces or premonitions of mediaevalism, and after mediaevalism was established it long retained, if it ever wholly lost, traces of the classical tradition. Thus, while the beginning of Latin literature may be definitely placed in a particular generation, and almost in a single year, there is no fixed point at which it can be said that its history concludes. Different periods have been assigned from different points of view. In the year 476, Romulus Augustulus, the last of the Western Emperors, handed over the name as well as the substance of sole power to the Herulian chief Odoacer, the first King of Italy ; and the Roman Senate, still in theory the supreme governing body of the civilised world, formally renounced its sovereignty, and declared its dominions a diocese of the Byzantine Empire. This is the date generally adopted by authors who deal with literature as subordinate to political history. But the writer of the standard English work on Latin grammar limits his field to the period included between Plautus and Suetonius ; while another scholar, extending his scope three centuries and a half further, has written a history of Latin literature from Ennius to Boethius. Suetonius and Boethius probably represent the extreme variation of limit which can be reasonably adopted ; but between them they leave room for many points of pause. Up to the end of the fourth century we have followed a stream of tendency, not, indeed, continuous, but yet without any absolute rupture. Between the writers of the fourth century and their few successors of the fifth there is no marked change in language or manner. Sidonius Apollinaris continues more feebly the style of poetry initiated a century before him by Ausonius. Boethius wrote his fine treatise *On the Consolation of Philosophy* half a century after the extinction of the Empire of the West. By a strange freak of history, it was at the Greek capital that Latin scholarship finally faded away. Priscian and Tribonian wrote at Constantinople; and the Western world received its most authoritative works on Latin grammar and Roman law, not from the Latin Empire, nor from one of the Latin-speaking kingdoms which rose on its ruins, but from the half-oriental courts of Anastasius and Justinian.

The two long lives of the great Latin fathers, Jerome and Augustine, cover conjointly a space of just a century. Jerome was born probably a few months after the main seat of empire was formally transferred to New Rome by Constantine. Augustine, born twenty-three years later, died in his cathedral city of Hippo during its siege by Genseric in the brief war which transformed Africa from a Roman province to a Vandal kingdom. The *City of God* had been completed four years previously. A quarter of a century before the death of Augustine, Jerome issued, from his monastery at Bethlehem, the Latin translation of the Bible which, on its own merits, and still more if we give weight to its overwhelming influence on later ages, is the greatest literary masterpiece of the Lower Empire. Our own Authorised Version has deeply affected all post-Shakespearian English; the *Vulgate* of Jerome, which was from time to time revised in detail, but still remains substantially as it issued from his hands, had an equally profound influence over a vastly greater space and time. It was for Europe of the Middle Ages more than Homer was to Greece. The year 405, which witnessed its publication and that of the last of the poems of Claudian to which we can assign a certain date, may claim to be held,

if any definite point is to be fixed, as marking the end of
ancient and the complete establishment of mediaeval
Latin.

In the six and a half centuries which had passed since
the Greek prisoner of war from Tarentum produced the
first Latin play in the theatre of the mid-Italian Republic
which was celebrating her victories over the formidable
sea-power of Carthage, Latin literature had shared the
vicissitudes of the Roman State; and the successive stages
of its development and decay are intimately connected with
the political and social changes which are the matter of
Roman history. A century passed between the conclusion
of the first Punic war and the tribunate of Tiberius
Gracchus. It was a period for the Republic of internal
tranquillity and successful foreign war. At its conclusion,
Italy was organised under Roman control. Greece,
Macedonia, Spain, and Africa had become subject provinces; a Roman protectorate was established in Egypt,
and the Asiatic provinces of the Macedonian Empire only
preserved a precarious and partial independence. During
this century, Latin literature had firmly established itself in
a broad and vigorous growth. Dramatic and epic poetry,
based on diligent study of the best Greek models, formed
a substantial body of actual achievement, and under Greek
impulse the Latin language was being wrought into a medium
of expression at once dignified and copious, a substance
capable of indefinite expansion and use in the hands of
trained artists. Prose was rapidly overtaking verse. The
schools of law, and the oratory of the senate-house and the
forum, were developing national forms of literature on
distinctively Roman lines : a beginning had been made in
the more difficult field of history; and the invention and
popularisation of the satire, or mixed form of familiar prose
and verse, began to enlarge the scope of literature over a
broader field of life and thought, while immensely adding
to the flexibility and range of the written language.

A century followed during which Roman rule was extended and consolidated over the whole area of the countries fringing the Mediterranean, while concurrently a long series of revolutions and counter-revolutions ended in the overthrow of the republican oligarchy, and the establishment of the imperial government. Beginning with the democratic movement of the Gracchi, this century includes the civil wars of Marius and Sulla, the temporary reconstitution of the oligarchy, the renewed outbreak of war between Julius Caesar and the senate, and the confused period of administrative anarchy which was terminated by the rise of Augustus to a practical dictatorship, and the arrangement by him of a working compromise between the two great opposing forces. During this century of revolution the whole attitude of Rome towards the problems both of internal and of foreign politics was forced through a series of important changes. The revolt of Italy, which, after bringing Rome to the verge of destruction, was finally crushed by the Asiatic legions of Sulla, was almost immediately followed by the unification of Italy, and her practical absorption into the Roman citizenship. With renewed and enlarged life, Rome then entered on a second extension of her dominions. The annexation of Syria and the conquest of Gaul completed the circle of her empire ; the subjugation of Spain was completed, and the Eastern frontier pushed towards Armenia and the Euphrates ; finally Egypt, the last survivor of the kingdoms founded by Alexander's generals, passed wholly into Roman hands with the extinction of its own royal house.

During this period of perpetual excitement and high political tension, literature, in the forms both of prose and verse, rapidly grew towards maturity, and, in the former field at least, reached its perfection. Oratory, the great weapon of politicians under the unique Republican constitution, was in its golden age. Greek culture had permeated the governing class. History began to be written by trained statesmen, whose education for the command of armies and the rule of provinces had been based on elaborate linguistic and rhetorical study. Alongside of grammar and rhetoric, poetry and philosophy took a place as part of the higher education of the citizen. The habit and capacity of abstract thought reached Rome from the schools of Athens; with the growing power of expression and the increased tension of actual life, the science of politics and the philosophy of life and conduct became the material of a new and splendid literature. Along with the world of ideas diffused by Athens there arrived the immense learning and high technical skill of the Alexandrian scholars and poets. Roman poetry set itself anew to learn the Greek lesson of exquisite form and perfect finish. In the hands of two poets of the first order, and of a crowd of lesser students, the conquest of poetical form passed its crucial point, and the way was prepared for the consummation of Latin poetry in the next age.

Another century carries us from the establishment of the Empire by Augustus to the extinction of his family at the death of Nero. At the opening of this period the Empire was exhausted by civil war, and welcomed any form of settled rule. The settlement of the constitution, based as it was on a number of elaborate legal fictions meant to combine republican forms with the reality of a strong monarchical government, left the political situation in a state of very unstable equilibrium; all through the century the government was in an uncertain or even a false position, and, when Nero's misrule had made it intolerable, it collapsed with a crash which almost shivered the Empire into fragments. But it had lasted long enough to lay the foundations of the new and larger Rome broadly and securely. The provinces, while still in a sense subordinate to Italy, had already become organic parts of the Empire, instead of subject countries. The haughty and obstinate Roman oligarchy was tamed by long years of proscription, confiscation, perpetual surveillance, careful exclusion from great political power. The municipal institutions and civic energy of Rome were multiplied in a thousand centres of local life. Internal peace allowed commerce and civilisation to spread; in spite of the immense drain caused by the extravagance of the capital and the expense of the great frontier armies, the provinces generally rose to a higher state of material welfare than they had enjoyed since their annexation.

The earlier years of this century are the most brilliant in the history of Latin literature. During the last fifty years of the Republic a series of Roman authors of remarkable genius had gradually met and mastered the technical problems of both prose and verse. The new generation entered into their labours. In prose there was little, if any, advance remaining to be made. In the fields of oratory and philosophy it had already reached its perfection; in that of history it acquired further amplitude and colour. But the achievement of the new age was mainly in verse. Profound study of the older poetry, and the laborious training learned from the schools of Alexandria, now bore fruit in a body of poetry which, in every field except that of the drama, excelled what had hitherto been known, and was at once the model and the limit for succeeding generations. Latin poetry, like the Empire itself, took a broader basis; the Augustan poets are still Romans, but this is because Rome had extended itself over Italy.

The copious and splendid production of the earlier years of the principate of Augustus was followed by an almost inevitable reaction. The energy of the Latin speech had for the time exhausted itself; and the political necessities of the uneasy reigns which followed set further barriers in the way of a weakening literary impulse. Then begins the movement of the Latin-speaking provinces. Rome had absorbed Italy; Italy in turn begins to absorb and coalesce with Gaul, Spain, and Africa. The first of the provinces in the field was Spain, which had become Latinised earlier than either of the others. At the court of Nero a single brilliant Spanish family founded a new and striking style, which for the moment eclipsed that formed by a purer taste amid a graver and a more exclusive public.

A hundred years from the downfall of Nero carry us down to the reign of Marcus Aurelius. The Empire, when it recovered from the collapse of the year 69, assumed a settled and stable organisation. Traditions of the old jealousies and discontents lingered during the reigns of the three Flavian Emperors ; but the imperial system had now got into permanent working order. The cataclysm which followed the deposition of Nero is in the strongest contrast to the ease and smoothness, only broken by a trifling mutiny of the praetorian guards, with which the principate passed into the hands of Nerva after the murder of Domitian.

This century is what is properly known as the Silver Age. A school of eminent writers, in whom the provincial and the Italian quality are now hardly to be distinguished, produced during its earlier years a large body of admirable prose and not undistinguished verse. But before the century was half over, the signs of decay began to appear. A mysterious languor overcame thought and art, as it did the whole organism of the Empire. The conquests of Trajan, the peace and material splendour of the reign of Hadrian, were followed by a series of years almost without events, suddenly broken by the appalling pestilence of the year 166, and the outbreak, at the same time, of a long and desperate war on the northern frontiers. During these eventless years Latin literature seemed to die away. The classical impulse was exhausted ; the attempts made towards founding a new Latin bore, for the time, little fruit. Before this period of exhaustion and reaction could come to a natural end, two changes of momentous importance had overtaken the world. The imperial system broke down under Commodus. All through the third century the civil organisation of the Empire was at the mercy of military adventurers. Twenty-five recognised emperors, besides a swarm of pretenders, most of them raised to the purple by mutinous armies, succeeded one another in the hundred years between Commodus and Diocletian. At the same time the Christian religion, already recognised under the Antonines as a grave menace to the very existence of the Empire, was extending itself year by year, rising more elastic than ever from each fresh persecution, and attracting towards itself all the vital forces which go to make literature.

The coalition between the Empire and the Church, which, after various tentative preliminaries, was finally effected by Constantine, launched the world upon new paths : and his transference of the main seat of empire to the shores of the Bosporus left Western Europe to pursue fragmentary and independent courses. The Latin-speaking provinces were falling away in great lumps. An independent empire of Britain had already existed for six or seven years under the usurper Carausius. After the middle of the fourth century Gaul was practically in possession of the Visigoths and the Salian Franks. During the reign of Honorius mixed hordes of Vandals, Suabians, and Alans poured through Gaul across the Pyrenees, and divided Spain into barbarian monarchies. A few years later the Vandals, called across the straits of Gibraltar by the treachery of Count Boniface, overran the province of Africa, and established a powerful kingdom, whose fleets, issuing from the port of Carthage, swept the Mediterranean and sacked Rome itself. Rome had, by the famous edict of Antoninus Caracalla, given the world a single citizenship ; to give organic life to that citizenship, and turn her citizens into a single nation, was a task beyond her power. So long as the Latin-speaking world remained nominally subject to a single rule, exercised in the name of the Senate and People of Rome, Latin

literature had some slight external bond of unity; after the
Western Empire was shattered into a dozen independent
kingdoms, the phrase almost ceases to have any real
meaning. Latin, in one form or another, remained an
almost universal language; but we must speak henceforth
of the literatures of France or Spain or Britain, whether the
work produced be written in a provincial dialect or in the
international language handed down from the Empire and
preserved by the Church.

For the Catholic Church now became the centre of
European cohesion, and gave continuity and common life
to the scattered remains of the ancient civilisation.   Already,
in the fifth century, Pope Leo the Great is a more important
figure than his contemporary, Valentinian the Second, for
thirty years the shadowy and impotent Emperor of the
West.   Christian literature had taken firm root while the
classical tradition was still strong; in the hands of men like
Jerome and Augustine that tradition was caught up from
the wreck of the Empire and handed down, not unimpaired,
yet still in prodigious force and vitality, to the modern world.

Latin is now no longer a universal language; and the
direct influence of ancient Rome, which once seemed like
an immortal energy, is at last, like all energies, becoming
slowly absorbed in its own results.   Yet the Latin language
is still the necessary foundation of one half of human
knowledge, and the forms created by Roman genius underlie
the whole of our civilisation.   So long as mankind look
before and after, the name of Rome will be the greatest of
those upon which their backward gaze can be turned.   In
Greece men first learned to be human: under Rome mankind first learned to be civilised.   Law, government, citizenship, are all the creations of the Latin race.   At a thousand
points we still draw directly from the Roman sources.
The codes of Latin jurists are the direct source of all
systems of modern law.   The civic organisation which it
was the great work of the earlier Roman Empire to spread

throughout the provinces is the basis of our municipal institutions and our corporate social life. The names of our months are those of the Latin year, and the modern calendar is, with one slight alteration, that established by Julius Caesar. The head of the Catholic Church is still called by the name of the president of a Republican college which goes back beyond the beginnings of ascertained Roman history. The architecture which we inherit from the Middle Ages, associated by an accident of history with the name of the Goths, had its origin under the Empire, and may be traced down to modern times, step by step, from the basilica of Trajan and the palace of Diocletian. These are but a few instances of the inheritance we have received from Rome. But behind the ordered structure of her law and government, and the majestic fabric of her civilisation, lay a vital force of even deeper import; the strong grave Roman character, which has permanently heightened the ideal of human life. It is in their literature that the inner spirit of the Latin race found its most complete expression. In the stately structure of that imperial language they embodied those qualities which make the Roman name most abidingly great — honour, temperate wisdom, humanity, courtesy, magnanimity; and the civilised world still returns to that fountain-head, and finds a second mother-tongue in the speech of Cicero and Virgil.

INDEX OF AUTHORS